HOLDING POLICE ACCOUNTABLE

Also of interest from the Urban Institute Press:

Trial and Error in Criminal Justice Reform: Learning from Failure,
by Greg Berman and Aubrey Fox

But They All Come Back: Facing the Challenges of Prisoner Reentry,
by Jeremy Travis

Juvenile Drug Courts and Teen Substance Abuse, edited by
Jeffrey A. Butts and John Roman

THE URBAN INSTITUTE PRESS
WASHINGTON, DC

EDITED BY
CANDACE MCCOY

HOLDING POLICE ACCOUNTABLE

INTRODUCTION BY
SAMUEL WALKER

THE URBAN INSTITUTE PRESS
2100 M Street, N.W.
Washington, D.C. 20037

Library of Congress Cataloging-in-Publication Data

Holding police accountable / edited by Candace McCoy ; with an introduction by Samuel Walker.
    p. cm. — (John Jay series on criminal justice)
  Includes bibliographical references and index.
  ISBN 978-0-87766-765-0
  1. Police misconduct. 2. Police—Professional ethics. 3. Police brutality. 4. Police training. I. McCoy, Candace.
  HV7936.C56H65 2010
  363.2'32—dc22
                    2010015328

Printed in the United States of America

12 11 10   1 2 3 4 5

THE URBAN INSTITUTE is a nonprofit, nonpartisan policy research and educational organization established in Washington, D.C., in 1968. Its staff investigates the social, economic, and governance problems confronting the nation and evaluates the public and private means to alleviate them. The Institute disseminates its research findings through publications, its web site, the media, seminars, and forums.

Through work that ranges from broad conceptual studies to administrative and technical assistance, Institute researchers contribute to the stock of knowledge available to guide decisionmaking in the public interest.

Conclusions or opinions expressed in Institute publications are those of the authors and do not necessarily reflect the views of officers or trustees of the Institute, advisory groups, or any organizations that provide financial support to the Institute.

The John Jay Series on Criminal Justice covers contemporary topics about criminal justice system operations and their impacts. Describing and analyzing social policy in action, the series is aimed at policymakers, justice officials, scholars, journalists, and citizens who value critical thinking about crime and the state's response to it.

An international leader in educating for justice, John Jay College of Criminal Justice of The City University of New York offers a rich liberal arts and professional studies curriculum to upwards of 15,000 undergraduate and graduate students from more than 135 nations. In teaching, scholarship and research, the College approaches justice as an applied art and science in service to society and as an ongoing conversation about fundamental human desires for fairness, equality and the rule of law.

Dedicated to Jim Fyfe—
"a cop's cop, a scholar's scholar, a writer's writer"

Contents

PART II. **The Use of Nondeadly Force**

PART III. **Methods to Encourage Police Accountability**

Foreword

Police scandals recur, and after each come demands for better ways to prevent brutality, or racial profiling, or corruption, or types of malfeasance. Considering that the problems periodically reappear, devising methods to prevent them might seem difficult. That is so, and yet, as several chapters in this book explain, the quality of policing in America has improved markedly over the past fifty years. While far from perfect, it is also far from what it was.

Progress occurred thanks to the hard work of a dedicated generation of police professionals. These thoughtful and courageous officials had been educated in justice—in the research on both the policing profession's operational aspects and the outcomes of social, political, and legal demands that must be fitted into a theory of what police are and what they may be required to do or prohibited from doing. Developing a theory of police accountability preoccupied an earlier generation of scholars who convinced a generation of police officials to grapple with it as well, and this healthy examination of standard police procedures palpably improved policing across the nation.

Today, the need to understand and effectuate accountability is as great as ever. Changes in the policing environment present opportunities to test previous theories and apply them to new circumstances. This book seizes this opportunity. Its authors address police accountability by recounting the history of scholarship on the issue and applying its lessons and insights to new problems. For example, organizational theorists examined accountability mainly in terms of administrative controls on police use of deadly force, and this history is recounted here. But *Holding Police Accountable* goes further, applying that research to nonlethal force: how to train officers to control it, or to measure it, or to reconfigure shift work to help officers make good decisions about it.

The history of scholarship on police accountability cannot be written without reference to the work of the late James Fyfe. His work inspired this book and the conference from which it grew. Most of the contributing authors participated in a conference on police accountability that Sam Walker organized and that John Jay College presented. Sam was so generous with his time and energy, and the speakers were so gracious in agreeing immediately to present their latest research, that the roadshow arrived in New York on its own steam. We here at John Jay sincerely thank Sam and his entourage, which included Bill Geller and Geoff Alpert. At John Jay, Dean James Levine and the extremely capable Mayra Nieves provided the essential support for producing the conference, which about a hundred scholars and police practitioners attended. Tom Brady and Yasmin Haug helped us plan and produce a fundraising dinner at which the Fyfe Fellowship for a doctoral student who previously served as a police officer was inaugurated at John Jay College. American University's Richard Bennett and Brian Forst made helpful suggestions for organizing this book.

Eminent police chiefs commented on these chapters, to the benefit of all. Sincere thanks go to John Timoney, Miami's chief of police, who was Philadelphia's police commissioner while Fyfe was writing op-eds there excoriating practices and policies that had not changed since the days of Frank Rizzo. Timoney's testimony to the power of research in encouraging police reform honored his Philadelphia "partner in noncrime" Fyfe. Tom Constantine, formerly superintendent of the New York State Police, offered a local perspective and a thoughtful analysis of how police policies change over time. Gil Kerlikowske, then the chief of police in Seattle and now the federal "drug czar," smoothly synthesized major ideas about police use of nondeadly force, explaining compellingly how Fyfe's scholarship and practice apply to today's problems.

Jerome Skolnick gets the "oft said, but n'er so well expressed" award for describing his coauthor James Fyfe as "a writer's writer, a scholar's scholar, and a cop's cop." Yet, anybody who knew him could give examples and recount "wacko" Jim stories, preferably delivered in a Brooklyn accent. Jim's writings and scholarship are partly chronicled in this book, as is the impact of his extensive work serving as an expert witness in *Monell* litigation. Less widely known, he worked as a "cop's cop" as a rookie in Brooklyn's 84th Precinct and, later, as a patrol officer on Times Square in the 1960s and as a young lieutenant assigned to the Police Academy in the 1970s.

Jim temporarily left the New York Police Department (NYPD) in 1971 to get a Ph.D. at the State University of New York at Albany. Later, he left again to become a professor at American University and to work with former NYPD Police Commissioner Patrick V. Murphy at the Police Foundation in Washington, D.C. What followed was a stellar academic career for the 6-foot-seven kid from Bay Ridge. After years of teaching at Temple University, Jim returned to New York as a distinguished professor at his undergraduate alma mater, CUNY's John Jay College of Criminal Justice, only to return—full circle—to policing in 2002, when Commissioner Raymond W. Kelly invited him back to the NYPD as deputy commissioner for training, partly to manage his beloved Police Academy, at that point training several thousand rookies a year. The "scholar's scholar" and "cop's cop" ended up in the job that most perfectly merged both aspects of this remarkable career.

It is fitting that Jim's academic legacy would be celebrated at his alma mater and the school in which he held a distinguished professor post at the time of his death. After decades of university teaching and research and mentoring, he taught his last class—a doctoral seminar on the police—at John Jay at night, while he was also serving as deputy commissioner during the day, and using a portable chemotherapy pump. Fyfe's grasp of the police role in society and the need to define it with utmost care shines through this book. He was an educator for justice, and this book is, too.

Jeremy Travis, President
John Jay College of Criminal Justice

Preface: Observations on the Study of Police Accountability

Candace McCoy

Police accountability is out of style. It was once a major concern, generally regarded as a primary spur for the systematic police reform efforts of the 1960s and 1970s.[1] Back then, "police accountability" was a codeword for the drive to bring state and local police procedures and practices into conformity with the U.S. Constitution, not only in such areas as searches and seizures or interrogations but in efforts to change a police subculture that was too often racist, violent, and dismissive of due process (Skolnick 1966). A herculean program of social change involving hotly contested cases from the U.S. Supreme Court and painful confrontations between police officials and citizens' groups ripened into shared agreement that some reform was necessary.

Eventually, a "professional model" of policing emerged and supplanted the old-style traditional "watchman" model. (Wilson [1968] coined these terms; see Walker [1977] for this history.) Accountability was universally understood to be an essential component of such police professionalism, and the term was assumed to mean "held to standards of law and internal departmental rules written in compliance with that law." An officer held accountable would be asked to "account" for his or her actions to determine whether they fit with established police department rules—rules that were themselves "held accountable" to the law (Murphy 1975). The buzzword "oversight" shares much of its meaning with the term "accountability," and it is currently in vogue as part of, or even as an alternative to, "regulation" (in hot debates about the unregulated excesses of Wall Street investment firms and lack of appropriate oversight in the subprime mortgage industry). But accountability is broader than oversight or regulation. It encompasses not only scrutiny by outside agencies but ethical vigilance from within the organization itself. Ultimately, it means that the organization must comply with the rule of law.

Perhaps the very success of the professionalism model slowly eroded concerns about police accountability. Because there was a serious and important movement to modernize and professionalize American police and because accountability was a part of that movement, reformers assumed that accountability would improve as professionalism proceeded. In the 1960s and 1970s, reformers focused on discovering police illegality, and professionalism insisted on implementing rules and guidelines to eradicate it. Once local police practices followed the law, reformers assumed that accountability would naturally be achieved. In turn, police scholarship would move on to new research challenges.

Mostly, that is indeed what happened. Professionalism changed American policing in fundamental ways, and police managers and officers today are more attuned to the requirements of law and ethics than they were prior to the 1970s. But it is possible that, precisely because the professionalism movement mostly succeeded in shaking police out of traditional practices and procedures, complacency about accountability to the law could set in—after all, the problem had been "dealt with." When serious legality problems arose in new ways in the 1990s—racial profiling, wrongful convictions, brutality by rogue police units—it became clear that accountability had not, in fact, been "dealt with" entirely successfully.

Police reformers and scholars of the 1970s and 1980s missed an important factor in their studies of accountability: political environments outside the police department can influence police policies, and these in turn produce actions that violate the law. (The influence of the federal government's "Operation Pipeline" on the New Jersey State Police, and subsequent racial profiling scandals, springs to mind.) How can there be accountability to the law when outside directives to the police, or expectations of the police, are antithetical to legal norms?

In the 1990s, concern about police illegality that was the result of outside political pressure played itself out on the front pages of newspapers more than in scholarly research, although there was some important scholarship about racial profiling (see, for example, Harris 1997, 1999, 2007; Zingraff et al. 2000; Weitzer and Tuch 2006; see also Holmes and

Smith 2008, arguing that police brutality against minorities will be reduced not by police organizational change but by wider social inter-group conflict reduction). The scandals were disheartening to advocates of police professionalism and the social science researchers who study the police—partly, perhaps, because they had hoped that the account-ability measures set into place in the 1980s would have prevented such widespread phenomena as racial profiling and wrongful convictions. But wrongful convictions, for example, are scarcely attributable solely to the police. Trial courts themselves, those bastions of "lawfulness," are ulti-mately responsible and present an example of the wider organizational environment that permits police to act irresponsibly. Police misconduct arises from factors outside the police organization as much as within it, and researchers should approach the problem of accountability anew, with an eye on this different source of misconduct.

But there has been no renewed wave of scholarship on police account-ability to the law. Why are so few researchers studying the conditions that gave rise to the accountability scandals of the 1990s and 2000s? Why is accountability to the law not more of an issue in contemporary evalu-ations of such innovations as community or problem-oriented policing? One way to understand the development of American police practices and scholarship about them, to explain why some topics have been deeply studied while others lie fallow, is to look at police scholarship over time as intellectual history. What ideas, theories, and research about police have been most prominent over the past half century, and how have they changed?

Police use of deadly force and the development of problem-oriented policing are two such ideas. Scholarship about the police responds to changes in policing, of course, but sometimes research has helped initi-ate those changes, which is the case with these two topics. The chapters in this book continually refer to research on police use of force, both deadly and nondeadly, because such research first developed the tem-plate for studying police accountability. This scholarship first blossomed in the 1980s and 1990s in the context of studies on controlling police dis-cretion to use force. Indeed, Sam Walker's excellent introductory chap-ter sets this topic into the broader history of the "central problem" in criminal justice organizations generally: how much discretion the law and policy should provide for each criminal justice decisionmaker, and how that discretion should be structured and controlled. Police discre-tion and accountability to the law and the police mission "to protect life" is but one of many examples of the need to structure justice officials' decisions.

Another reason this book continually refers to previous research on deadly force is that it grew out of a conference celebrating the scholarly legacy of James Fyfe, known to his jocular contemporaries as "Doctor Deadly Force." Fyfe's 1977 doctoral dissertation examined the effect of a policy the New York Police Department adopted that allowed officers to shoot a fleeing felon only if the suspect presented significant danger to the officer or bystanders (Fyfe 1978). (At that time, most states permitted such shooting.) Fyfe showed that, after adopting the policy, deaths of suspects dropped significantly but crime rates were unaffected, and he concluded that meaningful change in police operations could be achieved from within, through administrative controls, if administrators were attuned to broader social, legal, and ethical standards. In a lifetime of writing, teaching, and expert witnessing, Fyfe's was the preeminent voice of the police officer–scholar, explaining how accountability to the primary police mission "to protect life" could be achieved.[2] In chapter 2, Fridell explores this history in excellent detail. Her work is both historical and contemporary, because it demonstrates that police departments can change for the better even under strong internal and external resistance.

Fundamentally, early research on the use of deadly force was based on an explanation of accountability rooted in organizational theory. There was something about policing that produced excessive use of force, it was believed, so reform efforts aimed to change the organization and the officers. Beginning in the 1970s, a small industry was devoted to researching such subjects as whether there was a "police personality" that new hiring could screen out (McNamara 1967; Cecil and Lamberth 1974), whether more education improves police performance (Sherman 1978, 1980; Carter, Sapp, and Stevens 1989a, b; Kappeler, Sapp, and Carter 1993), whether opening the police ranks to women would be good or bad for police work (Ermer 1978; Martin 1980; Schultz 1995). (The answers were, respectively, no, there's not a personality, but yes, you can screen for particular unwanted psychological propensities; not necessarily; and opening ranks to women was good.) A research agenda to study law and national policy on understanding police use of deadly force proceeded from this organizational perspective (for overviews, see Matulia 1985; Fyfe 1988; Geller and Scott 1992) and usually concluded with the policy recommendation that police executives could and should control officers' illegal force within established command-and-control structures.

The first wave of research on police accountability, then, was based on the notion that accountability to the law and morality would be fostered when factors *internal* to the police organization were changed.

Subsequently, in the 1990s, research tracked the movement from professional policing to community-oriented and problem-solving policing, but there was little scholarship about accountability under these new approaches, perhaps because accountability scholarship primarily examined organizational controls and was less concerned with what occurs outside the police department—for instance, in the community. Community policing was enthusiastically heralded as an entirely new methodology (Goldstein 1986; Kelling and Moore 1998; Trojanowicz and Bucqueroux 1990), and the 1994 Crime Act placed thousands of new officers trained in community policing techniques into local police departments nationwide through the federal Community Oriented Policing Services (COPS) program. Supporters claimed that, by removing barriers between police and citizens and encouraging greater community involvement in defining appropriate police activities and strategies, the traditional police military-style subculture (Skolnick 1966) would finally give way to a new kind of policing. Further, in cities that rejected traditional methods in favor of a professionalism model, the unfortunate distance between police and citizens would be reduced. Police scholarship encouraged and evaluated these developments—indeed, it could be said that such scholarship provided the intellectual juice for invention of community policing at the outset (see Goldstein 1977; Skolnick and Bayley 1986).

There is no doubt that community policing has been and continues to be a force for progressive and truly community-empowering municipal activity (Skogan 2006). Research on the topic has concentrated on how community policing is implemented and with what effects, and an entire branch of research and practice known as problem-solving policing developed and has been widely researched. (See Goldstein [1990], Spelman and Eck [1987], subsequent publications by Eck, and four articles in *Criminology and Public Policy* in February 2010.) Accountability has seldom been a topic in this research, though. Perhaps this is because COPS is regarded as such a humane and progressive movement that it was assumed to be antithetical to the abuses of power so common in traditionalist policing. In 1993, Skolnick and Fyfe stated:

> community-oriented [and] problem-oriented policing should, above all, advocate a change in the philosophy of policing. The organization must be more flexible and willing to adapt to changing needs. The police officer, in turn, is required

> to be more of a generalist, more humanistic, more in tune with the underlying needs, problems, and resources of the areas being policed. Such an orientation is far less likely to generate police violence than traditional patrol policing, with which the familiar culture of policing . . . is associated. (Skolnick and Fyfe 1993, 258)

Seventeen years later, these new styles of policing have achieved much of the predicted effect of being more humanistic and generating less violence. But simply because their supporters were honest and progressive reformers did not mean that abuses of police authority disappeared. Skolnick and Fyfe had also warned

> If, in conveying an understanding that policing involves a range of problems and not just crime; that problems require analysis and differentiated responses; and that police are limited in their capacity to address these problems and need to involve the community, it would be paradoxical if police were to resort to the kind of aggressive patrolling that community-oriented and problem-oriented policing were supposed to eliminate, and that are often a prelude to violence. (Skolnick and Fyfe 1993, 258–59)

In the years after Skolnick and Fyfe wrote this, aggressiveness sanctioned by community- and problem-oriented policing was indeed a problem, though thankfully not worse than police violence had been under the traditionalist or professional policing models. As Skolnick and Fyfe predicted, in the late 1990s, government-sanctioned racial profiling and aggressive stop-and-frisk practices that pushed the bounds of the Fourth Amendment emerged. Vehement criticism and calls for reform appeared in the media. These focused on the practice of racial profiling but not on the organizational conditions that might have produced it. Strangely, there was not much scholarly research on the links between new techniques of policing and problems of accountability.[3] Yet scholars of community- and problem-oriented policing have always been concerned that the decentralization of authority necessary for these models to work might produce a situation in which police officers in local neighborhoods—and their bosses at headquarters—lose sight of the overarching legal standard to which they are accountable.

Indeed, in its zeal to convince police officers to respond to neighborhood concerns, community policing might give tacit approval to new forms of police lawlessness. The fundamental question that must be asked at the beginning of any inquiry into police accountability is, *accountable to what?* The established answer is, accountable to the law and representative democracy. But the community policing answer is often, accountable to the decentralized, neighborhood-oriented consensus formed between police and the communities policed. The problem is that sometimes community members or politicians want police to break the law. Sometimes police are expected to respond to insistent neighborhood concerns instead of following broader social policies that reflect civic participation by many different groups and interests. Sometimes city officials urge police to do things in the name of community responsiveness that, upon later analysis, are simply wrong. Sometimes police leaders order street cops to do things in some neighborhoods that would never be condoned in others. And even when good community-oriented policing produces a policing style that responds to local needs, inequality may result because "community policing assumes that policing problems and priorities vary from neighborhood to neighborhood" and therefore the outcomes will be different in different parts of a city (Skolnick and Fyfe 1993, 254).

In the 2000s, residents of poor and ethnic neighborhoods have chafed under search and stop-and-frisk policies aimed at finding terrorists or guns, while residents of more affluent neighborhoods have had no such experiences. Police officials explained that they concentrated their interdiction efforts in neighborhoods where people complained of gun violence or where intelligence indicated terrorism might "reside," but these people asked for safety, not for unequal treatment. The tensions persist. Might a fresh look at the issue of police accountability help explain and resolve such tensions? The goal of this book is to urge renewed concern about the issue and to offer some contemporary research as a first step in formulating a research agenda.

The National Research Council (NRC) of the Academy of Sciences recently called for just such an agenda. The Council published an excellent summary of policing research (2004) that sets out the intellectual history mentioned above. In 400 pages of text summarizing the major literature about police and policing, the Committee to Review Research on Police Policy and Practices categorized the literature into "the ten most important topics that police researchers studied" from 1960 to 2000. Ranked by how often they appeared in scholarly and practitioner journals, they were organization and management; crime; strategies (including community-oriented policing); drugs; policewomen; discrimination; evaluation; ethics, accountability, and discipline; international and comparative policing; and patrol. "Interestingly," the committee stated, "practitioners were as interested in ethics/accountability/discipline as scholars" (NRC 2004, 26).

But the topic was low on each list. "Accountability" had earlier been a critical component of the professionalism movement but, by the year 2000, had been mostly overtaken by other concerns—primarily crime prevention and community policing. Focus shifted from old notions of police accountability as an ethics-driven enterprise holding police accountable to the rule of law to a different approach: community-based accountability to lowering crime statistics. The CompStat model of information exchange and response relies on top police managers from each district being "accountable" for understanding and reducing crime statistics in their precincts. It is widely credited for crime reductions from the late 1990s to the present, though of course many other factors also explain some lowered crime throughout that period (Silverman 2001). The notion of accountability subtly shifted to a concern about crime reduction in neighborhoods rather than control of officers' behavior.

Skolnick and Fyfe in 1993 had been concerned about the possibility that aggressive patrol in the name of community responsiveness would undermine fairness and equality in policing practices, and in their incisive criticism of cops as "soldiers," they warned that unless the military model of policing and the numbers game that too often accompanies it can be changed, police reform will not advance (Skolnick and Fyfe 1993). Why are police departments organized as if they were the military, and what does this do to the police mind-set? If police see people as the enemy, they are unlikely to think protecting life is the most important police mission. Community-oriented police officers, for all their training in a new style of patrol, still work in a military-style organization.

In 2004, the National Research Council's Committee to Review Research on Police Policies and Practices reported that it "returned again and again to the twin issues of fairness and effectiveness in policing. Many of the controversies and challenges facing today's police reflect a perception that these may be to a certain extent antithetical goals, but the committee concluded otherwise" (vii). The task of scholarship is to explain how the goals can work together, and the task of police administration is to make them work.

Accordingly, the committee made a forceful recommendation (and did not make such recommendations in most other areas of inquiry):

> Not enough is known about the extent of police lawfulness, or police compliance with legal and other rules, nor can the mechanisms that best promote police lawfulness be identified. The committee recommends renewed research on the lawfulness of police and a coordinated research emphasis on the effectiveness of organizational mechanisms that foster police rectitude. (NRC 2004, 290)

This book represents one step to begin that renewed research. It is a collection of articles from established scholars who recently returned to the concept of police accountability as a fundamental principle for analyzing police roles, operations, and impacts. All these authors have published on other subjects, but they agreed to return to the topic and provide their perspectives. The occasion for this invitation was a conference held at John Jay College of Criminal Justice, City University of New York, in October 2006. Professor Sam Walker organized the conference as a tribute to the late Dr. James Fyfe, the renowned police scholar and practitioner who died in 2005. Taking a cue from a slogan that Fyfe often repeated in class, in court, and in print—"the primary purpose of the police is to protect life"—the conference was titled "To Protect Life: The Legacy of James Fyfe."

Walker asked researchers whose work had concentrated on accountability issues to present any new perspectives they might have. All the presenters had at some time in their careers worked with James Fyfe, as colleagues, students, or, in my own case, as the Fyfe Wyfe. They included young scholars who learned from Fyfe when he mentored them as students and who therefore make up a cohort of the next generation of researchers on police accountability. The topics they chose are rooted mostly in earlier assumptions about the origin of police misconduct— that is, that misconduct emerges from factors within the organization itself, and that police officials can use good policies, training, and supervision to prevent it. But the book also urges a return to fundamentals, a renewed inquiry into why police do what they do and how they can be accountable *to that mission* and to *a professional standard of care* rather than succumb to pressures either inside or outside the organization, especially in social circumstances that shift over time. "What mission is it, exactly, to which police are accountable?" It is not merely crime-fighting or service to the community. More fundamentally, it is the obligation to protect life. An article Fyfe published in 1993 was influenced by Herman Goldstein's and Egon Bittner's work. In it, Fyfe says that "in large measure, the presence or absence of crime has nothing to do with the police" but that the police are much more often on call to "do what nobody else does" when citizens need help. "Unfortunately," Fyfe said,

> in the areas most in need of high quality police services . . . the *community* and its needs are neither readily identifiable nor monolithic. Instead, as Wilson suggested, such neighborhoods are marked by great social, racial, and political cleavages and

by divergent views about law enforcement and order-maintenance policies and practices. As long as this is so, virtually every police policy or action will offend some interests in the community . . . as long as communities define the police role in the expectation that police will merely respond unquestioningly to their wishes, the police mandate will continue to be amorphous and unclear. (Fyfe 1993, 275)

Moreover, if accountability to the community is not the primary answer to the question "accountable to what?" neither is "accountable to a prioritized mission," nor "accountable to quantitative measures," nor "accountable to crime-prevention expectations." Fyfe considered and explained why each answer is insufficient and instead offered the first line of the New York City Police Department's *Patrol Guide:* "The primary purpose of the police is to protect life." Agreeing with such scholars as Mastrofski, Bayley, and Garofalo, Fyfe suggested that methods of holding officers accountable to this purpose can be developed by turning to police officers themselves. In both professional and community-oriented police departments, "good cops" are easily identified by their peers, and the officers can say what good police practices are. Two writers who contributed chapters to this book—David Klinger and Michael White—each independently call for officer involvement in setting internal standards as the beginning point for police accountability. It is not surprising that they were Fyfe's students.

Fyfe constantly repeated the slogan that "the primary purpose of the police is to protect life. All policy follows from that." He said this in class, in the media, and in hundreds of police-misconduct lawsuits in which he served as an expert witness. The questions of police mission and "accountability to what" emerge clearly in post-9/11 policing. How far should local police go in supporting federal antiterrorism efforts? Is the mission of protecting life weakened if local police must engage in counter-terrorism interdiction, and at what point is accountability to local law as well as the U.S. Constitution attenuated? Is the small chance of saving a great many lives through terrorism prevention to be given higher priority than the much more likely outcome of saving some individual lives under traditional crime-fighting principles? For instance, to get information for crime-fighting, local police need to work with illegal immigrants, and the immigrants must trust the police enough to help them protect life in immigrant neighborhoods. Will local police departments bow to external pressure to serve as immigration and antiterrorism officials, or will they concentrate on the crime problems of the people who live in their communities no matter what their ethnic or citizenship status?

When a "protect life" mission is matched to specific situations like this, often a rough cost-benefit analysis presents itself. However, by holding fast to the "protect life" mandate, clarity emerges and hard choices can be made. In the 1980s and 1990s, police use of deadly force showed a similar dynamic. Certainly crime-fighting is the established way that police protect life, but if the paradoxical result is to take life in pursuit of this mission, something is very wrong. Lori Fridell's comprehensive overview of the history of policies about deadly force and how they changed in the 1980s offers insight into the conditions necessary for radical questioning of the police role: Do crime-control measures work? If they do, do they create more misery than good? Do they allow police to cling to incorrect assumptions about their proper role? Fridell is a storyteller, and her subject is how revising deadly force policies caused policymakers to rethink the proper role of the police in America. It is a story with important lessons for contemporary police practices, as any glance at current headlines demonstrates. (Compare, for example, contrasting events in Oakland, California, in 2009. In the first, a transit police officer shot an unarmed man in the back with his semi-automatic handgun—he claimed he was reaching for his Taser but pulled the wrong weapon; in the second, a parolee killed two police officers who stopped him for a traffic violation, then ran and forced a shootout in which two more officers and the parolee died.) Fridell's chapter in part 1 chronicles how deadly force policies changed drastically in the 1980s, and how scholarship helped in that development. Reading this material today, we might ask, can the methodology of the deadly force research be applied to the use of *non*deadly force? What are the similarities, or the differences, and how might we expand our thinking about use of force to encompass both?

The chapters in part 2 all explore that issue. They offer contemporary research on the police use of force, though this time the subject is the use of *non*deadly force. It is a measure of the success of the efforts in the 1980s and 1990s in researching and controlling police use of deadly force that by the time this book was published 25 years later, available literature on the use of force is almost exclusively about the nonlethal variety. All three chapters proceed from a view of police accountability as achievable primarily through well-informed and well-designed internal departmental rules and guidelines, training, discipline, and supervision, which is the traditional organizational-theory approach.

For instance, conventional wisdom holds that illegal or simply inappropriate use of force can be reduced if police are trained correctly in how to respond to potentially violent situations. The police organization can mold its personnel to comply with rules set not only by the courts but by citizens' expectations. But how effective is violence reduction training, and perhaps more important, what *type* of training most helps officers learn to respond with only the force appropriate to the threat posed? In chapter 5, Klinger's project was a controlled experiment in which officers were randomly assigned to one of two groups: one that received violence reduction training—role-playing exercises in which officers were placed in simulated potentially violent situations and taught how to respond—and a control group in which officers did not receive the training. Such a gold standard of evaluation methodology is rare in social science research, and Klinger's findings support the traditional notion that the police organization can hold its personnel accountable to legal standards. The project is important not only for its methodology but because it trained police in the degree of coercion they may use in everyday police-citizen encounters, not just cops-and-robbers crime-fighting and "shoot, don't shoot" videogame-style training.

Indeed, that there is a coercion continuum on which proper police response to various situations can be arranged is, by now, conventional wisdom. William Terrill has studied and published on this topic, and his chapter 3 offers a comprehensive overview of the coercion continuum and how it can be translated into department rules and policies. It logically pairs with Klinger's chapter, because the continuum shows how force should be used proportionate to the threat posed—no more and no less. Terrill provides a very useful visual explanation of his model. White and Ready's chapter 4 about Tasers provides a specific example of the use of nonlethal force on such a continuum. All these studies are welcome additions to the literature on accountability because they are examples of excellent continuing inquiry into the control of force and the conditions under which force may be used appropriately.

In sum, the articles in part 2 are based on the idea that police accountability is achieved by developing internal department rules and guidelines and changing the organization to comply with them.[4] The chapters in part 3, by contrast, are concerned with the problem of how the *external* political and social environment affects what police departments do. Prior to the 1980s, there was no common professional standard of care in the policing profession. Departments varied widely in how they carried out their operations, and except for legal requirements governing arrests and interrogations (set by the Supreme Court in such famous cases as *Mapp v. Ohio* and *Miranda v. Arizona*), there was not a well-articulated standard of best practices for professional policing. Leaders of the movement to professionalize police, in the 1970s, thought that police executives and analysts would eventually develop a common professional standard of care. But that did not happen. This standard, at least as it related to the most serious violations of accountability, was developed by a force *outside* the police community: the courts. McCoy's chapter on lawsuits against the police (chapter 6) proceeds from the assumption that the political and social environment is a powerful force that can foster police accountability as well as undermine it. Without the litigation explosion of the 1980s, the accountability movement of that era would not have been successful, and the basic requirements of constitutional law would not have formed the common standards of professionalism under which all American police departments are expected to operate. Using statistics about types of lawsuits against the police and examples of specific groundbreaking cases, chapter 6 shows that lawsuits became a powerful accountability device—a device that would have been useless had the U.S. Supreme Court not expanded and strengthened it in *Monell v. Department of Social Services* (1978). Various devices for achieving accountability through internal and external pressures—exclusionary rules, consent decrees, internal rules and guidelines—are available, and all have their place, but the chapter concludes that the legal structure set in place in the 1980s under *Monell* has been the most powerful factor in achieving accountability since that time.

In chapter 7, Brian Vila identifies a problem not usually on the radar of people concerned about police accountability but that turns out to be practical and far-reaching: personnel policies that prevent police from following their own established rules and guidelines. In this case, those policies are shift work and overtime assignments that produce sleep deprivation. Sleepy cops make bad decisions, no matter how good their departments' rules are or how careful their training is. Vila places the blame for these work-assignment policies on the wider social and political environment in which labor leaders strive to get contracts providing lucrative overtime pay or, in another example, in which public expectations that police are on-call 24 hours a day, seven days a week, with guns ready, create stresses that can lead to poor decisions. Again, these policies should be examined in light of the primary police mission "to protect life."

Vila's work points to the idea that the political and social environment outside policing, when combined with self-serving but mistaken assumptions about public safety within the police community, can undermine accountability. Michael White's chapter 8 on "the data-driven police department," though, returns to the notion that accountability is best fostered within the police department when police personnel can learn and be influenced by their own evaluation findings. White's chapter is primarily methodological, arguing that transparency and accountability will place increasing pressures on police departments to account for their operations, and that therefore police officers should learn how to use and report quantitative data. This is not a CompStat program for captains and chiefs, but a skill to be acquired by line officers and applied "from the bottom up." White reports on a pilot project that trained officers in statistical analysis, an enterprise that could be useful in accounting for officer behavior inside and outside the organization. Whether outside organizations, such as media outlets, will be able to obtain such data, of course, is a topic currently under debate in the courts and important to the question of whether and how outside organizations may influence police actions in the future.

Samuel Walker, an esteemed American scholar of police accountability, began this book by putting all these ideas into a broader context: all organizations have discretion to achieve their goals, but how is that discretion to be controlled? This major question was researched extensively in the first wave of scholarship on police accountability, and Walker asks how these concepts can be re-examined as renewed scholarship on accountability moves forward. He notes that research and policy about controlling use of force relied on "the organizational/managerial explanation of police behavior," which turned out to offer powerful insight into the accountability problem and was so successful that it should be applied to justice organizations outside the police. Walker reviews the operations of other criminal justice agencies—prosecutors, judges, correctional officials—and concludes that they all would benefit from application of this organizational/managerial approach exemplified in administrative rule-making and rule-enforcing. The control of discretion is a topic that will never go out of style.

Walker also makes the important point that understanding criminal justice organizations and then holding them accountable to norms of legality and ethics can be achieved only if these organizations are open to research. In this, he agrees completely with the National Research Council's call for a renewed research agenda on police accountability. This book, we hope, will be one step in that direction.

NOTES

1. See the President's Commission on Law Enforcement and the Administration of Justice (1967), which spawned the Law Enforcement Assistance Administration.

2. The term is taken from the New York Police Department's Patrol Guide, which is a detailed statement of proper procedures for patrol officers to follow when encountering a wide variety of situations. For instance, in the section on "aided cases," standard operating procedure for responding to a mentally ill or emotionally disturbed person is spelled out. The section begins by stating "The primary duty of *all* members of the service is to preserve human life. The safety of *all* persons involved is paramount" (New York City Police Department, procedure No. 216-05, effective January 1, 2000). Similar statements to the effect that "the primary purpose of the police is to protect life" (including the officers' lives) are found throughout the patrol guide and NYPD regulations. Fyfe often mentioned while testifying in court or talking to criminal justice officials that he first concentrated on that phrase and realized its implications while studying for the sergeant's exam in 1975.

3. An exception is Lersch (2002), especially the chapter "Community Policing and Police Corruption" by Joseph Shafer. Also, there was a series of studies and reports from the federal COPS office on appropriate personnel practices under community-oriented policing. Though not regarded specifically as accountability measures, police performance evaluation under community-oriented policing begins to approach the problem (Alpert and Moore 1993). See also Weisburd, McElroy, and Hardyman (1989) for an early statement of the problem, and publications from the Police Executive Research Forum, such as *Personnel Performance Evaluations in the Community Policing Context* (1997). See also Oettmeier and Wycoff (1997).

4. Perhaps its best practical example is the operation of the Commission on Accreditation of Law Enforcement Agencies and police agencies across the nation that regularly train officers into compliance with CALEA-style guidelines.

REFERENCES

Alpert, Geoffrey P., and Mark H. Moore. 1993. "Measuring Police Performance in the New Paradigm of Policing." In *Performance Measures for the Criminal Justice System* (109–140). Washington DC: U.S. Government Printing Office.

Carter, David L., Alan D. Sapp, and Darrel W. Stephens. 1989a. "Higher Education as a Bona Fide Occupational Qualification." *American Journal of Police* 7: 1–28.

———. 1989b. *The State of Police Education: Policy Direction for the 21st Century.* Washington DC: Police Executive Research Forum.

Cecil, Joe S., and John C. Lamberth. 1974. *Alternative Methods for the Psychological Testing of Police Officers.* Norman: University of Oklahoma.

Ermer, Virginia B. 1978. "Recruitment of Female Police Officers in New York City." *Journal of Criminal Justice* 6 (Fall): 233–46.

Fyfe, James J. 1978. "Shots Fired: An Analysis of New York City Police Firearms Discharge." Ph.D. diss., State University of New York at Albany. Ann Arbor, MI: University Microfilms.

———. 1988. "Police Use of Deadly Force: Research and Reform." *Justice Quarterly* 5(June): 165–205.

———. 1993. " 'Good' Policing." In *The Socio-Economics of Crime and Justice*, edited by Brian Forst. New York: M.E. Sharpe.

Geller, William A., and Michael S. Scott. 1992. *Deadly Force: What We Know.* Washington DC: Police Executive Research Forum.

Goldstein, Herman. 1977. *Policing a Free Society.* Cambridge, MA: Ballinger.

———. 1986. "Toward Community-Oriented Policing: Potential Basic Requirements and Threshold Questions." *Crime and Delinquency* 33: 1–30.

———. 1990. *Problem-Oriented Policing.* New York: McGraw-Hill.

Harris, David A. 1997. "'Driving while Black' and All Other Traffic Offenses: The Supreme Court and Pretextual Traffic Stops." *Criminal Law and Criminology* 87(2): 544–82.

———. 1999. "The Stories, the Statistics, and the Law: Why 'Driving while Black' Matters." *Minnesota Law Review* 84(2): 265–326.

———. 2007. "The Importance of Research on Race and Policing: Making Race Salient to Individuals and Institutions within Criminal Justice." *Criminology and Public Policy* 6(1): 5–23.

Holmes, Malcolm D., and Brad W. Smith. 2008. *Race and Police Brutality: Roots of an Urban Dilemma.* Albany: State University of New York Press.

Kappeler, Victor E., Alan D. Sapp, and David L. Carter. 1993. "Police Officer Higher Education, Citizen Complaints, and Departmental Rule Violations." *American Journal of Police* 11: 37–54.

Kelling, George L., and Mark H. Moore. 1998. *The Evolving Strategy of Policing.* Washington, DC: National Institute of Justice.

Lersch, Kim M., ed. 2002. *Policing and Misconduct.* Upper Saddle River, NJ: Prentice Hall.

Martin, Susan E. 1980. *Breaking and Entering: Policewomen on Patrol.* Berkeley: University of California Press.

Matulia, Kenneth R. 1985. *A Balance of Forces,* 2nd ed. Gaithersburg, MD: International Association of Chiefs of Police.

McNamara, John H. 1967. "Uncertainties in Police Work: The Relevance of Police Recruits' Backgrounds and Training." In *The Police: Six Sociological Essays,* edited by David J. Bordua (162–252). New York: John Wiley and Sons.

Murphy, Patrick V. 1975. "Police Accountability." In *Readings on Police Productivity,* edited by Joan L. Wolfle and John F. Heaphy (35–46). Washington, DC: Police Foundation.

National Research Council. 2004. *Fairness and Effectiveness in Policing: The Evidence.* edited by Wesley Skogan and Kathleen Frydl. Washington, DC: The National Academies Press.

Oettmeier, Timothy N., and Mary Ann Wycoff. 1997. *Personnel Performance Evaluations in the Community Policing Context.* Washington, DC: Police Executive Research Forum.

President's Commission on Law Enforcement and the Administration of Justice. 1967. Washington, DC: Government Printing Office.

"Problem-Solving Policing." 2010. Symposium. *Criminology and Public Policy* 9(1): 135–195.

Schultz, Dorothy. 1995. *From Social Worker to Crimefighter: Women in United States Municipal Policing.* Westport, CT: Praeger Publishers.

Sherman, Lawrence. 1978. *The Quality of Police Education: A Critical Review with Recommendations for Improving Programs in Higher Education.* Washington, DC: Jossey-Bass.

———. 1980. "Causes of Police Behavior: The Current State of Quantitative Research." *Journal of Research in Crime and Delinquency* 17:69–100.

Silverman, Eli B. 2001. *NYPD Battles Crime in Innovative Strategies in Policing.* Boston: Northeastern University Press.

Skogan, Wesley G. 2006. *Police and Community in Chicago: A Tale of Three Cities.* New York: Oxford University Press.

Skolnick, Jerome H. 1966. *Justice Without Trial.* New York: John Wiley and Sons.

Skolnick, Jerome H., and David H. Bayley. 1986. *The New Blue Line: Police Innovation in Six American Cities.* New York: The Free Press.

Skolnick, Jerome H., and James J. Fyfe. 1993. *Above the Law: Police and the Excessive Use of Force.* New York: The Free Press.

Spelman, William, and John E. Eck. 1987. *Newport News Tests Problem-Oriented Policing.* Washington, DC: U.S. Department of Justice.

Trojanowicz, Robert, and Bonnie Bucqueroux. 1990. *Community Policing: A Contemporary Perspective.* Cincinnati: Anderson Publishing Co.

Walker, Samuel. 1977. *A Critical History of Police Reform: The Emergence of Professionalism.* Lexington, MA: Lexington Books.

———. 2005. *The New World of Police Accountability.* Thousand Oaks, CA: Sage Publications.

Weisburd, David, Jerome McElroy, and Patricia Hardyman. 1989. "Maintaining Control in Community-Oriented Policing." In *Police and Policing: Contemporary Issues,* edited by Dennis Jay Kenney. New York: Praeger.

Weitzer, Ronald, and Steven A. Tuch. 2006. *Race and Policing in America.* New York: Cambridge University Press.

Wilson, James Q. 1968. *Varieties of Police Behavior.* Cambridge, MA: Harvard University Press.

Zingraff, Matthew T, Marcinda Mason, William R. Smith, Donald Tomaskovic-Devey, Harvey L. McMurray, and C. Robert Fenton. 2000. *Evaluating North Carolina State Highway Patrol Data: Citations, Warnings, and Searches in 1998.* Raleigh: North Carolina Department of Crime Control and Public Safety.

1

Police Accountability and the Central Problem in American Criminal Justice

Samuel Walker

Research and policy development on controlling police use of deadly force began with the work of James J. Fyfe. His pioneering research, based on his 1978 dissertation, found that administrative controls effectively reduced discharges of officer firearms (Fyfe 1978, 1979). This point is well known to all students of American police, and his research has had a profound impact on police firearms policy. Today, virtually all police departments have put in place the administrative controls over the use of firearms use that Fyfe studied (Geller and Scott 1992).

Less well known is that the research and policy development inspired by Fyfe's work were but one part of a much broader evolution in policy and research that addresses what some see as the central problem in American criminal justice. At the time of his dissertation research, there was ferment throughout the criminal justice field over the use and misuse of official discretion (Walker 1993). The central thrust of policy change over the past 30 years has, in very broad terms, paralleled the developments related to police use of deadly force. Fyfe's findings on the effectiveness of administrative controls over police shooting discretion provided important support for the development of similar controls over discretion in other parts of the criminal justice system, including bail setting, plea bargaining, sentencing, and parole release.

The impact of Jim Fyfe's original work on the control of police use of firearms (see chapter 2) has another important dimension. Many cynics

1

dismiss academic research as a largely self-referential enterprise, without practical utility, in which academics talk only to themselves. To the contrary, Fyfe's work demonstrates that academic research—research that meets the highest scientific standards—does make a difference in the real world of criminal justice and as a consequence in the lives of all Americans (Walker 2004).

Original Research on Police Use of Deadly Force

Fyfe's original research on police use of deadly force was a landmark event in several respects. The issue of police shootings had been a bitter controversy for many years, particularly with respect to police-community relations. Many of the riots of the 1960s had been sparked by the fatal shooting of an African American by a white police officer (National Advisory Commission 1968). These events initiated a political and scholarly debate over police shooting practices. On the one side, many community activists, some scholars, and a number of elected officials saw a pattern of racial bias among persons shot and killed by the police. Some analysts found disparities of 6:1 or even 8:1 in the ratio of African Americans to whites fatally shot. On the other, the police and their allies argued that whatever racial disparities existed were the result of differential involvement in criminal activity by African Americans, not bias on the part of the police (Geller and Scott 1992).

Similar debates have occurred—and for that matter continue—with respect to racial disparities in traffic enforcement (Harris 2002), imprisonment (Blumstein 1982), the use of the death penalty (Paternoster 1991), and the entire criminal justice system (Walker, Spohn, and DeLone 2007). Thus, as it emerged into a political controversy in the 1960s, the debate over the racial aspects of police shootings was directly related to larger questions of race and criminal justice that continue to animate public debate.

The debate over police shootings in the 1960s, in what we can call the pre-Fyfe era, was inconclusive because it was based on completely inadequate data. Critics of the police did not have access to official police files on shooting incidents and based their analyses on other available data, such as published aggregate police data or media accounts, both of which we now recognize are often unreliable and certainly not adequate for a meaningful analysis of police shooting patterns (Kobler 1975; Robin

1963). For their part, the police and their supporters were not about to conduct detailed analyses of internal police files, either—a task for which few police officials were equipped and which in any event would have opened up the data to independent inquiry.

One important collateral contribution of Fyfe's research on police use of firearms, with enormous long-term consequences for police research in general, was helping open police departments to research by independent investigators. Younger scholars today probably do not fully appreciate the closed nature of American police departments through the mid-1960s. The first systematic observation of police patrol work involved Albert Reiss and Donald Black's study for the President's Crime Commission in 1966 (Black 1980; President's Commission on Law Enforcement and Administration of Justice 1967a; Reiss 1971). Even this project encountered problems both in gaining access for the field research and in reporting any observations of questionable police conduct. Suffice it to say that within a very few years, an increasing number of police departments accepted the principle of openness to research, discovering that solid research is an important component of professional development and improved policing. The net result over the past few decades has been an impressive body of research (National Research Council 2004).

Openness with regard to patrol work was one thing (even when it included observations of officer use of force), but the highly sensitive issue of police use of deadly force was another matter altogether (Geller and Scott 1992). The great breakthrough occurred almost simultaneously in two locations in the mid-1970s. At nearly the same time that Fyfe gained access to the New York City data, William A. Geller obtained access to the shooting files of the Chicago Police Department. His report appeared about the same time as Fyfe's first scholarly article (Geller and Karales 1981).

The findings of Jim Fyfe's research are well known and need only a brief summary here (see chapter 2). He investigated the impact of Temporary Order of Policy 237 (TOP 237) on firearms discharges by New York City police officers between 1971 and 1972. Police Commissioner Patrick V. Murphy issued TOP 237 in August 1972. (Interestingly, Murphy does not mention this historic step in his memoirs; see Murphy and Plate 1977.) The new policy restricted the use of deadly force to situations involving the defense of life, replacing the traditional "fleeing felon" rule. The policy also prohibited discharging firearms as warning shots, as calls for assistance, or at or from moving vehicles, as well as in other situations. In addition to the substantive policy, TOP 237 added an accountability process. Officers were required to complete a report after each firearms discharge, and those reports were subject to an automatic review by a firearms discharge review board (FDRB) comprising high-ranking supervisors (Fyfe 1979).

Examining firearms discharges in the NYPD between 1971 and 1975, Fyfe found that TOP 237 has had a significant and positive impact. The weekly mean of officers' discharging their weapons declined by 29.9 percent. In addition, the policy had no unintended or adverse consequences: no increase in officer injuries or deaths followed implementation of the policy, nor did serious crime increase. As best as could be measured, compliance with the policy was high. While there was some increase in the number of accidental shootings reported, the overall percentage of discharges remained relatively low (9 percent of all discharges in the post-237 period) (Fyfe 1979).

The data also indicated that the principal factor associated with shootings in New York City was the environment of the precinct in which the officer worked. Not surprisingly, shootings were highest in high-crime areas and lowest in low-crime areas (Fyfe 1981). The most important corollary of this finding was that the officer's race was not a significant factor in police shootings.

Policy Impact and Theoretical Implications

Fyfe's research had a dramatic impact on police policy (chapter 2). When Commissioner Murphy introduced the defense-of-life policy in 1972, it was a radical innovation. To be fair, there were undoubtedly other law enforcement agencies that already had restrictive policies. The FBI, for example, adopted a restrictive defense-of-life policy in the 1940s (Geller and Scott 1992). The important point, however, is that none had the lasting national impact on policy that New York City's had. Within a matter of a few years, the defense-of-life policy was the standard policy in major cities across the country (Geller and Scott 1992; Sherman 1978). Today, deadly force policy varies somewhat from department to department, with some a bit more permissive in situations when an armed felon is believed to pose a risk of committing another crime. Departments also vary with regard to the specific prohibited actions. With regard to the principle of a required report and an automatic review, however, there is basically no variation, despite considerable differences in how those reviews are conducted. The standard policy on police use of deadly force that exists today stands in sharp contrast to the great variations in policy that existed in the era before TOP 237, including the virtual absence of any meaningful policy in some agencies (Uelmen 1973).

Although in his original research on police use of firearms, Fyfe did not explore the theoretical implications of his findings, they make a significant contribution toward explaining police behavior and support the organizational-managerial interpretation. This view holds that officer behavior is in part (an important qualification) influenced by organizational factors, in this case formal policies and the administration of those policies. Support for the organizational-managerial perspective has important policy implications, because it suggests that certain important aspects of police behavior can be controlled through the development and enforcement of meaningful administrative policies. Walker (1993) argues that this principle has been extended to other components of the criminal justice system.

This perspective stands in contrast to individual explanations for police behavior, which focus on the characteristics of individual officers, particularly race and ethnicity, gender, and education. As noted earlier, Fyfe did not find that an officer's race explained shooting rates (Fyfe 1981), nor has other research supported such explanations of behavior (National Research Council 2004). Although many reformers have assumed that police behavior can be improved through increased employment of racial and ethnic minorities, women, and officers with higher levels of education, the evidence does not indicate that such changes are likely to be an effective reform strategy (Fyfe 1981; National Research Council 2004).

The organizational-managerial perspective also differs from sociological perspectives that attempt to explain police behavior in terms of the external environment and situational factors of particular police-citizen encounters (National Research Council 2004). Unlike the organizational-managerial viewpoint, the sociological perspective is inherently pessimistic with regard to policy for the simple reason that the police do not control either their community environment (e.g., levels of poverty or social disorganization) or situational factors (e.g., victim-offender relationships or substance abuse by the citizens they encounter).

The organizational-managerial perspective has important policy implications, because unlike the individual or sociological explanations, it suggests that certain important aspects of police behavior can be controlled through the development and enforcement of meaningful administrative policies. Walker (1993) argues that this principle has been extended to other components of the criminal justice system.

Discretion: The Central Problem in Criminal Justice

The research on police use of deadly force arrived at a critical moment in the history of American criminal justice. Administrators, elected officials, judges, and scholars alike were wrestling with the problem of controlling the discretion of criminal justice officials (Gottfredson and Gottfredson 1988; Walker 1993). The various stakeholders had different policy objectives. Some wanted to reduce racial disparities; others wanted to close alleged loopholes and eliminate leniency toward serious offenders; others simply wanted a more rational and transparent justice system. Fyfe's research made an extremely important contribution to this active policy debate to the extent that he provided empirical evidence of the effectiveness of a particular method of controlling discretion. While it would be overreaching to suggest that he launched or inspired this development, the point is that his contribution goes beyond the relatively specialized area of police use of firearms and is part of a larger public and scholarly concern about the functioning of the entire justice system.

The Discovery of Discretion

The exercise of discretion was a neglected issue in American criminal justice until the late 1950s and early 1960s. The pivotal event was the American Bar Foundation Survey of 1956–57, which conducted the first observational studies of criminal justice officials at work: police, prosecutors, judges, correctional officials, and so on (Walker 1992). The project began with a research agenda of gathering data, most of which involved purely administrative factors (e.g., the number of patrol cars) (American Bar Foundation 1955). The field research quickly shattered the assumptions underlying the original research agenda as the research team made observations with staggering implications. In the case of policing, criminal events involved a relatively small portion of their activities. Most was devoted to what we now call order maintenance and problem solving: public drunkenness, mentally ill people, domestic disturbances, and so on. Moreover, officers exercised broad discretion in handling these situations and, even worse, frequently ignored legal considerations altogether. Officers often ignored clear violations of the law and at other times used the law for purposes unrelated to punishment (e.g., locking up the chronic drunk). The survey generated similar revelations on plea negotiations, sentencing, and other observed parts of the system. Pleas of guilty, for example, were the product of a variety of organizational and sociological factors that generally had little to do with the rule of law, strictly speaking (Goldstein 2005; Newman 1966).[1]

The findings of the bar foundation demolished the traditional view of the administration of criminal justice in which officials operated in a "ministerial" fashion, executing the law as written. In its place, the foundation developed a "law-in-action" perspective focusing on the various sociological, organizational, and personal factors that influence decision-making. The eventual result was a new paradigm for the criminal justice system, one that has served as a guide to teaching, research, and policy-making over the past half century (Walker 1992).

The Legitimacy Crisis of the 1960s

A political and legal crisis over the legitimacy of the justice system spurred recognition of the central problem in criminal justice. The crisis was a product of two separate but overlapping developments. First, the Supreme Court—with an activist, civil libertarian orientation—probed the previously hidden realms of the justice system (Walker 1992, 1998). Second—and most famously and controversially—were Supreme Court decisions related to police search-and-seizure and interrogation practices (*Mapp v. Ohio*, 367 U.S. 643 [1961]; *Miranda v. Arizona*, 1966). The Court also issued a landmark decision on the right to counsel for all accused felons (*Gideon v. Wainwright*, 372 U.S. 335 [1963]), and the NAACP launched its constitutional attack on the death penalty, which culminated in *Furman v. Georgia* in 1972.

The revolution in constitutional law over criminal justice coincided with the escalating national race crisis. A series of urban riots swept the nation's cities from the summer of 1964 through 1968 (National Advisory Commission on Civil Disorders 1968). At the same time, growing concern about the justice system prompted President Lyndon Johnson to create the

President's Crime Commission in 1965, the first national study of the criminal justice system since the Wickersham Commission of 1929–1931 (National Commission on Law Observance and Enforcement 1931; President's Commission on Law Enforcement and Administration of Justice 1967a). Following the fourth summer of urban riots in 1967, Johnson created the Kerner Commission to study the riots and make recommendations for reform (National Advisory Commission on Civil Disorders 1968).

The racial crisis and the Supreme Court decisions inspired other criticisms of the criminal justice system. Constitutional challenges to the death penalty were a direct outgrowth of the civil rights movement (Meltsner 1974), as was the prisoners' rights movement (Walker 1998). A variety of factors, meanwhile, fueled a profound discontent with the indeterminate sentence (see below).

Searching for the Effective Control of Discretion

The various criticisms of the justice system increasingly focused the attention of policymakers and scholars on the problem of discretion and prompted a search for effective means of controlling it. The result was, in effect, a debate over alternative means of control. Although police experts rarely talked with sentencing or prison experts, they were all wrestling with essentially the same set of issues—what can be seen as the central problem in criminal justice.

The traditional approach to controlling discretion—that is, the professional model—relied on the education and training of officials. It sought to emulate established practices in professions of medicine, law, and education. Applied to criminal justice, however, the professional model was clearly inadequate. With respect to the police, recruitment standards, educational levels, and training programs did not begin to meet even the minimal levels expected of a profession (President's Commission on Law Enforcement and Administration of Justice 1967b). With respect to court officials—judges, prosecutors, defense attorneys—the emerging research on the criminal process, derived from the American Bar Foundation Survey, indicated that, despite their professional training as lawyers, their decisions as justice officials were heavily influenced by sociological factors—often with undesirable effects (Newman 1966).

In the 1960s, many liberals and civil libertarians placed their hopes for the control of discretion in the U.S. Supreme Court. The net effect of such decisions as *Mapp, Miranda,* and other decisions was that the

Court wrote a set of administrative rules for the police. In subsequent years, the Court's decisions represented a set of rules for applying the death penalty. Perceptive critics, including some who fully supported the intent and effect of the Court's various rulings, argued that the Supreme Court was an inadequate instrument for governing day-to-day decisions in the justice system (Amsterdam 1973–74, H. Goldstein 1967). The Supreme Court has no mechanism for enforcing its own decisions, there are ample opportunities for evading the intent of decisions (Leo and Thomas 1998; Oaks 1970), and too many decision points are left untouched by Court rulings. In the area of policing, Herman Goldstein (1967) made the strongest argument about the limits of all forms of external control, concluding that internal administrative controls were likely to be the most effective.

Some scholars responded by arguing that police discretion should be abolished, as in Joseph Goldstein's 1960 pathbreaking article. As later parts of this chapter explain, there were similar proposals for abolishing plea bargaining (National Advisory Commission on Criminal Justice Standards and Goals 1973, 46) and for "flat time" sentencing that would eliminate judicial discretion on criminal sentencing (Task Force on Criminal Sentencing 1976). As is explained below, the idea of abolishing discretion never won any serious support, and policy development moved in the direction of administrative controls—the model investigated by Fyfe in his research on deadly force.

Administrative Control of Other Police Actions

Administrative controls over police use of deadly force represented an application of the general principle of administrative rule making. As elaborated by administrative law expert Kenneth Davis (1971, 1975), rule making seeks to control discretion by structuring, confining, and checking its exercise (Walker 1993). The next section explains its application to other critical police actions.

High-Speed Pursuits

The most elaborate application of rule making involves high-speed vehicle pursuits. The process of policy development on this aspect of policing parallels that of deadly force very closely. For decades, vehicle pursuits by police officers were completely ungoverned by any formal policy. Basically, officers pursued fleeing vehicles at their own choosing. Concern about the risks and consequences of pursuits began to arise in the 1970s, primarily because of the costs of litigation over pursuit-related deaths and injuries. The initial studies found that high-speed pursuits were extremely dangerous police actions, resulting in high rates of accidents and injuries and of deaths to police officers, pursued drivers, and innocent bystanders. Subsequent research provided a refined picture of these consequences, and if some of the earliest findings appear to be exaggerated, the risks are nonetheless now recognized as significant and worthy of control (Alpert and Dunham 1990).

Policies for controlling vehicle pursuits have followed the administrative rule-making model already applied to deadly force:

- First, controls take the form of written policies that specify when pursuits are permitted or forbidden; this effort represents structuring discretion in Davis's 1971 model.
- Second, policies allow for the exercise of discretion but guide it by specifying factors that an officer should take into account: the seriousness of the suspected offense and the risks posed by road conditions, time of day, the social environment (e.g., residential neighborhood, school zone, and the like), and so on. The policies ask officers to weigh the benefits of apprehension against the risk of injury or death. This step represents confining discretion in the Davis model.
- Third, officers are required to complete an incident report after each pursuit.
- Fourth, these reports are then reviewed by either a supervisor or a committee to determine whether the officer's actions complied with official policy (Alpert and Dunham 1990).

These latter two steps represent checking discretion in the Davis model.

Evaluations of police vehicle pursuits have found restrictive policies effective in reducing the incidence of accidents, injuries, and deaths. As with Fyfe's research on deadly force policies, moreover, administrative controls limiting pursuits have not been found to have adverse unintended consequences (Alpert and Dunham 1990).

Nonlethal Force

The principle of administrative control over the use of deadly force has been extended to police use of nonlethal force and essentially to all forms of police use of force (Alpert and Dunham 2004). Policies closely parallel the deadly force model: a written policy that specifies when force can and cannot be used; the requirement of a written report of each incident; and an automatic review of each report by either a supervisor or a review committee. In response to considerable community protests, for example, the model is currently being applied to the use of electroconductive devices, popularly known by the trademarked name Tasers (Police Executive Research Forum 2005; see White and Ready, chapter 4).

Research on the impact of administrative controls over nonlethal force is far less developed than in the area of deadly force (National Institute of Justice 1997). There are no studies paralleling Fyfe's original study that would investigate the impact of administrative controls over the use of force. As a result, while a strong consensus of opinion in the law enforcement profession holds that restrictive controls are necessary, no empirical evidence supports the belief that they are in fact effective in limiting the use of force.

Domestic Violence

The women's rights movement in the 1970s identified domestic violence as a serious national problem and directed particular attention to the failure of police to arrest men who assaulted their wives or partners. Research, including data from the ABF survey, found that police officers were less likely to make arrests when the parties involved were married (Black 1980; Sherman 1992).

Lawsuits against the police in Oakland and New York City alleging discrimination against women resulted in settlements that included written departmental policies designed to guide the discretion of officers in handling domestic disputes (Loving 1980). As other departments adopted similar policies and a number of states enacted laws related to police handling of domestic violence, a rough consensus on policy emerged. That consensus included a presumption of arrests when a felonious assault had occurred and standards to guide the arrest discretion in the absence of that presumption. These policies are generally characterized as mandatory arrest or arrest preferred. In many departments, the new domestic violence policies also included the requirement that officers complete a special domestic violence incident report separate from the standard incident or arrest reports.

In short, the 1970s witnessed a revolution in police policy related to domestic violence that closely paralleled the revolution in policy on deadly force. The traditional practice of leaving arrest discretion completely unregulated was rejected and replaced by controls representing the administrative rule-making model that followed policy developments on deadly force and high-speed pursuits. It is worth noting that domestic violence is virtually the only arrest situation where officer discretion is regulated.

Unlike the areas of deadly force and high-speed pursuits but like the area of less lethal force, no empirical studies have investigated the impact of arrest preferred or mandatory arrest policies with respect to domestic violence.

The Control of Discretion in the Courts

The effort to control discretion in the courts took place mainly through the movement to reform bail and the attempt to control plea bargaining.

Two Bail Reform Movements

Bail practices also came under heavy attack during the 1960s. The traditional money bail system in America meant that innumerable poor defendants remained in jail awaiting trial (Goldfarb 1965; Wice 1974). Caleb Foote's pioneering research in the 1950s found that detaining people before trial not only was a punishment in and of itself but also hindered the defendant's ability to prepare his or her case, thereby increasing the probability of both conviction and a sentence of incarceration. Civil libertarians were concerned about violations of the Eighth Amendment right to bail, while social justice liberals focused on the impact of detention on the poor. Unnecessary pretrial detention of many people, meanwhile, imposed significant financial costs on county or city budgets (President's Commission on Law Enforcement 1967a, 326). In addition to the unfairness of the money bail system, reformers also began to question the arbitrariness of bail decisions. Most courts had no standards for guiding judges' decisions about whether to require money bail at all and, if ordered, how much bail to require.

Credit for initiating reform of the American bail system at both the federal and the local level in the 1960s belongs to the Kennedy administration and to Attorney General Robert Kennedy in particular. The attorney general developed an interest in the issue as part of his larger concern about poverty and the plight of poor African American criminal defendants in particular. In New York City, meanwhile, the Vera Foundation developed a pioneering bail release program. An evaluation found that released defendants were no more likely to commit crimes on bail or to fail to appear at trial than were defendants who remained in jail (Botein 1964). Kennedy convened a national conference on bail in Washington, D.C., that involved virtually all the leading experts on the subject and featured an opening address by Chief Justice Earl Warren, who spoke passionately about the need to ensure justice for the poor (National Conference on Bail and Criminal Justice 1965).

Attorney General Kennedy's initiatives led to a wave of bail law reform. The 1966 federal bail reform act rejected the money bail paradigm and replaced it with a presumption of pretrial release, generally through release on recognizance. Meanwhile, states revised their bail laws along the same lines, with most adopting a presumption of release, typically including release on recognizance or 10 percent bail plans (Thomas 1976).

For the purpose of this chapter, the important aspect of the new bail procedures was the development of bail release "schedules" specifying the criteria to be used in determining eligibility for release on recognizance. These criteria were based on the likelihood of a defendant's appearing at trial, as well as employment, family ties, and the like. A defendant would be assigned points for each criterion he or she met, and the resulting point total would be used to determine eligibility for release. Here, as with other emerging controls in the justice system, the goal was to limit and guide the discretion of judges to provide greater consistency in decisions and to reduce, if not eliminate, discrimination based on class, race, or gender (Goldkamp and Gottfredson 1985).

A second bail reform movement occurred in the 1970s, however, with the opposite purpose. The conservative political mood of the nation included increased public fear of crime by repeat offenders. Conservatives argued that too many dangerous offenders were released on bail and that crime could be reduced by detaining them before trial. The result was a new wave of bail laws that sought to detain defendants who posed a risk to public safety. The Supreme Court upheld preventive detention in 1987 (*Salerno v. United States*). Although the policy goals of preventive detention are completely different from those of the first bail reform movement, it is significant that both movements relied on the same technique for controlling bail decisions.

Goldkamp and Gottfredson's 1985 research on bail guidelines in Philadelphia reveals the extent to which those guidelines resemble the administrative rule-making model for controlling discretion. They structure and confine discretion through a decisionmaking grid that embodies two factors: the severity of the immediate offense and factors that indicate dangerousness (e.g., demeanor in the courtroom or threat to victims or witnesses). The guidelines seek to control discretion, moreover, to achieve broad public policy goals: protection of public safety and rationality and equity in bail setting (Goldkamp and Gottfredson 1985).

Goldkamp and Gottfredson found that the bail guidelines in Philadelphia were generally effective in achieving their intended goals. Judges conformed to the guidelines in 76 percent of all cases. The amount of bail set by judges subject to the guidelines was lower than that set by judges in a control group. Particularly important, bail decisions were "markedly more consistent" (Goldkamp and Gottfredson 1985, 198) than those by judges in the control group, indicating an increase in equity in bail decisions.

The Goldkamp and Gottfredson findings support both the theoretical and the policy implications of Fyfe's research on deadly force. They suggest that judicial discretion in bail setting can be controlled by formal written guidelines. This supports the organizational-managerial theory of judicial behavior. It does not support the view that judicial decisionmaking is shaped by individual characteristics, particularly the race or gender of judges. It also casts doubt on the professional model of controlling discretion, which relies on professional training of judges.

Attempts to Control Plea Bargaining

Plea bargaining was another key decision point in the criminal justice system that involved completely unfettered discretion. Even worse, unlike sentencing or parole release, the process of plea negotiations was hidden behind closed doors, with pleas announced in court only after the deal had been done. As with sentencing reform, critics of plea bargaining had different policy perspectives. Liberals saw arbitrariness and possible patterns of discrimination, while conservatives saw excessive leniency. Many critics believed that prosecutors deliberately overcharged defendants so that the ensuing plea negotiations would result in an appropriate charge. Civil libertarians were particularly concerned that the process appeared to coerce defendants into waiving their Fifth Amendment protection against self-incrimination (McDonald 1985). All the various criticisms of plea bargaining highlighted the larger point that prosecutorial discretion, like police discretion, had traditionally been almost completely unchecked (McDonald 1985).

These criticisms finally coalesced in the early 1970s in a movement to abolish plea bargaining altogether (McDonald 1985). The National Advisory Commission on Criminal Justice Standards and Goals (1973) called for the abolition of the practice within five years. Needless to say, this proposal was almost completely ignored. The state of Alaska was the only major jurisdiction to attempt to abolish plea bargaining. Because of the centralized structure of the state's criminal justice system, abolition could be accomplished by administrative order from the attorney general directing prosecutors to "refrain from engaging in plea negotiations with defendants" or to achieve a guilty plea "in return for a particular sentence." In addition, prosecutors should not reduce charges in return for a guilty plea (Rubinstein, Clarke, and White 1980).

The Alaska ban was subject to a formal evaluation funded by the U.S. Justice Department. The evaluation found that, contrary to both proponents and opponents, the ban had little impact on the processing of cases through the system. Most important, the dire predictions of opponents did not come true: the criminal courts did not "collapse," and there was no huge backlog of cases. Most surprising and contrary to the expectations of just about everyone, there was only a small increase in the number of trials (Rubinstein et al. 1980). The surprising findings only confirmed the durability of the process leading to guilty pleas, whether overt or covert. A similar ban in the district court in El Paso, Texas, however, found mixed results of a prosecutor-initiated ban on plea bargaining (Callan 1979; Holmes, Daudistel, and Taggart 1992).

The failure to abolish plea bargaining has led to reforms based on the administrative rule-making model, including written policies to guide the practice. Such guidelines have been developed through a variety of means. Some have been developed at the initiative of prosecutors themselves. In New Jersey, however, the state supreme court, holding that differential plea bargaining practices across counties were unconstitutional, ordered the state attorney general to develop uniform statewide guidelines (New Jersey Attorney General 2004). In Minnesota, state law requires each county attorney to adopt "written guidelines governing . . . plea negotiation policies and practices," which are to include "the circumstances under which plea negotiation agreements are permissible . . . [and] the factors that are considered in making charging decisions and formulating plea agreements" (Minnesota Statutes Sec. 388.051, 2006).

Plea negotiation guidelines consist of several elements. Many local rules prohibit bargaining over charges in the case of certain high-profile crimes, usually sex offenses or those involving use of weapons. This practice represents an attempt to limit the discretion of prosecutors to ensure the appropriate punishment of serious offenders. Some guidelines also involve closer supervision of staff prosecutors, usually in the form of administrative review by the head prosecutor or a deputy head. This practice represents a check on plea bargaining, similar to the review of officer reports on firearms discharges, although in the case of plea bargaining, there is the obvious advantage of being able to review negotiated agreements before they are executed rather than after the fact.

Empirical research on the impact of plea bargaining guidelines has not produced any definitive findings. The traditional view has been that any attempt to limit the discretion of either prosecutors or judges in the processing of criminal cases will simply displace discretion "upstream" or "downstream," in what some experts have characterized as a "hydraulic" or "zero sum" effect. Miethe regards this view as "firmly entrenched" in a skeptical attitude toward reform efforts (1987, 155). In that study of the impact of the Minnesota Sentencing Guidelines, however, Miethe did not find any significant "hydraulic displacement of discretion" onto prosecutors as a result of placing significant limits on the discretion of judges.

The Attack on the Indeterminate Sentence

In their discussion of bail guidelines, Goldkamp and Gottfredson noted the very "clear parallels" between bail reform and concurrent efforts to reform both criminal sentencing and parole decisionmaking (1985, 36–37). Another part of the growing discontent with the American criminal justice system in the 1960s was a profound disillusionment with the indeterminate sentence. Adopted in the great reform period before

World War I, the indeterminate sentence was essentially universal by the 1960s, and as one scholar has pointed out, it was possible to talk about *the* American system of sentencing (Tonry 1988). By the 1990s, though, that was no longer the case, and the indeterminate sentence has been replaced in a number of jurisdictions by some form of determinate sentencing (Bureau of Justice Assistance 1996). Determinate sentencing, whatever its specific form, embodies the principles of administrative rule making (Davis 1971).

The general public, scholars, and civil rights activists alike shared a discontent with indeterminate sentencing, although they had very different perspectives on the exact nature of the problem. Some argued that sentencing decisions were simply arbitrary, with no rhyme, reason, or pattern. One convicted robber went to prison while another was sentenced to parole; one convicted robber was sentenced to 15 years in prison while another was sentenced to only 5 years. Some liberal critics, however, saw not arbitrariness but a pattern of discrimination, particularly with regard to race. Some liberal critics also argued that the original humanitarian goals of the indeterminate sentence—namely, individualizing punishment and providing correctional treatment—had become perverted in practice and actually resulted in longer sentences than were reasonable (American Friends Service Committee 1971; Morris 1974).

Conservative critics, in contrast, believed the unfettered discretion of the indeterminate sentence resulted in a pervasively weak system that failed to punish serious criminal behavior properly. Judges, they argued, improperly placed some serious offenders on probation and gave others inappropriately light sentences, while parole boards released offenders too early (Wilson 1975). This view was the same one that fueled the movement for preventive detention in setting bail.

Despite their very different social policy agendas, both liberal and conservative critics of the indeterminate sentence agreed on one basic point: the system was dishonest. Criminal codes advertised certain punishments for crime (say, up to 50 years for certain offenses), and judges might sentence offenders to, for example, 3 to 10 years in prison; the reality of actual time served, however, was much less. Unfettered discretion, in the words of one critic, had led to a system of "law without order" (Frankel 1972). The emphasis of federal sentencing guidelines on "truth in sentencing" was one response to this view (U.S. Sentencing Commission 1987). Observers generally agreed that the heart of the problem was the nearly unfettered discretion exercised by judges in sentencing and by parole officials in making decisions on parole release. A general consensus emerged that the appropriate solution was to limit judicial discretion to a greater or lesser degree.

The criticisms directed at sentencing decisions were directed at parole decisions with equal force. Liberal critics argued that parole release decisions were either wholly arbitrary or systematically discriminatory. Conservative critics, meanwhile, argued that early release on parole put dangerous criminals back on the street where they would again victimize law-abiding citizens. Studies of parole found that release decisions were shaped in part by institutional needs, particularly the threat of denying early release as a means of controlling the inmate population. Studies also suggested that release criteria corrupted the treatment programs offered within prisons. Inmates participated in group therapy or other activities simply because doing so would help to earn release. As a result, some critics argued, instead of instilling habits of good behavior, treatment programs only cultivated cynicism and manipulative skills (Allen 1959; Morris 1974).

It is important to recognize that, at the time the indeterminate sentence was created, the grant of broad discretion was seen as a great scientific advance, one that would not only reduce crime but also treat criminal offenders in a more humane fashion than in the past—primarily by individualizing sentences. The rise of the indeterminate sentence was fueled in large part by the emergence of the social and behavioral sciences (Walker 1998), precisely the point that aroused many critics. Decisions that were essentially therapeutic in nature were being made without any scientific basis.

By the early 1970s, the various criticisms of the indeterminate sentence converged to create a powerful movement for sentencing reform. Initially, however, this convergence brought together those with very different objectives, and consensus quickly came apart. The initial reform idea was something called "flat-time" sentencing. The idea was that sentencing statutes would provide a fixed sentence for each crime—say, three years for burglary (Task Force on Criminal Sentencing 1976). In effect, this approach involved abolishing judicial discretion altogether. After a brief flurry of interest among scholars, the idea of flat time quickly died, as was the case with respect to plea bargaining. Abolishing sentencing discretion was recognized as impractical, given the variety of factors (seriousness, prior record, and other mitigating or aggravating factors) that enter (or should enter) a sentencing decision. In addition, the political coalition supporting flat time came apart as the conflicting goals of liberals and conservatives became apparent (Law Enforcement Assistance Administration 1978).

The debate over flat-time sentencing, however short, was a very fruitful exercise because it illuminated the practical aspects of sentencing, including the problem of controlling judicial discretion. Out of this debate emerged the idea of structured sentencing or sentencing guidelines (Tonry 1988). For the purpose of this chapter, the relevant point is that structured sentencing embodies the essential features of the administrative controls over police use of deadly force. These elements include a recognition that discretion cannot be abolished, both as a practical and as a philosophical matter; that discretion can be effectively limited by establishing broad parameters of permissible outcomes; and that formal criteria can guide decisionmaking within those parameters.

The sentencing guidelines operating in the federal courts, Minnesota, and an estimated 15 other states embody the same basic models, although they differ with respect to goals and some important details (Bureau of Justice Assistance 1996). A sentencing matrix is employed based on the seriousness of the current offense and the offender's criminal history. Based on these two factors, the matrix indicates the presumptive sentence. The Minnesota Sentencing Guidelines specify certain offenses as presumptively probation and some as presumptively incarceration. Where incarceration is the presumptive sentence, the guidelines specify a range of months within which the judge can set the actual sentence. In addition, judges may depart from the presumptive sentence, either upward or downward in terms of severity, but must justify the decision in a written sentencing memorandum. These elements of the guidelines follow the basic elements of the administrative rule-making model by structuring, confining, and checking judicial discretion.

The impact of sentencing guidelines is mixed, primarily because of significant variations in the purpose and specific requirements of the guidelines in different jurisdictions. On the one hand, the Federal Sentencing Guidelines have the stated purpose of ensuring punishment, and the increase in the population in federal prisons indicates that they have achieved that result. The Minnesota guidelines, on the other hand, have the stated purpose of limiting imprisonment, and they appear to have achieved that result (Bureau of Justice Assistance 1996; Miethe and Moore 1985). The fact that two very different sentencing guidelines systems, with opposite purposes, can both achieve their intended objectives lends powerful support to the idea that judicial sentencing decisions are malleable and subject to control by formal rules.

The evidence on the impact of sentencing guidelines, while mixed, lends further support to the organizational-managerial view of official behavior in criminal justice. Discretionary decisions can be shaped by formal rules and regulations. The evidence does not support individual theories of official behavior, focusing on the race, ethnicity, or gender of decisionmakers.

Conclusion

Jim Fyfe's major contribution to American policing involved his research finding that administrative controls effectively reduced firearms discharges by police officers. Evidence from his work and others indicates that such controls have extremely positive social policy benefits. They greatly reduce the number of unnecessary shootings of unarmed people. They also reduce the racial disparity in persons shot and killed by the police. Moreover, he found that these gains are achieved without adverse unintended consequences. The collateral social benefits of these results include a reduction in incidents that inflame racial tensions and a consequent improvement in police-community relations.

The purpose of this chapter has been to argue that Fyfe's contributions were not confined to policing or even to the limited subject of police use of firearms. His work was directly connected to a broad stream of research and policymaking throughout the American criminal justice system and addressed what I call the central problem in criminal justice: the exercise of discretion by criminal justice officials, the adverse consequences of unfettered discretion, and the movement to institute controls over that discretion. I have argued that this movement embraces other critical incidents involving the police, bail setting, plea negotiations, sentencing (including the death penalty), and parole release decisions.

The trend toward the control of discretion in all these areas of criminal justice involves the model of administrative rule making found in the NYPD shooting policy investigated by Fyfe in his dissertation. That model attempts to limit but not abolish discretion through written guidelines that specify permissible and impermissible actions, factors to be considered in making decisions within those limits, and a process of accountability, including written incident reports and supervisory review of those reports. Jim Fyfe did not initiate or necessarily influence the parallel efforts in the other parts of the justice system. But his work was a very important part of this larger reform movement, and it provided one of the relatively few examples of empirical evidence indicating the effectiveness of the controls in question.

As already suggested in this chapter, Fyfe's original research on police use of deadly force made contributions to criminal justice policy and research that reach far beyond the immediate subject of police use of firearms. With respect to theoretical explanations of police behavior, his work lends support to the organizational-managerial argument that officer behavior is malleable in some important (but not necessarily all) respects. Formal rules can shape officer decisionmaking, and those rules can have positive social policy benefits. This view stands in contrast to theories of police behavior based on the characteristics of individual officers and sociological theories of police-citizen encounters. As suggested in this chapter, the organizational-managerial theory of official behavior can also be applied to other components of the criminal justice system.

In its time, the new work on police use of firearms was also extremely important in helping open police departments to serious research by independent investigators. It demonstrated to police that independent research would not destroy their organizations and that research can actually be an important element of professional development and better policing.

Finally, the research on police use of firearms challenged the widespread cynicism about academic research. Many people, both within and outside the academic world, believe that research has no relevance to the real world of people's lives. Fyfe's work proved that the best research can make a real difference in social policy and can help support change efforts that have a direct impact on the well-being—indeed the lives—of countless people. Thirty years after he defended his dissertation and published his first seminal article, probably thousands of people—most of them African American males—are alive today because of policies that are based on this work. That fact is probably the greatest tribute to the importance of policy-related social science research. It also points the way for future research and policy review aimed at controlling discretion, which itself is the fundamental goal of any effort to achieve accountability.

NOTE

1. Interview with F. Remington, 1988, and Herman Goldstein, July 13, 1988. The files of the American Bar Foundation Survey are housed in the library of the University of Wisconsin Law School. They are a fascinating and incredibly rich source of information on criminal justice agencies in three communities in the 1950s.

REFERENCES

Allen, Francis A. 1959. "Legal Values and the Rehabilitative Ideal." *Journal of Criminal Law and Criminology, and Police Science* 50:226–32.

Alpert, Geoffrey P., and Roger G. Dunham. 1990. *Police Pursuit Driving: Controlling Responses to Emergency Situations.* Westport, CT: Greenwood Press.

———. 2004. *Understanding Police Use of Force.* New York: Cambridge University Press.

American Bar Foundation. 1955. *Plan for a Survey.* Chicago: American Bar Foundation.

American Friends Service Committee. 1971. *Struggle for Justice.* New York: Hill and Wang.

Amsterdam, Anthony G. 1973–74. "Perspectives on the Fourth Amendment." *Minnesota Law Review* 58(3): 349–477.

Black, Donald J. 1980. *The Manners and Customs of the Police.* New York: Academic Press.

Blumstein, Alfred. 1982. "On the Racial Disproportionality of United States' Prison Populations." *Journal of Criminal Law and Criminology* 73(3): 1259–81.

Botein, B. 1964. "Toward Justice for the Poor: The Manhattan Bail Project." *Criminology* 2(1): 14–16.

Bureau of Justice Assistance. 1996. "National Assessment of Structured Sentencing." Washington, DC: Department of Justice.

Callan, Sam W. 1979. "An Experience in Justice without Plea Negotiation." *Law and Society Review* 13(2): 327–47.

Davis, Kenneth C. 1971. *Discretionary Justice: A Preliminary Inquiry.* Urbana: University of Illinois.

———. 1975. *Police Discretion.* St. Paul, MN: West Publishing.

Foote, Caleb. 1954. "Compelling Appearance in Court: Administration of Bail in Philadelphia." *University of Pennsylvania Law Review* 12:1031–79.

Frankel, Marvin E. 1972. *Criminal Sentences: Law without Order.* New York: Hill and Wang.

Fyfe, James J. 1978. "Shots Fired: An Analysis of New York City Police Firearms Discharges." Ph.D. diss., State University of New York at Albany.

———. 1979. "Administrative Interventions on Police Shooting Discretion: An Empirical Examination." *Journal of Criminal Justice* 7 (Winter): 309–24.

———. 1981. "Who Shoots? A Look at Officer Race and Police Shooting." *Journal of Police Science and Administration* 9(4): 367–82.

Geller, William A., and Kevin Karales. 1981. *Split Second Decisions: Shootings of and by Chicago Police.* Chicago: Chicago Law Enforcement Study Group.

Geller, William A., and Michael S. Scott. 1992. *Deadly Force: What We Know*. Washington, DC: Police Executive Research Forum.

Goldfarb, Ronald. 1965. *Ransom: A Critique of the American Bail System*. New York: McGraw-Hill.

Goldkamp, John S., and Michael R. Gottfredson. 1985. *Policy Guidelines for Bail: an Experiment in Court Reform*. Philadelphia: Temple University Press.

Goldstein, Herman. 1967. "Administrative Problems in Controlling the Exercise of Police Authority." *Journal of Criminal Law, Criminology, and Police Science* 58(2): 160–72.

———. 2005. *The Origins of Problem-Oriented Policing: An Interview with Samuel Walker*. DVD. Omaha: Police Professionalism Initiative.

Goldstein, Joseph. 1960. "Police Discretion Not to Invoke the Criminal Process." *Yale Law Journal* 69(4): 543–94.

Gottfredson, Michael R., and Don M. Gottfredson. 1988. *Decision Making in Criminal Justice: Toward the Rational Exercise of Discretion*, 2nd ed. New York: Plenum.

Harris, David A. 2002. *Profiles in Injustice: Why Racial Profiling Cannot Work*. New York: The New Press.

Holmes, Malcolm D., Howard C. Daudistel, and William A. Taggart. 1992. "Plea Bargaining Policy and State District Court Caseload: An Interrupted Time Series Analysis." *Law and Society Review* 26(1): 139.

Kobler, A. 1975. "Figures (and Perhaps Some Facts) on Police Killing of Civilians in the United States, 1965–1969." *Journal of Social Issues* 31(1): 185–91.

Law Enforcement Assistance Administration. 1978. *Determinate Sentencing: Reform or Regression?* Washington, DC: U.S. Department of Justice.

Leo, Richard A., and George C. Thomas, eds. 1998. *The Miranda Debate: Law, Justice, and Policing*. Boston: Northeastern University Press.

Loving, Nancy. 1980. *Responding to Spouse Abuse and Wife Beating: A Guide for Police*. Washington, DC: Police Executive Research Forum.

McDonald, William F. 1985. *Plea Bargaining: Critical Issues and Common Practices*. Washington, DC: U.S. Department of Justice.

Meltsner, Michael. 1974. *Cruel and Unusual: The Supreme Court and Capital Punishment*. New York: William Morrow.

Miethe, Terance D. 1987. "Charging and Plea Bargaining Practices under Determinate Sentencing: An Investigation of the Hydraulic Displacement of Discretion." *Journal of Criminal Law and Criminology* 78(1): 155–76.

Miethe, Terance D., and Charles A. Moore. 1985. "Socioeconomic Disparities under Determinate Sentencing Systems: A Comparison of Preguideline and Postguideline Practices in Minnesota." *Criminology* 23(May): 337–63.

Morris, Norval, ed. 1974. *The Future of Imprisonment*. Chicago: University of Chicago Press.

Murphy, Patrick V., and Thomas G. Plate. 1977. *Commissioner: A View from the Top of American Law Enforcement*. New York: Simon and Schuster.

National Advisory Commission on Civil Disorders. 1968. *Report*. New York: Bantam Books.

National Advisory Commission on Criminal Justice Standards and Goals. 1973. *Courts*. Washington, DC: U.S. Department of Justice.

National Commission on Law Observance and Enforcement. 1931. *Reports*. Washington, DC: Government Printing Office.

National Conference on Bail and Criminal Justice. 1965. *Proceedings*. New York: Arno Press.

———. *1974 Proceedings* [1964, 1965]. New York: Arno Press.

National Institute of Justice. 1997. *Police Use of Force*. Washington, DC: Department of Justice.

National Research Council. 2004. *Fairness and Effectiveness in Policing: The Evidence*. Washington, DC: National Academy Press.

New Jersey Attorney General. 2004. *Brimage Guidelines (2004 Revisions)*. Trenton: Office of the Attorney General.

Newman, Donald J. 1966. "Sociologists and the Administration of Justice." In *Sociologists at Work*, edited by Arthur B. Shostak (177–87). Homewood, IL: Dorsey Press.

Oaks, Dallin H. 1970. "Studying the Exclusionary Rule." *University of Chicago Law Review* 37:665–757.

Paternoster, Raymond. 1991. *Capital Punishment in America*. Lexington, KY: Lexington Books.

Police Executive Research Forum. 2005. *PERF Conducted Energy Device Police and Training Guidelines for Consideration*. Washington, DC: Police Executive Research Forum.

President's Commission on Law Enforcement and Administration of Justice. 1967a. *The Challenge of Crime in a Free Society*. New York: Avon Books.

———. 1967b. *Task Force Report: The Police*. Washington, DC: Government Printing Office.

Reiss, Albert J. Jr. 1971. *The Police and the Public*. New Haven: Yale University Press.

Robin, Gerald D. 1963. "Justifiable Homicide by Police Officers." *Journal of Criminal Law, Criminology, and Police Science* 54(2): 225–31.

Rubinstein, Michael L., Stevens H. Clarke, and Teresa J. White. 1980. *Alaska Bans Plea Bargaining*. Washington, DC: Department of Justice.

Sherman, Lawrence W. 1978. "Restricting the License to Kill—Recent Developments in Police Use of Deadly Force." *Criminal Law Bulletin* 14 (November): 577–83.

———. 1992. *Policing Domestic Violence*. New York: Free Press.

Task Force on Criminal Sentencing. 1976. *Fair and Certain Punishment*. New York: McGraw-Hill.

Thomas, Wayne H. 1976. *Bail Reform in America*. Berkeley: University of California Press.

Tonry, Michael. 1988. "Structuring Sentencing." In *Crime and Justice: A Review of Research*, vol. 10, edited by Michael Tonry and N. Morris. Chicago: University of Chicago Press.

Uelmen, Gerald F. 1973. "Varieties of Police Policy: A Study of Police Policy regarding the Use of Deadly Force in Los Angeles County." *Loyola-LA Law Review* 6:1–61.

U.S. Sentencing Commission. 1987. *Sentencing Guidelines and Policy Statements.* Washington, DC: Sentencing Commission.

Walker, Samuel. 1992. "Origins of the Contemporary Criminal Justice Paradigm: The American Bar Foundation Survey, 1953–1969." *Justice Quarterly* 9 (March): 201–30.

———. 1993. *Taming the System: The Control of Discretion in Criminal Justice, 1950–1990.* New York: Oxford University Press.

———. 1998. *Popular Justice: A History of American Criminal Justice,* 2nd ed. New York: Oxford University Press.

———. 2004. "Science and Politics in Police Research: Reflections on Their Tangled Relationship." *Annals* 593 (May): 137–55.

Walker, Samuel, Cassia Spohn, and Miriam DeLone. 2007. *The Color of Justice: Race, Ethnicity and Crime in America.* Belmont: Wadsworth.

Wice, Paul B. 1974. *Freedom for Sale: A National Study of Pretrial Release.* Lexington, KY: Lexington Books.

Wilson, James Q. 1975. *Thinking about Crime.* New York: Basic Books.

PART I
Accountable to What?

2

Deadly Force Policy and Practice

The Forces of Change

Lorie A. Fridell

Forty years ago, law enforcement agencies had minimal policies on deadly force or none at all. As a result, shooting incidents such as the following described by the American Bar Foundation researchers in the late 1950s took place: "A foot patrolman signaled to a speeding driver to stop. When the driver continued moving, the officer fired his weapon five times" (LaFave 1965, 213). Major cities had policies that merely told officers to "use your best judgment," and in 1974 in Memphis, it was neither a violation of department policy nor of state statute to fatally shoot an unarmed 8th-grader for fleeing from an empty house with $10 and a purse. Today, agency policies place strong limits on police authority to shoot. These policies reflect either the standard set down by the U.S. Supreme Court in 1985 or the even more restrictive "defense-of-life" model.

This chapter explores the changes in policy on deadly force over this 40-year period and the impact of those changes on police practice. A number of forces led agencies to adopt policies that significantly reduced officer discretion to shoot at citizens:

- the general movement within policing to control discretion
- the call for racial justice in the context of the civil rights movement
- the expanded civil liability of municipalities for the actions of their officers

- social science research on the impact of deadly force policy on various outcomes
- the U.S. Supreme Court decision in *Tennessee v. Garner*

In the next section, I review policies on deadly force then and now to show the nature and degree of the change over time. Following that policy chronology, I review some of the forces of change. Finally, I look at how the changes in agency policies across the nation affected both the extent to which police use deadly force and the demographics of their subjects.

Deadly Force Policies: Then and Now

Before the 1950s, agencies paid very little attention to use-of-force issues; training, documentation, and even policy were nonexistent or minimal. Two sources from 1967 provide information about deadly force policies at that time in our history: *The Task Force Report: The Police* produced by the President's Commission on Law Enforcement and Administration of Justice and a review of departmental policies by Samuel Chapman.

The task force commented that "it is surprising and alarming that few police departments provide their officers with careful instruction on the circumstances under which the use of a firearm is permissible" (p. 189). The task force reported the results of a 1961 survey of Michigan police departments, which found that 27 of the 49 had no firearms policies.[1] The task force also described the 1964 survey results on firearms policies received from 45 of the 51 U.S. cities with populations greater than 250,000.[2] While several had "comprehensive policy statements," three had no written policies whatsoever, and the majority had policies that were "quite limited" (p. 189). Regarding the latter group, one policy read in full, "no warning shots." Another advised officers to "exercise the greatest possible caution." Ten agencies had policies that merely instructed officers to "use good judgment."

Chapman (1967) made the observation that some departments might not have written policies but could have "oral policies" instead. He commented, however, that "oral policy too often means no policy at all" (p. 232). He describes some of the written policies produced from his review. In one midsize agency, for example, the policy read, "Never take me out in anger, never put me back in disgrace." Another agency, Chapman tells us, had eight pages of rules and regulations on uniform allowances and specifications and yet had less than one page on firearms. Even this page, however, did not specify the circumstances of firearms use. Others read in their entirety (p. 232–33):

- "Leave the gun in the holster until you intend to use it."
- "It is left to the discretion of each individual officer when and how to shoot."

The most controversial aspect of police shooting powers was the ability to shoot "any fleeing felon." This authority reflected common law, a major basis of American law, and was consistent with the execution of felons under common law up to the nineteenth century (see Binder and Fridell 1984). Some challenges to this law were made as early as the 1920s, but significant changes in policies—including limits to the any-fleeing-felon doctrine—did not occur until the 1960s.

Changes in policies over time can be traced through the model firearms policies advocated by the International Association of Chiefs of Police (IACP) in 1940, 1966, and 1980. In 1940, the IACP statement on this topic was insistent that agencies *have* deadly force policies and that those policies allow deadly force only against people who had committed a "very serious crime," were fleeing from one, or both. Presumably because this "very serious crime" could be interpreted, consistent with common law, as at least a felony, the IACP model would be in accord with the common law "any-fleeing-felon" policy. The 1966 policy was not much more restrictive, still allowing the use of firearms against any person "whom the (officer) has reasonable cause [to believe] has committed a felony," except someone committing a felonious motor vehicle violation. It was not until 1980 that the IACP changed its model in a manner that significantly restricted use of deadly force. The 1980 directive allowed for officer use of deadly force only when under an immediate threat of death or serious bodily injury to the officer or another person. In evaluating the threat when dealing with a fleeing felon, the officer could consider whether the subject "previously demonstrated threat to or wanton disregard for human life" (IACP 1980).

We learn about the flux in police policies during the early and mid-1970s from Uelmen (1973) and Sherman (1978). Uelmen reviewed the policies and shootings of most of the 50 agencies in the Los Angeles metropolitan area in the early 1970s. One finding was that the policies were "surprisingly diverse" (1973, 7). The most important difference at the time was whether the policy allowed for the shooting of any fleeing felon. Sherman (1978) chronicles the adoption of more restrictive firearms policies in New York, Kansas City, and Atlanta in 1972, 1973, and 1976, respectively.

Agencies that did not rid their policies of the shoot-any-fleeing-felon authority by 1985 were required to do so when the U.S. Supreme Court decided *Tennessee v. Garner* (471 U.S. 1 [1985]). Through this case, the U.S. Supreme Court set a minimum standard that reduced the breadth of authority for using deadly force and thus the range of variation across agencies.

Today, virtually every agency has a comprehensive policy on the use of force, including, of course, deadly force. These policies are often lengthy and detailed; they are supplemented with force models (e.g., a continuum of force) and extensive training. Most important, the modern-day policies greatly limit the circumstances under which police can use their firearms. For the most part, these circumstances reflect either a strict defense-of-life policy or the *Garner* standard.[3]

All models, consistent with the general law of self-defense, allow officers to use deadly force to prevent "imminent" or "immediate" death or serious bodily harm to themselves or others. An agency with policy reflecting a defense-of-life model allows deadly force only in these circumstances. In *Garner,* the U.S. Supreme Court held that deadly force can be used not only in self-defense but also when necessary to prevent the escape of certain dangerous felons—specifically those felons who have "committed a crime involving the infliction or threatened infliction of serious physical harm" (*Tennessee v. Garner* 11). Some agencies have policies that reflect this *Garner* standard.

After discussing the various factors that helped produce the changes to police policies on deadly force, I will describe the impact of those policies on the nature and extent of police shootings.

Factors Producing Change in U.S. Deadly Force Policy

Several factors were especially significant in changing policies on police use of deadly force from "use good judgment" to the very detailed, restrictive policies of the present day. These factors were not discrete but rather came together collectively and dynamically to produce change. Below,

I describe these important events or phenomena; they include (1) the general movement within policing to control discretion, (2) the racial minority call for fairness and justice in the context of the civil rights movement, (3) the expanded civil liability of municipalities for the actions of their officers, (4) social science research on the impact of deadly force policy on various outcomes, and (5) the U.S. Supreme Court decision in *Tennessee v. Garner*.

Movement to Control Police Discretion

The changes to policies governing deadly force described above were not isolated but rather were individual aspects of a wider movement in the police profession and other parts of the criminal justice system to impose greater controls on the broad discretion of employees (see Walker's introduction). But first, reports Sam Walker, discretion had to be "discovered." He writes, "Before you can address a problem, you have to know that it exists. Discretion was not always seen as a problem in criminal justice. Prior to the late 1950s, the leading experts in the field barely acknowledged its existence, much less saw it as a central problem" (1993, 6). According to Walker, discretion was brought to light by the American Bar Foundation Survey of the Administration of Criminal Justice. The researchers set out to look into how justice was administered in the United States and determined that "to a large extent, the administration of criminal justice can be characterized as a series of important decisions from the time a crime is committed until the offender is finally released from supervision" (Remington 1956). According to Walker, "What stunned the survey's field research team was the fact that the routine business of criminal justice involved the making of critical decisions without either formal controls or reference to legal norms" (1993, 10).

The move to implement various mechanisms for controlling discretion in policing and other components of the criminal justice system achieved momentum in the 1960s as concerns about increasing crime and the fair administration of justice came to the fore. Sam Walker (introduction, this volume) describes the various mechanisms that were used to control discretion. For instance, a major source of control during this period was the U.S. Supreme Court and its decisions, such as *Miranda v. Arizona* (384 U.S. 436 [1966]) and *Mapp v. Ohio* (367 U.S. 643 [1964]). According to Walker, the Court's rulings prompted reforms beyond the specific holdings in the cases: "They stimulated a broad reform movement within policing that encompasses improvements in recruitment standards, training, and supervision—including measures designed to control discretion" (1993, 19).

Another important source of control was administrative rule making: a model that attempts "to limit but not abolish discretion through written guidelines that specify permissible and impermissible actions, factors to be considered in making decisions within those limits, and a process of accountability, including written incident reports and supervisory review of those reports" (Walker, introduction, 20–21). Thus, within this wider move to reduce discretion, agencies adopted policies to limit the discretion officers have in shooting their firearms at people. According to Walker and Fridell (1992, 108), "The available evidence suggests that the process by which most big city police departments revised their deadly force policies in the pre-Garner years was not unique. Rather, it was part of a larger trend toward greater administrative rule making in police administration."

Calls for Racial Justice

The newly discovered discretion became more important and relevant once concerns about crime and the fair administration of justice became salient. The latter manifested in the form of nationwide calls for equal treatment of racial minorities in the justice system.

As Walker and Fridell report, "Conflict between the police and racial minorities has been one of the most important aspects of American policing since the early 1960s" (1992, 104). Police behavior generally and use-of-force policies and practices in particular were very much a part of the pool of concerns that precipitated the civil rights movement. Police were the symbol of a repressive, unfair, and unjust society; perceptions of the minority communities that police had unjustly or excessively used force precipitated many of the riots in the 1950s and 1960s. According to Walker, "Police shootings have always been a civil rights issue" (1993, 26).

Alpert and Fridell compared the change process across both deadly force policies and pursuit policies. They suggest that the earlier and arguably faster rate and greater degree of change in force policies compared to pursuit policies were due in part to the fact that minorities were, first, disproportionately represented among subjects of police use of deadly force and, second, a cohesive and organized activist group. They claim that "the primary agents of change were the minority communities. These communities had unity and organization which facilitated their challenge of police practices when they perceived that these practices were being misused to their collective detriment" (1992, 148). The innocent victims (or their families) of police pursuits (e.g., the innocent "bystanders" harmed or killed by the person being pursued or the police in pursuit) who would be most likely to challenge pursuit policies were not a cohesive, activist group with salient common characteristics.

The impact of minority challenges to law enforcement policies and practices has been documented at the jurisdictional level by several researchers. For instance, the policy changes in the New York Police Department (NYPD) described below were affected by minority community protests and eventually by riots over a shooting of a black male. According to Sherman (1983), before the shooting, Commissioner Murphy had called on command staff to develop a more restrictive policy with more effective enforcement methods. Broad participation in the development of the policy down to, but not including, line personnel led to buy-in at the upper levels of the department and lack of buy-in on the part of line personnel. The concerns of line personnel stalled policy adoption. Sherman (1983) describes the events that led to its formal adoption:

> When an eleven-year-old black male . . . was shot and killed while fleeing from a stolen car after a police chase . . . , a small riot involving some two hundred persons occurred in Staten Island's black community. . . . The community uproar over the shooting near the end of a very hot summer (which had already witnessed record numbers of homicides) created what the police commissioner later called an opportunity for implementing and deflecting criticism of the new policy.

Sherman also describes the race-related shootings that led to policy changes in Kansas City, Missouri. As was the case in New York, various city leaders in Kansas City carefully reviewed the policy on firearms even before the critical incident occurred that spurred the policy change. In November 1973, a police officer shot and killed an unarmed 15-year-old black male who was fleeing from a house burglary with two stolen watches. No rioting ensued, but both the local and the national NAACP strongly criticized the shooting. Within days, the new chief, Joseph McNamara, announced a more restrictive firearms policy.

Sherman summarizes this force of change that manifested itself across the country: "Massive protests in many black communities after killings of unarmed (black) youths posed a political problem for many mayors, and provided a continuing source of pressure for restraint in shootings at blacks" (1986, 11).

Expanded Civil Liability of Police

Title 42 of the U.S. Code, Section 1983, makes officers civilly liable for committing unconstitutional acts during the course of their law enforcement work. This law, passed in 1871, became more potent in 1961 as a result of a U.S. Supreme Court ruling.[4] Excessive force—a violation of the Fourth Amendment—is encompassed by these provisions. This liability for *individual officers,* however, did not prompt police executives and other jurisdictional officials to review their firearms policies. Rather, it was the expansion of civil liability to *municipalities* that caught their attention.

The expanded civil liability of local governments for the actions of their officers was a major factor in precipitating change in force policies. In *Monell v. Department of Social Services* (436 U.S. 658 [1978]), the U.S. Supreme Court held that a municipality can be held liable if an employee's unconstitutional action was taken as a part of an official policy or custom.[5] According to *Monell,* municipalities could be sued for unreasonable use of force on the part of officers made in line with the agency's written or unwritten policies. According to a subsequent U.S. Supreme Court case (*Pembauer v. City of Cincinnati,* 475 U.S. 469 [1986]), this constitutional violation could be a single decision (rather than a "pattern of decisions").

In an article written in the early years following this important U.S. Supreme Court decision, Fyfe commented on how *Monell*-based lawsuits led to policy changes in agencies that were defendants and how policy improvement was the best way to prevent becoming a defendant. Fyfe reported that some chiefs had "instituted restrictive firearms policies in response to judgments against them for shootings of unarmed fleeing nonviolent felony suspects that were justified by law" (1981, 387). Further, Fyfe noted that "the trend of court decisions is likely to make the institution of a restrictive deadly force policy the best insurance against wrongful death litigation" (1981, 387). McCoy (chapter 6), confirming the heightened law enforcement attention to policies following *Monell,* writes, "After *Monell* opened the door in 1978 to lawsuits alleging police illegality, police chiefs and city managers responded by reviewing their 'customs, policies, and practices' so as to bring them into compliance with the Constitution." McCoy describes civil litigation before and after *Monell,* providing strong support for the contention that civil litigation has been a major factor in police policy reform—particularly that pertaining to use of force.

In addition to its direct impact on policies referenced above, *Monell* had important ramifications for the subsequent *Tennessee v. Garner. Monell* was decided while *Garner* was working its way through the courts. The Federal District Court ruled before the *Monell* decision was handed down and held in favor of the defendants. The Sixth Circuit handed down its decision after *Monell;* it affirmed for all defendants except the City of Memphis. The court remanded the case to determine whether the city was liable in light of the *Monell* decision. The district court ruled that no violation of the Constitution had occurred and therefore that *Monell* was not relevant. The Sixth Circuit reversed, however, saying that Garner's constitutional rights had been violated and that the city was therefore liable for the actions of Officer Hymon. According to Fyfe and Walker, "Absent *Monell,* all the defendants in Garner would have escaped liability, and the case would have resulted in no change in the constitutional status of the fleeing felon rule" (1990, 173).

Social Science Research

Articles in law journals addressed the legal aspects of police deadly force as early as the 1920s (e.g., Boatwright 1929; Bohlen and Shulman 1927), but the first major social science study to receive significant attention was not conducted until the 1960s. Robin (1963) examined justifiable police homicides in Philadelphia from 1950 to 1960. Lamenting the lack of attention paid to this topic by social scientists, Fyfe commented,

> Criminology and criminal justice scholars apparently did not notice that police officers in most states were authorized by law and by their departments to kill people whom they suspected of bicycle theft; with . . . slight exceptions . . . they left us no clues as to how often or in what circumstances the police shot suspected bicycle thieves or anybody else. (1988, 166)

As outlined in Alpert and Fridell (1992) and Binder and Fridell (1984), the number of studies and their sophistication increased during the 1970s and 1980s (e.g., Knoohuizen, Fahey, and Palmer 1972; Kobler 1975; Milton et al. 1977; Geller and Karales 1981; Binder, Scharf, and Galvin 1982). Much of this research merely described the nature and extent of police use of deadly force and the people (officers, subjects) involved and, as such, was not a major force in policy change. Two subsets within this range of research, however, seem to have influenced agency policy: research that looked at whether and how changes in policy affected various key outcomes, such as shooting frequency, crime, and officer safety, and research that highlighted and attempted to explain the disproportionate representation of blacks among the subjects shot by police.

The Impact of Revised Firearms Policies on Enforcement Effectiveness, Crime, and Officer Safety. The various forces described in this chapter were pushing agency executives to reconsider their firearms policies, and yet these chiefs and sheriffs had important questions regarding the potential impact of changed policies on key outcomes, such as felony apprehensions and arrests, crime, and officer safety. At a critical juncture in this movement toward narrower firearms policies, James Fyfe conducted an important study that helped answer those questions.

Fyfe had left the NYPD as a lieutenant to complete his Ph.D. in criminal justice at the State University of New York at Albany. For his dissertation research, he examined various aspects of police use of deadly force by the NYPD; a key component of his study was his assessment of the impact of a new firearms policy.[6]

As described above, the new NYPD policy—known as TOP 237—was developed by command staff at the direction of Commissioner Murphy and implemented in August 1972 after the shooting of a young black male. TOP 237 restricted the circumstances in which officers could use deadly force. Before its adoption, NYPD shootings were constrained by a state statute that allowed deadly force only to defend life or make arrests for various "violent felonies." The new policy specified that firearms would be used only as a last resort "when arresting, preventing, or terminating a felony or for the defense of oneself of another." The policy also forbade warning shots, shots at or from moving vehicles (except in narrow circumstances), and shots that might endanger innocent bystanders. What Fyfe describes as of "equal significance" were the aspects of TOP 237 that increased accountability for the use of firearms. Per TOP 237, the Firearms Discharge Review Board was developed that would, as the title indicates, review and evaluate all firearms discharges.

Fyfe was able to measure the frequency of both firearms discharges and serious assaults against police both before and after the adoption of TOP 237. He also gathered before-and-after information on the number of felony arrests made and the number of criminal homicides. As expected, Fyfe found that shootings decreased following the adoption of the more restrictive policy. Significantly, he also found that the more restrictive policy, which reduced shootings, did not reduce officer safety and that the reduction in shootings could not be explained by reduced criminal activity.

In terms of shooting frequency during the period 1972–75, Fyfe reports a weekly mean of 18.4 officers reporting firearms discharges before TOP 237 compared to 12.9 after the policy adoption, a 30 percent decrease. The nature of the shootings changed in expected ways. The percentage of all shootings to "prevent/terminate crime" (often a fleeing-felon situation) decreased substantially from 21.9 to 4.6 percent. The weekly means of "prevent/terminate crime" discharges fell from 3.9 to 0.6. The percentage of defense-of-life shootings increased from 65.8 to 70.5 percent. Consistent with what Uelmen (1973) had found in southern California (discussed more fully below), even defense-of-life shootings decreased following the policy adoption (falling from 11.9 to 9.0).[7] Subjects killed before and after TOP 237 fell to a weekly mean of 1.0 from 1.6. Injuries to subjects declined as well from a weekly mean of 3.9 before the policy adoption to 2.3 after.

To assess the impact of TOP 237 on officer injury, Fyfe looked at before-and-after data for officer injuries and deaths sustained in the line of duty, including injuries or deaths of officers who were taking police action while technically off duty. Fyfe reports that the weekly means of both injuries and deaths declined after the adoption of TOP 237. Before TOP 237, officers suffered nonfatal injuries at a rate of 4.4 officers per week; after TOP 237, the figure dropped to 2.5. The rate at which officers were killed declined to one every 10 weeks from one every 5 weeks.

Fyfe assessed whether the reduction in the use of firearms by NYPD during his study reference period could have been attributable to reduced criminal activity as measured by felony arrests and criminal homicides. He found that criminal homicides remained relatively constant over the study period and that arrests increased annually. Fyfe produced measures of the relationship between police shootings and felony arrests and between police shootings and criminal homicides. He reports that the annual ratio of arrests to shootings "nearly doubled" over the course of the reference period (moving from 47.62 felony arrests per shooting to 86.88). The ratio of homicides to shootings increased as well: "In 1971," Fyfe notes, "there were 2.33 reported criminal homicides for every police shooting in New York City; this ratio declines slightly (to 2.11) in 1972, then increases considerably over 1973 and 1974 to a high of 3.67 in 1975" (1979, 313). Fyfe summarizes his results as follows:

> In the most simple terms . . . the New York City experience indicates that considerable reductions in police shooting and both officer and citizen injury and death are associated with the establishment of clearly delineated guidelines and procedures for the review of officer shooting discretion. (1979, 322)

Fyfe's dissertation research was conducted at a critical time for the law enforcement profession. The profession was reducing officer discretion in many realms, racial minorities were demanding changed force policies, and municipalities faced increased liability for the actions of their officers. Even with this pressure, however, some executives wondered about the potential negative impacts of more restrictive shooting policies. Would crime go up? Would felony arrests go down? Would officers be in more danger? Fyfe's results provided important answers to those questions—results that, along with the other change factors, had significant effects on deadly force policies and practices in the United States.

The Racial Aspects of Shootings. As noted above, that minorities were disproportionately the subjects of police shootings was a major cause for concern during the civil rights era (and, indeed, to this day). The early study by Robin (1963) found that blacks predominate among people killed by police. Virtually all research projects confirmed disproportionate black victimization relative to representation in the residential population of the jurisdiction, including studies conducted by Harding and Fahey (1973) in Chicago; Milton et al. (1977) in seven cities; Fyfe (1979) in New York City; Meyer (1980) in Los Angeles; Blumberg (1983) in Atlanta and Kansas City; and Binder et al. (1982) in Birmingham, Miami, Newark, and Oakland. Additional research attempted to determine whether this disparity was due to police bias or racism or to the disproportionate involvement of blacks in violent crime. Thus, many of the same researchers mentioned above compared the proportion of blacks killed by police to the proportion of blacks arrested for felonies or violent crime. Harding and Fahey, for example, reported that 75 percent of the people killed by police in Chicago over a two-year period were black. The percentage of blacks in the residential population was 33; the percentage of blacks among people arrested for murder, robbery, aggravated assault, felony weapons offense, and felonious burglary was 73. Because arrest figures might also reflect police racism, some studies looked instead at the race of suspects as reported by victims (see e.g., Goldkamp 1976 and Blumberg 1983).

Another method used to disentangle the potential factors of black criminality and police racism in explaining disproportionate black victimization was to look at the features of incidents. Blumberg took this approach, reasoning that if police do have, as Takagi claimed, "one trigger finger for whites and another for blacks" (1974, 30), then we would find blacks being shot under conditions of less threat. In his research in Atlanta and Kansas City, he found no difference in threat to officers in black and white shootings (as measured by subject weapon and assaults on officers) or in the level of response by police (e.g., number of officers who fired their weapons, number of bullets fired, or whether the subject was injured or killed). Blumberg goes on to say that these "findings which indicate that blacks are shot and/or killed under circumstances that are similar to those involving white citizens must be seen as suggestive of the probability that the police in a particular city are no more likely to shoot blacks than they are to shoot whites in a given situation" (1983, 263–64). Similar findings were reported by Geller and Karales (1981) and Binder et al. (1982).

Meyer (1980), too, compared threat levels across demographic groups of subjects against whom deadly force was used, but he found differences in shooting circumstances across race. He used data on the shootings by Los Angeles Police Department officers during 1974 through 1979, including information on the subjects' race and ethnicity and on their actions before the police shot them. Subject actions were divided into seven categories based on the weapon (if any) they possessed and their use of it. Regarding the latter, Meyer distinguished between, for instance, subjects who displayed a weapon and subjects who used the weapon against the officer. He reports that a greater percentage of black opponents (28 percent), compared to white opponents (20 percent), were unarmed when shot by the police.

Fyfe (1982) sought to explain the differential findings across various jurisdictions. Why did some researchers find that shooting circumstances were similar across racial groups and others find that the circumstances were different? He conjectured that jurisdictions with policies that gave officers broader discretion to shoot might produce greater and unjustified racial disparities. Those agencies that gave officers broad powers to shoot at citizens, he noted, for the most part had not volunteered to be studied by researchers. The Memphis Police Department had a broad (and vague) firearms policy in place during the period 1969–74, the period that corresponded to the shooting data that the agency was forced to turn over as part of a lawsuit.

Fyfe developed a typology of shootings that—like the categorization scheme used by Meyer—was based on the immediate hazard to officers (a "hazard-based typology") and applied it to the Memphis data to see if whites and blacks were shot under different threat circumstances. As seen in figure 2.1, the threat circumstances for white and black subjects were quite different. Over 60 percent (62.5 percent) of the white subjects shot and killed by Memphis police were assaultive and armed compared to under 30 percent (26.9 percent) of the black subjects. Conversely, 50 percent of the black subjects who were killed by police were non-

Figure 2.1. Threat Circumstances in Which Black and White Subjects Were Killed by Memphis Police, 1969–74

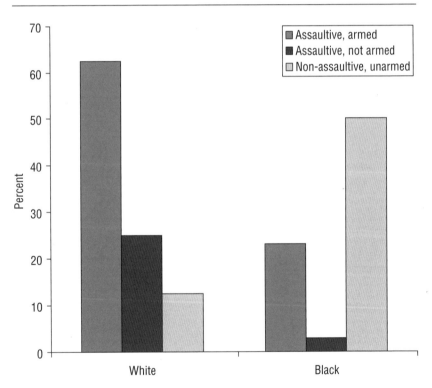

Source: Fyfe (1982)

Note: N = 255

assaultive and unarmed; the corresponding figure for white subjects was 12.5 percent.

A potent finding came from his calculation of the rates (per 100,000 population) at which Memphis police shot black and white unarmed, nonassaultive suspects: the death rate of unarmed and nonassaultive blacks from police shootings was "18 times higher than the comparable white rate" (Fyfe 1982, 720).[8]

Fyfe's study results were different from those found in most other cities (Los Angeles being the exception) and appeared to confirm his belief that those findings were based on the fact that most of the jurisdictions studied had restrictive policies. He showed that the results from those cities could not necessarily be generalized to cities that did not have restrictive policies.

The social science research that assessed the impact of restrictive policies on crime, enforcement, and officer safety and on racial disparities was influential in the context of the national discussion of police firearms policies. Policymakers learned from Fyfe's dissertation research that a restrictive policy with a meaningful enforcement mechanism could reduce police shootings without jeopardizing officer safety or reducing police effectiveness. Researchers showed these policymakers that racial disparities in shootings were not always explained by the degree of threat and that broad, high-discretion policies were more likely to produce unjustified disparities. These important findings came at a time when agency policies were in flux and chiefs were making key decisions.

Tennessee v. Garner

By the mid-1980s, many departments, particularly the largest ones, had modified their policies to reduce significantly the circumstances in which officers could use their firearms against citizens. A number of agencies, however, still allowed for the use of deadly force against "any fleeing felon," including the Memphis Police Department.

A call came into this agency on October 3, 1974, from a Memphis resident reporting a break-in at her next-door neighbor's home. Officers Hymon and Wright responded to this "prowler inside call" at 10:45 p.m. Officer Hymon was heading to the backyard when he heard a door slam and saw someone running across the yard. The officer shined his flashlight on the fleeing Edward Garner, who stopped briefly at the six-foot-high fence. Hymon saw Garner's face and hands and was "reasonably sure" that Garner was unarmed (*Tennessee v. Garner et al.*, 1). He yelled, "Police, halt" to this 5' 4" male and ran toward him as Garner started over the fence. Believing that if Garner made it over the fence, he would elude capture, the officer shot him fatally in the back of the head. Garner, an 8th grader, had taken $10 and a purse from the house.

Garner's father brought suit alleging that his son's constitutional rights had been violated. He lost at the district court level but won at the Court of Appeals for the Sixth Circuit.[9] This court held that the use of deadly force was a "seizure" governed by the reasonableness standard of the Fourth Amendment. The any-fleeing-felon law as applied to these facts did not pass the reasonableness test (*Garner v. Memphis P.D.*, 710 F. 2d 240 [1983]). The state of Tennessee appealed to the U.S. Supreme Court.

The U.S. Supreme Court affirmed the holding of the Sixth Circuit and held the any-fleeing-felon rule unconstitutional. The Court ruled that deadly force could be used by police if necessary to prevent an escape when "the officer has probable cause to believe that the suspect poses a significant threat of death or serious physical injury to the officer or others" (*Garner v. Memphis P.D.*, 1). The Supreme Court had been influenced in part by the social science research as well as by the fact that many agencies had already adopted more restrictive policies. The Court explained that it would not declare a police practice "unreasonable" if "doing so would severely hamper law enforcement" (*Garner v. Memphis P.D.*, 19). Here the Court acknowledged the research findings that showed the adoption of restrictive shooting policies did not hamper crime fighting nor reduce officer safety. The Court noted that if broad powers to shoot at fleeing felons were essential to effective policing, then police departments would not be moving away from such policies—but they already were.

The six-three decision by the Court is characterized most poignantly with the following quotation from the majority opinion:

> It is not better that all felony suspects die than that they escape. Where the suspect poses no immediate threat to others, the harm resulting from failing to apprehend him does not justify the use of deadly force to do so. It is no doubt unfortunate when a suspect who is in sight escapes, but the fact that the police arrive a little late or are a little slower afoot does not always justify killing the suspect. (p. 11)

When the *Garner* decision was announced, the media conveyed to its audience that this decision would have a major impact on agency policies around the nation. In fact, *Garner* had an important *but limited* impact on agency policies. While it is true that Garner struck down 21 state statutes, by then many police agencies had already restricted their use of deadly force beyond that required in their statutes. As indicated in the decision itself, many agencies had already abandoned the any-fleeing-felon rule even before the U.S. Supreme Court required them to do so.

Walker and Fridell (1992) assessed the impact of the *Garner* decision on the policies of the police departments in the 100 most populous municipalities in the United States. Of the 96 agencies that responded to the survey, two-thirds (69.8 percent) reported that they did not have to revise their deadly force policies following the U.S. Supreme Court decision. These agencies had already adopted policies that were at least as restrictive, if not more so, as the *Garner* standard. The remaining third reported that *Garner* required a change to their policies. Based on other surveys conducted before *Garner,* however, Walker and Fridell suggested that even this group of agencies likely did not have to make major changes to policy. Few of these would have had the any-fleeing-felon rule in place at the time of *Garner.* Instead, it is likely that these agencies had to transform forcible felony statutes into *Garner*-approved provisions.[10]

The study by Walker and Fridell focused on the agencies in the largest municipalities, as they were responsible for the vast majority of police shootings nationwide. The greatest impact of *Garner,* suggested Fyfe and Walker (1990), was on small and medium departments.

The Impact of Restrictive Policies on Shootings by Police. Research starting in the early 1970s has shown that reducing discretion within firearms policies affects shooting rates and the aggregate racial makeup of victims. To produce this information, researchers compared agencies with more restrictive and less restrictive policies or compared the same agencies before and after policy changes.

Uelmen's review of firearms policies and practice in the Los Angeles area was mentioned above in the context of the changes in policies starting in the 1960s. Uelmen compared the number and nature of shooting incidents across agencies with any-fleeing-felon policies to agencies with more restrictive policies. As expected, he found that agencies with restrictive policies reported fewer incidents involving firearms discharges. Interestingly, officers in agencies with more restrictive policies not only shot less frequently at fleeing felons, but "they also [shot] less frequently in asserted self-defense" (1973, 49).

Fyfe, as described above, found fewer police shootings following the adoption by NYPD of a more restrictive firearms police. Sherman (1983) found the same results in Kansas City, Missouri, and Atlanta. Thus, for instance, in Atlanta he found that the quarterly average number of incidents in which a citizen was shot fell from 7.6 before a policy change to 2.7 after it.[11]

Sherman and Cohn surveyed police departments that served populations of 250,000 or more to determine the number of citizens killed by police in those agencies for 1970 through 1984. As indicated in figure 2.2, between 1971 and 1984 the number of people killed by police decreased by 51 percent. Reduced crime could not explain the reduction, as homicide and violence did not decline in these cities during the period. Sherman and Cohn suggested that the reduction in shootings over this period was caused, "at least in part, by explicit changes in police policy" (1986, 13). They pointed to some of the factors already described in this chapter (civil liability and issues of racial justice) and cited as well the "training and discipline" that accompanied policy changes. They cumulative effect, they explained, was a change in the culture of policing: "The combined pressures of black protest, restrictive policies, training and discipline, and civil litigation may have created a new perspective on shootings within the police culture" (15).

Tennebaum (1994) specifically sought to investigate the impact of *Tennessee v. Garner* on officer shootings at citizens. For this purpose, he

Figure 2.2. Citizens Killed by Police in Large Cities, 1971–84

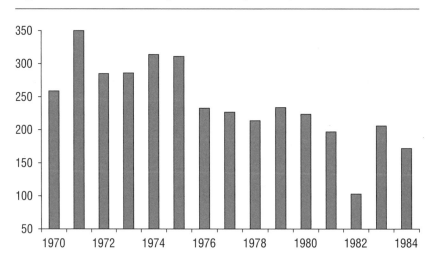

Source: Sherman and Cohn (1986)

Note: Data from 50 cities with populations of 250,000 or more.

used interrupted time series and the Uniform Crime Reports Supplemental Homicide Reports for the period 1976–88 for all UCR-submitting agencies. He reports that, following *Garner*, police homicides decreased by 16 percent or approximately 60 shootings per year.

For the Urban League, Mendez (1983) examined the race of shooting subjects during the time when policies were changing and use of deadly force was declining. In 1971, the ratio of black to white subjects was 7 to 1; by 1979, after many departments had changed their policies and practices, the ratio was 2.8 to 1. Mendez reports that the rate of white citizens killed per 100,000 remained basically unchanged during the period under study. The changed ratio was due to the decrease in the shooting by police of black citizens. Walker summarized the research:

> Administrative rules have successfully limited police shooting discretion, with positive results in terms of social policy. Fewer people are being shot and killed, racial disparities in shootings have been reduced, and police officers are in no greater danger because of these restrictions. (1993, 32)

Conclusion

Common law defined deadly force policy in this country for many years. According to this legal doctrine, not only could police shoot someone in self-defense, but also they could shoot any person fleeing from a crime defined in statute as a felony. Mikell asked compelling questions as they relate to an auto thief:

> May I ask what we are killing [the suspect] for when he steals an automobile and runs off with it? Are we killing him for stealing the automobile? . . . It cannot be . . . that we allow the officer to kill him because he stole the automobile, because the statute provides only three years in the penitentiary for that. Is it then . . . for fleeing that we kill him? Fleeing from arrest . . . is punishable by a light penalty, a penalty much less than that for stealing the automobile. If we are not killing him for stealing the automobile and not killing him for fleeing, what are we killing him for? (1931, cited in Fyfe and Walker 1990)

Law enforcement policies providing no or only meaningless guidance to officers began being replaced in the 1960s, with considerable policy revisions occurring during the 1970s. A minimal standard was set by the U.S. Supreme Court in 1985, and today all agency policies reflect a strict defense-of-life policy or the *Garner* standard.

A number of factors were key to this change process and include, as discussed in this chapter, the more general movement to reduce officer discretion, the call by racial minorities for more restrictive policies on deadly force, increased liability on the part of municipalities for the actions of their officers, results from social science research, and the U.S. Supreme Court decision in *Tennessee v. Garner.* As observed by Walker and Fridell, "Changes in police policy do not result from any single factor; many forces are at work simultaneously and they interact with each other in a dynamic and complex fashion" (1992, 106; see also Walker 1986). There was a complex and dynamic interaction among factors during this change. Thus, for instance, the more general movement to reduce discretion and the call for racial justice led to more restrictive policies, and those more restrictive policies helped persuade the Court in *Tennessee v. Garner.* The *Monell* decision increasing municipal liability was a change in its own right, but it was also key to the ultimate success of the *Garner* case. The municipal executives who may have been *inclined* toward policy change due to the race and liability issues may have ultimately been persuaded to act by the social science research that reported positive effects of reducing officer discretion and negative effects (racial disparity) of allowing officers broad discretion. The U.S. Supreme Court, too, was influenced by the research findings.

It seems obvious to us today that there are no valid reasons to shoot a fleeing felon who poses no physical danger to others, and yet it took many years and varied forces of change before reason took hold. That we no longer kill the auto thief described earlier is attributable to the factors just mentioned as well as to the general movement within policing to control discretion. Dynamically, these forces of change led to revisions in policy and the culture of policing that, in turn, led to a significant reduction in the number of people killed by police across the nation and, in particular, to a reduction in the number of racial minorities killed by police authorities. The conditions under which these many factors combined to challenge the conventional wisdom that people fleeing from the scene of crimes should be shot may present a lesson for police reformers who wish to challenge conventional wisdom about other subjects in the future.

NOTES

1. Citing Chapman and Crockett (1963).

2. Citing Cincinnati P.D. (1964).

3. Brave and Peters (1992) argue that there are six different deadly force policy models in use in the United States.

4. This case, *Monroe v. Pape* (365 U.S. 167 [1961]), is described by McCoy in chapter 6.

5. As explained by McCoy, in chapter 6, the U.S. Supreme Court held in this case that a local government was a "person" according to Section 1983 of the U.S. Code.

6. The evaluation of the NYPD changes in policy and accountability was only one component of Fyfe's 560-page dissertation. He produced a tremendous amount of information regarding officers who shoot and the nature of shootings, and he measured the impact of a change in drug enforcement policy on firearms discharges.

7. When Fyfe reassessed the changes in shootings with warning shots excluded, the before-and-after differences shrank but were still significant.

8. The rate of police killings of black unarmed, nonassaultive subjects is 5.4 per 100,000 black residents in the Memphis population. The rate for whites is 0.3.

9. I refer here to the rehearing at the Sixth Circuit Court of Appeals following *Monell*.

10. Forcible felony statutes and policies did not allow the use of deadly force against any fleeing felon but rather only against certain, primarily violent, fleeing felons.

11. There were not a sufficient number of incidents to test for the significance of change in Kansas City.

REFERENCES

Alpert, Geoff, and Lorie A. Fridell. 1992. *Police Vehicles and Firearms: Instruments of Deadly Force.* Prospect Heights, IL: Waveland Press.

Binder, Arnold, and Lorie A. Fridell. 1984. "Lethal Force as a Police Response." *Criminal Justice Abstracts* 16:250–80.

Binder, Arnold, Peter Scharf, and Raymond Galvin. 1982. "Use of Deadly Force by Police Officers." Washington, DC: National Institute of Justice.

Blumberg, Mark. 1983. "The Use of Firearms by Police Officers: The Impact of Individuals, Communities, and Race." Ph.D. diss., State University of New York at Albany.

Boatwright, H. Lee. 1929. "Legalized Murder of a Fleeing Felon." *Virginia Law Review* 15: 582–86.

Bohlen, Francis H., and Harry Shulman. 1927. "Arrest with and without a Warrant." *University of Pennsylvania Law Review* 75:485–504.

Brave, Michael A., and John G. Peters. 1992. "What's Your Use-of-Deadly-Force Standard?" Liability Assessment and Awareness International, Inc.

Chapman, Samuel G. 1967. "Police Policy on the Use of Firearms." In *Readings on Police Use of Deadly Force,* edited by James J. Fyfe (224–57). Washington, DC: Police Foundation.

Chapman, Samuel G., and Thompson S. Crockett. 1963. "Gunsight Dilemma: Police Firearms Policy." *Police* (May–June): 54. Quoted in President's Commission on Law Enforcement and Administration of Justice, 1967.

Cincinnati P. D. 1964. "Police Regulations Governing Use of Firearms Survey." Quoted in President's Commission on Law Enforcement and Administration of Justice, 1967.

Fyfe, James J. 1979. "Administrative Interventions on Police Shooting Discretion: An Empirical Examination." *Journal of Criminal Justice* 7:309–23.

———. 1981. "Observations on Police Deadly Force." *Crime and Delinquency* July 27(3): 376–89.

———. 1982. "Blind Justice: Police Shootings in Memphis." *Journal of Criminal Law and Criminology* 83:707–22.

———. 1988. "Police Use of Deadly Force: Research and Reform." *Justice Quarterly* 5:164–205.

Fyfe, James J., and J. T. Walker. 1990. "*Garner* plus Five Years: An Examination of Supreme court Intervention into Police Discretion and Legislative Prerogatives." *American Journal of Criminal Justice* 14 (2): 167–88.

Gain, Charles. 1971. "Discharge of Firearms Policy: Effecting Justice through Administrative Regulation—A Position Paper." Oakland Police.

Geller, William A., and Kevin J. Karales. 1981. *Split-Second Decisions: Shootings of and by Chicago Police.* Chicago: Chicago Law Enforcement Study Group.

Goldkamp, John. 1976. "Minorities as Victims of Police Shootings: Interpretations of Racial Disproportionality and Police Use of Deadly Force." *The Justice System: A Management Review* 2:169–83.

Griswold, David B. 1985. "Controlling the Police Use of Deadly Force: Exploring the Alternatives." *American Journal of Police* 4:93–109.

Harding, Richard W., and Richard P. Fahey. 1973. "Killings by Chicago Police, 1969–1970: An Empirical Study." *Southern California Law Review* 46(2): 284–315.

International Association of Chiefs of Police. 1980. "Model Policy: Use of Force." Alexandria, VA: International Association of Chiefs of Police.

Knoohuizen, Ralph, Richard P. Fahey, and Deborah H. Palmer. 1972. *Police and Their Use of Fatal Force in Chicago.* Chicago: Chicago Law Enforcement Study Group.

Kobler, Arthur L. 1975. "Figures (and Perhaps Some Facts) on Police Killing of Civilians in the United States, 1965–1969." *Journal of Social Issues* 31:185–91.

LaFave, Wayne R. 1965. *The Decision to Take a Suspect into Custody.* Boston: Little Brown.

Mendez, Garry A., Jr. 1983. *The Role of Race and Ethnicity in the Incidence of Police Use of Deadly Force.* New York: National Urban League.

Meyer, Marshall W. 1980. "Police Shootings at Minorities: The Case of Los Angeles." *Annals of the American Academy of Political and Social Sciences* 452:98–110.

Mikell, William E. 1931. Statement made during the proceedings of the American Law Institute. *ALI Proceedings* 9:186–87. Quoted in Fyfe, 1988.

Milton, Catherine H., Jeanne W. Halleck, James Lardner, and Gary L. Abrecht. 1977. *Police Use of Deadly Force.* Washington, DC: The Police Foundation.

National Advisory Board on Civil Disorders. 1968. *Report.* New York: Bantam Books.

Police Foundation. 1983. Amicus brief submitted to the U.S. Supreme Court in the case of *Tennessee v. Garner.*

President's Commission on Law Enforcement and Administration of Justice. 1967. *Task Force Report: The Police.* Washington, DC: U.S. Government Printing Office.

Remington, Frank. 1956. Memorandum to field staff, September 24, American Bar Foundation papers. Cited in Walker, 1993.

Robin, Gerald D. 1963. "Justifiable Homicide by Police Officers." *Journal of Criminal Law, Criminology, and Police Science* 54:225–31.

Sherman, Lawrence. 1978. "Restricting the License to Kill: Recent Developments in Police Use of Deadly Force." *Criminal Law Bulletin* 14(6): 577–83.

———. 1983. "Reducing Police Gun Use: Critical Events, Administrative Policy and Organizational Change." In *The Management and Control of Police Organizations,* edited by Maurice Punch (98–125). Cambridge, MA: MIT Press.

Sherman, Lawrence, and Ellen G. Cohn. 1986. *Citizens Killed by Big City Police, 1970–1984.* Washington, DC: Crime Control Institute.

Takagi, Paul. 1974. "A Garrison State in a 'Democratic' Society." *Crime and Social Justice: A Journal of Radical Criminology* 5 (Spring–Summer): 27–33.

Tennebaum, Abraham. 1994. "The Influence of the 'Garner' Decision on Police Use of Deadly Force." *Journal of Criminal Law and Criminology* 85(1): 241–60.

Tennessee Advisory Committee to the U.S. Committee on Civil Rights. 1978. *Civil Crisis—Civic Challenge: Police Community Relations in Memphis.* Quoted in Fyfe, 1982b.

Uelmen, Gerald F. 1973. "Varieties of Public Policy: A Study of Policy regarding the Use of Deadly Force in Los Angeles County." *University of Loyola at Los Angeles Law Review* 6:1–65.

Walker, Samuel. 1986. "The Dynamics of Change in American Criminal Justice: Towards an Understanding of 'Reform.' " In *European or North-American Juvenile Justice Systems—Aspects and Tendencies,* edited by J. Kerner et al. (155–77). Munich: Schriftenreihe der Deutschen Vereinigung fur Jugendgerichte und Jugendgerichtschilfen.

———. 1993. *Taming the System: The Control of Discretion in Criminal Justice, 1950–1990.* New York: Oxford University Press.

Walker, Samuel, and Lorie Fridell. 1992. "Forces of Change in Police Policy: The Impact of *Tennessee v. Garner." American Journal of Police* 11(3): 97–112.

PART II
The Use of Nondeadly Force

3

Police Use of Nondeadly Force

From Determining Appropriateness to Assessing the Impact of Policy

William Terrill

I n 1985, the U.S. Supreme Court set a defense-of-life standard for the use of deadly force by police officers. The resulting decision—stemming from *Tennessee v. Garner,* 471 U.S. 1 (1985)—prohibited police officers from using deadly force on fleeing felons, with only narrow exceptions made for threats that pose substantial risk to others should the police fail to seize a suspected offender. This landmark case was anticlimactic in many larger departments, since similar provisions were already in place. Nonetheless, those departments that still had some version of a fleeing-felon rule needed to alter their policies to conform to the new legal standard.

Four years after the *Garner* case, the Supreme Court attempted to clarify the standard for nondeadly force in *Graham v. Connor,* 490 U.S. 386 (1989).[1] The court ruled that the use of force by police officers must be judged under a standard of "objective reasonableness." Of course, applying this standard in either deadly or nondeadly force situations still requires some interpretation. In terms of deadly force, however, at least one key element offers guidance: defense of life. No such centering mechanism is in place for judging nondeadly force cases. In effect, there was, and is, no applicable standard for these cases that is equal to the defense-of-life rule for use of deadly force. Consequently, the effect of *Graham v. Connor,* in contrast to *Tennessee v. Garner,* has been less evident in terms of policy application.

This chapter begins with a discussion at the heart of all use-of-force decisions: determining appropriate force and the applicable standard that should be applied. The chapter then looks at the force continuum and how that mechanism may serve as a guidepost in the'quest to remove some of the vagueness surrounding the legality of objective reasonableness. The chapter concludes with a call for a better understanding of nondeadly force administrative policies. Fyfe's early work (1978, 1979, 1980, 1981, 1982) demonstrated the power of restrictive deadly force policies and stimulated a monumental shift in policy development that had national implications with local consequences. The effect of varying types of *nondeadly* force policies on police behavior, however, is still an unaddressed empirical question.

Determining Appropriate Force within the Context of Varying Standards

The author's initial experience with police use of force occurred while he was serving as a military police officer in the early 1980s. Although academy instructors taught much about how to use various types of force (e.g., how to strike a suspect with a flashlight, use mace, and fire a handgun), little guidance was offered on when such tactics should be used. Instructors simply stated "follow the policy," which indicated little more than "use the necessary force required." It quickly became apparent that not all officers were adequately prepared to determine just how much force was necessary. In particular, it often seemed—at least to those applying the force—that more force was generally better than less force.

Fast forward to the early 1990s, when the author had his first experience as an academic working on a project involving allegations of excessive force. While examining a large number of force reports looking for varying types of patterns, he found that many police officers did not appear to be sufficiently skilled at determining just how much force was necessary. Whether one is applying force as a practitioner in the field or whether one is studying it as an academic or a supervisor, it became apparent that assessing others' application of force post hoc raises the same *issue:* how to determine the appropriate amount of force in any given situation. Moreover, the *challenge* is the same: devising a measure by which appropriate force can be determined (i.e., the measuring stick). This challenge prompts the question, What framework would allow us to determine appropriateness?

Legal scholars, researchers, police administrators, academy trainers, patrol officers, and citizens all have insight into what constitutes the appropriate use of force in a given incident. Legal scholars tend to concentrate on the concept of reasonableness. This orientation naturally fits with the direction set by the high court and requirements in Fourth Amendment case law that police officers' actions be judged from a standard of objective reasonableness. Police administrators and trainers often emphasize procedural application. Here, the nuts and bolts of force application become a driving factor. For good reasons, patrol officers tend to focus primarily on neutralizing the immediate threat as effectively as possible, especially in relation to officer safety. Finally, the public (lay persons and juries) may emphasize the importance of what a suspect did before engaging the police in a forceful encounter or the extent to which the incident shocks the conscience.

Essentially, the focal points on which to assess the appropriateness of force vary. There is a legal standard, which is vague at best; there are professional standards, which can vary substantially; and there are public standards, which can vary even more. Unfortunately, all leave a degree of dissatisfaction.

From an academic standpoint, the concept of differing standards by which to assess the appropriateness of the use of force may be somewhat exciting, since variation offers a researcher something to study and attempt to explain. However, it can also be quite unsatisfying because of the degree of subjectivity involved: wide variation opens the door for the infusion of opinion. Invariably, when a high-profile force incident occurs, some pundits and news commentators will argue that appropriate force was used, and others will declare the opposite. Interestingly, while this divergence of opinion often occurs in panelists with differing professional orientations (e.g., a police trainer and a college professor), it also occurs within categories (e.g., trainer versus trainer or professor versus professor). When the issue arises in the courtroom and so-called experts are brought in to help determine appropriate force, Alpert and Smith aptly state that "the objectivity assessment for the police use of force has become a 'guided tour' with a different guide for each tour" (1994, 486).

The question thus becomes, If we cannot agree on the appropriateness or inappropriateness of more serious or egregious types of nondeadly force incidents, how might we generate consensus for those more common types of force applications (the macing of a suspect, for instance)? Incidents without baton wielding, Tasering, or all-out physical beating? And incidents that may not be shocking nor repulsive on the face of it but that nonetheless fall under the category of what Fyfe (1997) refers to as "unnecessary force" (i.e., force used by well-meaning officers ill equipped to handle various incidents)? In short, the nondeadly force standard (objective reasonableness) is much more elastic than the deadly force standard (defense of life) and thereby illustrates the need to explore ways to assess appropriateness better.

The Force Continuum

Social scientists in general tend to prefer objective determinations over subjective ones when possible. Where, though, do we find a more objective standard? The Connor case calls for assessing force within the confines of "objective reasonableness." Of course, there is still the application of subjectivity no matter how any one person might attempt to determine appropriateness. Nonetheless, it becomes apparent that while the various stakeholders have differing conceptions of what constitutes appropriate force, the underlying themes or elements are similar in content (e.g., reasonableness, no more force than necessary, force commensurate with the resistance faced, and so forth). The challenge then is to understand how each of these elements can be considered as a collective whole and placed into some type of meaningful form. The use of a force continuum provides a potential mechanism for meeting this challenge.

The Practitioner Side

Well established within the policing community, a force continuum is specifically designed to guide officers toward controlling suspects with an appropriate degree of force by laying out varying levels of force in response to varying levels of citizen resistance. As noted by McLaughlin, "A force continuum gives an officer a clearer picture of the type of force that may be used legitimately in a given situation, which usually is not accomplished through the reading of the appropriate legal statute" (1992, 65). A continuum structure offers a potential measuring stick that can satisfy the differing standards stemming from the legal, professional, and public domains. Essentially, a force continuum is designed as a policy and training tool concerned with offering a bridge between the vagueness of the law and the realities of street-level practice. In academic terms, it operationalizes "objective reasonableness."

Over the years, several versions incorporating the notion of a force continuum have been proposed. One of the earliest, the linear design (figure 3.1), is modeled in the form of a ladder or hierarchical steps where subject resistance is placed into one of several levels and force options for escalation (and de-escalation) are presented within each level. According to McEwen, this type of "continuum approach is to rely first on the officer's presence to quell a situation, and if that fails, to move to increasingly severe types of force" (1997, 49; see also Connor 1991). Other, less linear designs are laid out in matrix form (see figure 3.2) or depicted by a wheel (see figure 3.3 and Hoffman, Lawrence, and Brown 2004). In the matrix approach, varying forms of suspect resistance are presented vertically while varying police responses appear on a horizontal axis.

Figure 3.1. Example of Linear Design of the Force Continuum

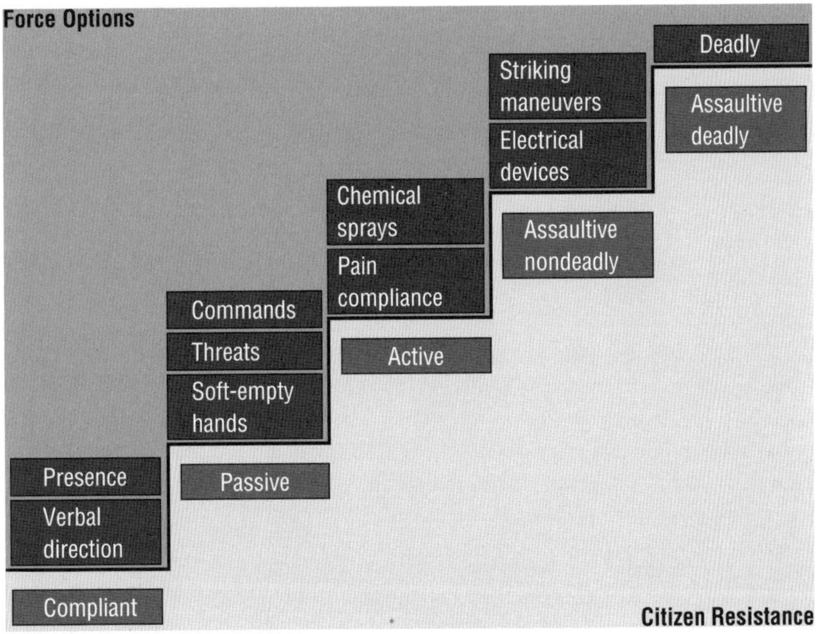

Figure 3.2. Example of Matrix Design of the Force Continuum

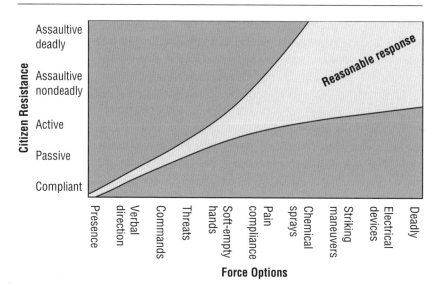

Figure 3.3. Example of a Wheel Design of the Force Continuum

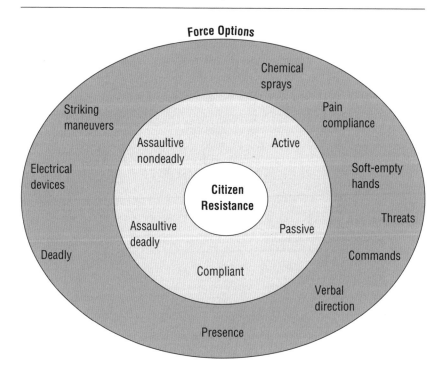

The wheel design is often presented by a series of concentric circles, with citizen resistance as the core, followed by an outer circle displaying appropriate forms of police force.

Agencies that select a linear design generally prefer the implied step-by-step approach to force application, prompting officers to start low on the continuum and work their way up based on resistance. Within this context, the use of the "least amount" of force is stressed by trainers and administrators. Those agencies preferring a wheel design emphasize using a "reasonable" force approach rather than the "least" amount of force, fearing that the linear model presents safety concerns because officers might believe they should start low on the continuum (e.g., verbal commands) even when suspects start high (e.g., assaulting the officer).[2] The matrix design option offers something of a middle ground. The precise type of force that should be used in response to a given level of resistance is less specific. The advantage here is that officers are aware of what may be egregious force (e.g., the use of a baton strike on a passively resistant suspect) but still given flexibility in what force options may be appropriate in the face of a certain type of resistance (e.g., the use of control holds, or pain compliance techniques, or chemical agents, on a physically resistant suspect).

Regardless of the type of continuum design a particular agency chooses (if any), the placement of different forms of force within the continuum structure can vary. For example, one department may place an electro-muscular disruption (EMD) weapon, such as the Taser, low on the continuum right after verbal direction, while another agency may place it high on the continuum just before deadly force. Of course, the implication is that some agencies view Taser use more as a "first resort," while other agencies encourage Taser use as a "last resort" before turning to deadly force. To date, there is no consensus on whether certain continuum designs or tactical placement within varying designs (e.g., Taser high or low on the continuum) offer tangible benefits, such as fewer citizen or officers injuries. An agency's decision to choose one design over another, and the location of varying tactics on the continuum, is driven solely by individual preference.

The Academic Side

Only in the past decade or so have researchers become interested in exploring the force continuum from an academic standpoint. In the mid-1990s, Klinger (1995) offered an early glimpse into how the force continuum might be used to analyze force application. In particular, he noted the importance of accounting for varying levels of severity by force types. That same year, Garner and colleagues (1995) went one step further by looking at levels of suspect resistance. A few years later, Alpert and Dunham (1997) proposed the use of "force factor" scores (subtracting the highest level of resistance from the highest level of force) to assess relative degrees of force in relation to suspect resistance.

Despite somewhat limited academic interest in the force continuum per se, there was certainly a clear link to previous work conducted by researchers investigating the evolving dynamics of police-citizen encounters. Al Reiss (1971), relying on observations of police in Boston, Chicago, and Washington during the mid-1960s, was one of the earliest researchers to discuss the importance of understanding police encounters with citizens as an interactive process. Some years later, Sykes and Brent (1983)— in an attempt to decipher how officers regulate or control encounters— sought to explore the process of interactions between officers and citizens in the context of individual sequences. In a similar vein, Bayley and Garofalo (1989) looked at the interactional process and proposed that police-citizen encounters move through three stages: contact, processing, and exit. Finally, Fyfe (1989), in his work with Miami Metro-Dade, examined how the unfolding of a police-citizen incident, over time or in stages, can affect the outcome.[3] In particular, he looked at police actions before the point of mobilization, as well as the effects of training. Interestingly, Fyfe found that in certain situations some officers may not have been aggressive enough in handling potentially violent encounters. That is, they failed to take charge when "it was clearly appropriate to take charge" (1989, 22). Taken as a whole, this body of prior work suggests that researchers who seek to explain or predict use-of-force decisions should, when possible, take into account the developmental nature of the police-citizen encounter.

Merging Practitioner and Academic Interests

If practitioners use the force continuum as a means to guide officer decision-making and researchers acknowledge the importance of accounting for varying types of force and the interactive nature of police-citizen encounters, why not merge the two and examine whether officers do, in fact, apply force within a continuum as an encounter evolves from beginning to end? Despite insights from practitioners and the research community, a disconnect still remained at the conclusion of the 1990s. Surprisingly, no one had yet attempted such a task. The academic research that had been done using the force continuum (Alpert and Dunham 1997; Garner et al. 1995; and Klinger 1995) still treated police-citizen interactions as if they were static rather than dynamically evolving events.

As argued elsewhere (Terrill 2001, 2005), the force continuum is a policy framework that is explicitly norm based, that attempts to capture some of the subtleties of coercion (types and levels), and that acknowledges that coercion in the police-citizen encounter is a dynamic process. What makes the force continuum attractive from both an application and an analysis perspective is that it contains two inherent principles that move us closer toward identifying appropriate use of force: *proportionality* and *incrementalism.* A suspect's polite refusal to obey an officer's command is a much smaller threat than an assault on the officer, although both constitute resistance that would justify police coercion, albeit at markedly different levels. The police are to apply a level of force proportional to the resistance that precedes it. Further, a continuum structure anticipates the possibility that a given level of police force may not produce the desired result and thus specifies how to proceed incrementally. For instance, if a given level of police coercion fails to make the suspect comply, officers may escalate the force, but they should do so in small increments.

A force continuum constitutes a simple standard against which police practice may be measured, modeled, and evaluated. As such, it offers a mechanism for developing more useful analyses of police use of force. By using a force continuum as a measuring standard, one can assess the extent to which police apply force proportionally and when applicable (i.e., multiple sequences are present), incrementally, throughout an encounter (escalation or de-escalation). In other words, one can assess the extent to which officers follow or deviate from a continuum structure. Both the theoretical and the practical relevance of this distinction lie within the notion of control. Applying force that falls within a continuum structure—that is, proportionate and incremental force—lends credence to the claim that the intended purpose is control in response to the threat posed. Behaviors that deviate from the continuum and exceed the force necessary for controlling the threat, though, may have some other purpose. For example, force may used to punish an offender. But just as important is that the continuum approach offers insights into cases at the opposite end of the spectrum: instances when citizen resistance calls for an escalation of police use of force but fails to prompt that response. These cases are particularly interesting in light of how much attention has been given to excessive force in the past. Measuring response against a continuum structure provides an opportunity to learn more about what prompts officers to use less rather than more force. Simply put, the force continuum is a mechanism for examining why and how officers use force and can provide the foundation for beginning to assess force appropriateness. Before one can begin to *judge* the appropriateness of police force, one must *measure* the extent to which force has been applied in a proportional and incremental manner.

In sum, researchers have observed that the best police work is accomplished when carried out in the least coercive manner possible (Bittner 1970; Klockars 1995; Muir 1977). Applying force sparingly ultimately enhances the legitimacy of the institution as a whole. The norm inherent within a force continuum is that force will be applied proportionally and incrementally. By examining force within this context, we can better measure and identify use of force and only then by extension can we begin to judge appropriate or inappropriate force.[4]

Early Evidence for Determining Appropriateness Using the Force Continuum

Using observational data from the Project on Policing Neighborhoods (POPN) study in Indianapolis and St. Petersburg, Terrill (2001, 2003, 2005) relied on a force continuum approach to measure the way in which officers applied force proportionately and incrementally. This early work was the first to examine how police officers and citizens respond to one another, in a temporally sequenced manner, within the context of a force continuum approach. It was the first attempt to quantify and analyze the interactive nature of multiple police-citizen encounters in this type of micro-oriented process since Sykes and Brent's (1983) pioneering work. Terrill found that officers did not leap at the opportunity to apply force to a resistant citizen but generally went to great lengths to resolve such encounters in the most noncoercive manner possible (often giving suspects multiple opportunities to comply). Conversely, the issue of appropriateness was more problematic when officers dealt with nonresistant suspects, as they were more likely to uses higher forms of force than the resistance called for.

Fortunately, other researchers have since offered additional studies that follow a somewhat parallel approach. Alpert and Dunham (2004), using official data from the Miami-Dade police department, followed Terrill's (2001) call for further refinement of an interactive approach. Their work offered a second look at how police officers and citizens respond to one another in terms of force and resistance as police-citizen encounters evolve. Among their findings was that the longer an encounter lasted, even nonviolent citizen resistance, the more likely the police were to use force. They also reported that "preemptive force seemed to be effective and produced an overall decrease in the number of incidents involving the use of force. Once a cycle of force is initiated, however, there appears to be only a limited opportunity to de-escalate the level of force" (Alpert and Dunham 2004, 122). Terrill (2001) found somewhat contradictory results with the POPN data, in that preemptive force led to greater uses of force later in the encounter and that officers were actually quite skilled at de-escalation when citizens raised the stakes through resistant behavior. Such findings reveal a greater need for additional research along these lines.

Researchers have also attempted to assist police practitioners with suggestions on how force continuum analyses can benefit an organization. For example, Terrill et al. (2003) have laid out a step-by-step guide detailing various methods for collecting, measuring, and assessing the application of force. They show how incorporating a force continuum into a force reporting system enables departmental administrators to track and assess everyday use of force by individual officers as well as by groups of officers (e.g., by shift or unit), which in turn gives a clearer picture for determining appropriate and inappropriate levels of force. Such an approach affords police managers an opportunity to create comparisons among different groups, based on, for example, gender, age, employment length, educational level, different types of units (e.g., patrol versus street crimes), or shifts. As data are collected over time, officials can longitudinally track both individuals and groups of individuals and compare them with past findings.

Limitations

The use of a force continuum is clearly not the only standard by which police use of force can be measured and analyzed. Perhaps the greatest difficulty is that it may be too mechanical in nature. In addition, the approach, on the face of it at least, fails to get at the preliminary frames Fyfe (1979) noted in his research and fails to identify when officers do something during an encounter to make force necessary. An advantage of the continuum approach, however, is that it may help identify "skilled" police officers, the standard that Klockars (1995) held up for judging appropriate police use of force. Relying on street-level officers (as Fyfe and others have advocated) can help identify *good policing* at the micro level and set the stage for defining good policing at the macro level. Certainly, using a force continuum may assist in such an endeavor, and developing detailed analyses of microlevel police practice may enable policymakers to further refine departmental policies that ultimately produce better officer practice in the use of force.

Assessing the Impact of Nondeadly Force Policies

Although researchers have begun to assess whether police officers apply force within a continuum framework, they have not asked nor answered the question of whether force continuum policies actually enhance officer decisionmaking, control suspects, or reduce the likelihood of injuries, shootings, complaints, and civil lawsuits. The closest researchers have come is to examine the impact of specific force tactics located on a force continuum scale. These studies are generally most interested in the "effect" of certain tactics (i.e., incapacitative abilities and injury rates). Chemical irritant sprays, such as oleoresin capsicum (O.C.), have perhaps been subject to the most inquiry (see Kaminski, Edwards, and Johnson 1999). In general, there is evidence that O.C. spray offers a moderate to high degree of incapacitative effect with a fairly low probability of long-term injuries; however, there is some debate over whether O.C. spray should be used in response to verbal resistance (see Adang and Mensink 2004, as well as Smith and Alpert 2000). A more contemporary concern centers on the use of another technology—EMD devices, such as the Taser. While there is anecdotal evidence in relation to the Taser's effectiveness (i.e., high control, low injury), Amnesty International (2004) previously reported that 74 people have died after being shocked by the Taser.[5] This raises the question of exactly where the Taser should be placed on the continuum of available force; perhaps it is more deadly than originally thought. Evidence on the extent to which other types of tactics offer high control and low injury, including physical forms of control (e.g., pain compliance techniques, martial art forms, and the like) and intermediate or less-deadly weapons (e.g., baton, pepperball, bean bag, and so forth) is lacking on the whole (for one limited review see Bertomen 2003).

Unfortunately, previous work (including the author's) has at best overlooked, and at worst failed to consider, the critical overlap of exploring the nature in which force is applied within a force continuum framework, the degree to which various tactics used to control suspects achieve their purpose without detrimental effects, and the broader policy environment. That is, researchers have generally looked at policy on nondeadly use of force in a narrow and disjointed fashion. Some studies have focused on the dynamics of force escalation and de-escalation separately and apart from examining such outcomes as officer or suspect injuries. Other research has focused on various tactics like the O.C. spray to determine their incapacitative effects and resulting injuries but not within the context of how such tactics fit into specific types of policies, most notably those employing a force continuum. In essence, little is known about the broader implications of how policies on nondeadly force affect officers' decisionmaking and the resulting outcomes of such decisions. Studies that examine any particular tactic or purported less-lethal technology (such as the Taser) apart from the broader application of such tactics, within varying policy contexts, unnecessarily limit potential insight. It is the merging of varying policy types with varying tactics, which include less-lethal technologies, which offers the most potential and ultimately useful information for policymakers and practitioners.

It has been some 30 years since Fyfe demonstrated the benefits of restrictive deadly force policies. Yet, researchers have not yet sought to determine empirically the extent to which various types of nondeadly force policies might also result in beneficial outcomes. In terms of policy development, we have not yet applied what we learned from research on deadly force to our understanding of nondeadly force. Although a majority of police agencies throughout the country employ a force continuum within their administrative policy (Terrill and Paoline 2006), the scientific community has no idea whether such an approach results in something of value. Given the wide variation in continuum approaches and even in the tactical placement of weapons (Taser as a first resort or a last?) within these varying designs, we clearly need to assess whether differences in certain policies matter and, if so, in what way.

It is now time for researchers to begin considering the role of nondeadly force policy on officer behavior to determine which types of policies might offer more beneficial outcomes to police practitioners. While tactic-specific or application-specific (e.g., escalation/de-escalation) inquiries will, and should, continue to merit further study, it is time to move beyond isolated attempts and look toward the connections between policy and outcomes. In particular, future research should focus on three areas of inquiry: improving decisionmaking, establishing control, and reducing injuries and complaints.

- First, researchers should examine whether certain types of force policies are more useful to officers in guiding their decisionmaking. For example, there is now some debate on whether force continuum policies help or hinder decisionmaking. Clearly, support for continuum policies comes from practitioners (Rogers 2001), but such support is not universal. For instance, according to Petrowski (2002), "The force continuum purports to provide a mechanical application when officers should be making a subjective threat assessment" (see also Aveni 2003; Williams 2002). Simply put, while the force continuum is often embedded in force policies, no evidence indicates that the approach actually enhances officer decisionmaking.
- Second, researchers should seek to uncover whether certain types of policies enable officers to establish or maintain control of suspects more effectively, which is the intended purpose of a forceful act. For instance, no research has identified whether a linear continuum design offers more control than a nonlinear or wheel design or even whether continuum approaches are more effective at controlling suspects than noncontinuum approaches. Moreover, no evidence exists on how and where less lethal technologies like the Taser fit into varying types of policies and the resulting effect on control. Further, an officer may know his or her policy and believe the policy offers guidance with respect to "what to do and when to do it." Nevertheless, while officers may feel certain policies are clear and offer guidance, such policies may be ineffective in controlling suspects.
- Third, researchers should assess whether certain types of policies reduce the number and extent of citizen and officer injuries, police shootings, citizen complaints, and lawsuits. The purpose here is to determine not only whether certain policies lend themselves more readily to issues of guidance and control but to discern the inter-

play between issues of guidance and control while considering injuries, shootings, complaints, and civil litigation. This is also the proper place to examine how more restrictive nondeadly force policies affect the use of force. Are policies that explicitly specify that officers should use the "least amount of force necessary" as effective, or even more effective, as those that call for officers to simply use "reasonable force"? Are departments that use a linear force continuum approach, which emphasizes progression in escalation and de-escalation, more likely to avoid problems than those that do not? Are policies that restrict Taser use to physically resistant suspects more beneficial than those that permit the Taser to be used on physically *and* verbally resistant suspects? There is a whole host of empirical questions that need to be asked and tested.

Research findings in these areas will offer valuable insight into how different policies actually influence police use-of-force outcomes. Such research will provide practitioners a guide for policymaking and development. Police administrators will have something on which to draw in deciding to employ a force continuum approach (or not) in their agency's use-of-force policy. More specifically, they will have empirical data on which policies are associated with lower rates of injuries or citizen complaints. Moreover, they will be able to discern which policy types provide officers greater degrees of control, and even those policies that might offer greater control but lead to more complaints and lawsuits. In short, such research will permit informed policy decisionmaking based on independent empirical assessment. Simply put, there needs to be a movement toward understanding varying degrees of restrictive nondeadly force policies, just as there was with deadly force policies in the 1970s.

NOTES

1. Graham, suffering from the onset of a diabetic seizure, was driven by a friend (Berry) to a convenience store to buy orange juice. Upon entering the store and witnessing a line of customers, Graham and Berry quickly left the store and began driving to a friend's house. Police officer Connor witnessed this suspicious behavior and conducted a traffic stop. Despite claims from Berry regarding Graham's diabetic state, he was physically detained until a check was conducted with store employees to ensure no wrongdoing had occurred. Graham filed suit alleging excessive force. The district court and court of appeals ruled against Graham, but the Supreme Court granted *certiorari* finding (9-0) that the

lower courts did not apply the appropriate standard (i.e., Fourth Amendment objective reasonableness). The case was remanded to district court, which subsequently ruled in Graham's favor.

2. Some police officials emphasize that there is no legal requirement to use the "least amount of force" only "reasonable force" (Terrill and Paoline 2006).

3. See chapter 5 in this volume for more on the Metro-Dade project.

4. Of course, appropriateness from a legal perspective (i.e., within the realm of objective reasonableness) and the use of "good force" do not always equate. There are certainly uses of force that are essentially "lawfully awful." This presents a challenge for police administrators attempting to chart a policy course. On the one hand, administrators need to be conscious of how juries interpret the objective reasonableness standard set in the Connor case. There are very real consequences if they do not. However, there is anecdotal evidence (Terrill and Paoline 2006) indicating that some jurisdictions have become so worried about liability that the issue of good policing squarely takes a back seat. In fact, several agencies that employed the use of force continuums in the past have now reversed course and cut any mention of a continuum approach in their policy or the use of language specifying that officers should use the least amount of force, solely for fear of liability.

5. See the chapter 4 in this volume for more on the Taser.

REFERENCES

Adang, Otto M. J., and Jos Mensink. 2004. "Pepper Spray: An Unreasonable Response to Suspect Verbal Resistance." *Policing: An International Journal of Police Strategies and Management* 27(2): 206–19.

Alpert, Geoffrey P., and Roger G. Dunham. 1997. *The Force Factor: Measuring Police Use of Force Relative to Suspect Resistance*. Washington, DC: Police Executive Research Forum.

———. 2004. *Understanding Police Use of Force: Officers, Suspects, and Reciprocity*. New York: Cambridge University Press.

Alpert, Geoffrey P., and William C. Smith. 1994. "How Reasonable Is the Reasonable Man? Police and Excessive Force." *Journal of Criminal Law and Criminology* 82(2): 481–501.

Amnesty International. 2004. "Excessive Use of TASERs in the USA." *The Wire*. November.

Aveni, Thomas J. 2003. "Force Continuum Conundrum." *Law and Order* 51(12): 74–77.

Bayley, David H., and James Garofalo. 1989. "The Management of Violence by Police Patrol Officers." *Criminology* 27(1): 1–27.

Bertomen, Lindsey. 2003. "Less-Deadly Toolbox: Law Enforcement Officers Test the Products on the Use-of-Force Continuum." *Law Enforcement Technology* 30(10): 64–69.

Bittner, Egon. 1970. *The Functions of Police in Modern Society*. Washington, DC: U.S. Government Printing Office.

Connor, Gregory. 1991. "Use of Force Continuum: Phase II." *Law and Order* 39(3): 30–32.

Fyfe, James J. 1978. "Shots Fired: An Analysis of New York City Police Firearms Discharges." Ph.D. diss., State University of New York at Albany.

————. 1979. "Administrative Interventions on Police Shooting Discretion: An Empirical Examination." *Journal of Criminal Justice* 7:303–23.

————. 1980. *Philadelphia Police Shootings, 1975–78: A System Model Analysis.* Washington, DC: U.S. Department of Justice.

————. 1981. "Who Shoots? A Look at Officer Race and Police Shooting." *Journal of Police Science and Administration* 9(4): 367–82.

————. 1982. "Blind Justice: Police shootings in Memphis." *Journal of Criminal Law and Criminology* 73(2): 707–22.

————. 1989. "Police-Citizen Violence Reduction Project." *FBI Law Enforcement Bulletin* 58:18–25.

————. 1997. "Good Policing." In *Critical Issues in Policing: Contemporary Readings,* 3rd ed., edited by R. G. Dunham and G. Alpert (194–213). Long Grove, IL: Waveland Press.

Garner, Joel H., Thomas Schade, John Hepburn, and John Buchanan. 1995. "Measuring the Continuum of Force Used by and against the Police." *Criminal Justice Review* 20:146–48.

Hoffman, Ron, Chris Lawrence, and Greg Brown. 2004. "Canada's National Use-of-Force Framework for Police Officers." *The Police Chief* 71(10).

Kaminski, Robert K., Steven M. Edwards, and James W. Johnson. 1999. "Assessing the Incapacitative Effects of Pepper Spray during Resistive Encounters with the Police." *Policing: An International Journal of Police Strategies and Management* 22(1): 7–29.

Klinger, David A. 1995. "The Micro-Structure of Nondeadly Force: Baseline Data from an Observational Study." *Criminal Justice Review* 20:169–86.

Klockars, Carl B. 1995. "A Theory of Excessive Force and Its Control." In *And Justice for All: Understanding and Controlling Police Abuse of Force,* edited by William A. Geller and Hans Toch (11–29). Washington, DC: Police Executive Research Forum.

McEwen, Thomas. 1997. "Policies on Less-Than-Deadly Force in Law Enforcement Agencies." *Policing: An International Journal of Police Strategy and Management* 20(1): 39–59.

McLaughlin, Vance. 1992. *Police and the Use of Force: The Savannah Study.* Westport, CT: Praeger.

Muir, William K., Jr. 1977. *Police: Streetcorner Politicians.* Chicago: University of Chicago Press.

Petrowski, Thomas D. 2002. "Use-of-Force Polices and Training: A Reasoned Approach." *The FBI Law Enforcement Bulletin.* October.

Reiss, Alpert J., Jr. 1971. *The Police and the Public.* New Haven: Yale University Press.

Rogers, Donna. 2001. "Use of Force: Agencies Need to Have a Continuum and Officers Need to Be Able to Articulate It." *Law Enforcement Technology* 28(3): 82–86.

Smith, Michael R., and Geoffrey P. Alpert. 2000. "Pepper Spray: A Safe and Reasonable Response to Suspect Verbal Resistance." *Policing: An International Journal of Police Strategies and Management* 23(2): 233–45.

Sykes, Richard E., and Edward E. Brent. 1983. *Policing: A Social Behaviorist Perspective.* New Brunswick, NJ: Rutgers University Press.

Terrill, William. 2001. *Police Coercion: Application of the Force Continuum.* New York: LFB Scholarly Publishing.

———. 2003. "Police Use of Force and Suspect Resistance: The Micro-Process of the Police-Suspect Encounter." *Police Quarterly* 6:51–83.

———. 2005. "Police Use of Force: A Transactional Approach." *Justice Quarterly* 22(1): 107–38.

Terrill, William, and Eugene A. Paoline III. 2006. "Police Use of Force Policy Types: Results from a National Agency Survey." Paper presented at the American Society of Criminology conference. Los Angeles, California, November 3.

Terrill, William, Geophrey P. Alpert, Roger D. Dunham, and Michael R. Smith. 2003. "A Management Tool for Evaluating Police Use of Force: An Application of the Force Factor." *Police Quarterly* 6:150–71.

Williams, George T. 2002. "Force Continuums: A Liability to Law Enforcement?" *FBI Law Enforcement Bulletin.* June.

4

Don't Taze Me, Bro'

Investigating the Use and Effectiveness of the Taser

Michael D. White and Justin Ready

Police agencies are deploying conducted energy devices (CEDs)—most notably the Taser—on a broad scale. Despite their adoption by approximately 10,000 law enforcement agencies in the United States, serious questions have been raised about the Taser's use and effectiveness, as well as its physiological impact. The ongoing discourse on police use of the Taser has been widely publicized, perhaps best illustrated by the famous YouTube video of a University of Florida student saying, "Don't taze me, bro," to police officers right before he is struck with the device, at an event where Senator John Kerry was speaking. The controversy surrounding the Taser came to a head in 2004 when Amnesty International issued a report describing 74 cases in the United States and Canada in which a suspect died after being stunned by a Taser. The report called for a moratorium on police use of the device until more research had been conducted on its physical effects. By March 2007, Amnesty International noted that more than 200 Taser-related deaths had been documented by police agencies and the media. Although a growing body of research has examined the physiological effects of the Taser (Maier et al. 2005; Ho et al. 2006; McDaniel et al. 2005), empirical research investigating the use and effectiveness of the weapon by officers in the field has been limited.

This chapter seeks to add to the scientific knowledge base through an examination of all Taser incidents involving officers in the New York

73

City Police Department (NYPD) from 2002 to 2005. After a descriptive analysis of the incidents, the authors use logistic regression to identify predictors of Taser effectiveness, measured as both the termination of suspect resistance and the officer satisfaction with the weapon. The chapter also provides a comparative analysis of the NYPD data with national and regional media reports describing Taser incidents, identified through Internet searches on the *New York Times* (regional level) and *LexisNexis* (national level). The comparative analysis explores whether incidents described in the two data sources differ with regard to (1) the circumstances in which the weapon is typically deployed; (2) the characteristics of the suspects involved in the Taser incidents; and (3) the significant predictors of continued suspect resistance and repeated use of the Taser by an officer. Overall, the chapter seeks to characterize typical incidents, identify factors related to positive outcomes in Taser incidents, and test whether media coverage and police reports of those incidents differ substantially on key characteristics. The chapter concludes with a discussion of the implications for the ongoing public discourse on the Taser, as well as those for police training, policy, and practice.

The Controversy Surrounding the Taser

The Taser, an acronym for *Thomas A. Swift Electric Rifle*, "is a conducted energy weapon that fires a cartridge with two small probes that stay connected to the weapon by high-voltage, insulated wire" (Wrobeleski and Hess 2003, 87). The electrical charge that is delivered through the probes (50,000 volts) overrides the central nervous system of the suspect, causing the loss of neuromuscular control, which gives the officer time to gain control of the suspect and apply handcuffs. As adoption of the Taser has become more common, serious questions have emerged about the appropriate conditions for using the device, its effectiveness, and the risk of death. Both the Police Executive Research Forum and the International Association of Chiefs of Police have recently published guidelines for use of the Taser, but there is still significant departmental variation in deployment and use patterns across the United States (Government Accountability Office 2005). For example, the Sacramento Police Department allows for use of the Taser during harmful situations, such as when a suspect is combative. The Phoenix and San Jose Police Departments permit use of the Taser at a lower level of force, such as when a suspect is actively resisting arrest but not assaulting an officer. Other departments, such as the Orange County Sheriff's Department, allow use of the Taser when a suspect is passively resisting the commands of an officer. News reports describing incidents in which police officers have used the weapon against the elderly, children, and the mentally ill have made national headlines. The three examples below illustrate the primary areas of controversy surrounding the Taser.

- *Use:* In fall 2005, police officers in Miami used a Taser on a 6-year-old boy who was cutting himself with a piece of glass and on a 12-year-old truant fleeing police.
- *Effectiveness:* In September 2003, a police officer in Adams County, Colorado, involved in a Taser incident wrote in his report, "By the 12th cycle, he [the suspect] appeared physically exhausted and wasn't a problem" (*Denver Post,* September 19, 2004).
- *Physiological impact:* Amnesty International issued a report in 2004 describing 74 cases in the United States and Canada in which a suspect died after being stunned by a Taser. The organization cites these deaths, recent biomedical research, and news reports of incidents involving the questionable use of Tasers to support a moratorium on their use.

In its 2004 report, Amnesty International concluded:

> In its recommendations . . . *Amnesty International* is reiterating its call on federal, state, and local authorities and law enforcement agencies to suspend all transfers and use of electro-shock weapons, pending an urgent rigorous, independent, and impartial inquiry into their use and effects. (Amnesty International 2004, 3)

The conclusions of the Amnesty International report underscore the controversy and debate among CED manufacturers and human rights organizations over the expanded use of the device among police agencies in the United States. In 2010, the debate continues with little in the way of empirical research to inform it.

The Origins of a Research Agenda

At about the same time the Amnesty International report was issued, Dr. James Fyfe—deputy commissioner of training for the NYPD and Distinguished Professor at the John Jay College of Criminal Justice—

asked one of the authors to teach a unique data analysis course to police officers on his staff. The course was designed to train officers in the practical use of SPSS (the Statistical Package for the Social Sciences) and provide officers with fundamental skills for engaging in statistically and methodologically sound research, including advanced bivariate and multivariate analysis.[1] Dr. Fyfe provided four data sets for the course, including hard copies of all Taser and stun device reports from 2003. Dr. Fyfe was acutely aware of the growing controversy over police use of the Taser, and he viewed this course as an opportunity to begin a thorough examination of the NYPD's use of the device, particularly in situations involving "emotionally disturbed persons" or EDPs.[2] Several weeks of the class were devoted to analysis of Taser data, and Dr. Fyfe subsequently requested that we expand the work by examining incident reports from additional years (2002–2005).

As part of this expanded effort, we searched the literature for other empirical studies on police use of the Taser. To our surprise, we found little independent research that was not published by CED manufacturers and police agencies, on the one hand, or by civil rights groups on the other. This discovery led to the realization that, like many other innovations in policing, researchers had failed to keep pace with the diffusion of this rapidly spreading technology. As a result, the data analysis class for NYPD officers initiated our research agenda on the Taser, which is described below.[3]

Data and Methods

The following section provides a description of the data and methods used for three sets of analyses: a descriptive analysis of the NYPD's Taser policy and deployment practices, a multivariate analysis examining predictors of suspect resistance, and a comparative analysis of news reports and police records on Taser deployments.

The Study of the NYPD

The NYPD has issued the Taser to officers in a limited manner with restrictive policies for its deployment, almost exclusively to officers assigned to the Emergency Service Unit (ESU), a group of several hundred specially trained officers who function as the department's SWAT or emergency response team. In addition, all officers who are promoted to the rank of sergeant or above are trained in its use and are authorized to carry it, and each precinct has at least one Taser that may be signed out by a supervisor, although they are not required to carry it. The patrol guide details the specific circumstances in which it is appropriate for a supervisor or ESU officer to use a Taser:

> Patrol supervisors or uniformed members of the service assigned to the Emergency Services Unit may utilize a TASER electronic stun device or stun device to assist in restraining emotionally disturbed persons if necessary. The TASER/stun device may be used:
>
> a. To restrain an EDP who is evincing behavior that might result in physical injury to himself or others, or
> b. To restrain person(s) who, through the use of drugs, alcohol or other mind-altering substances, are evincing behavior that might result in physical injury to himself or others.
>
> Emergency Service Unit personnel will obtain the permission of the Emergency Service Unit Supervisor prior to utilizing a TASER/stun device, except in emergencies. (NYPD 2000)

Thus, in accordance with the policy, the Taser is typically used in situations involving an EDP or person under the influence of drugs or alcohol who is posing a threat of physical injury, where either Emergency Service officers are deployed or a supervisor is present and has a Taser in his or her possession.[4]

Data for this research are obtained from the Taser/Stun Device Report, a one-page form that is completed after every Taser deployment. The form documents information relating to the suspect, officer, and circumstances in which the device was deployed. Much of the form requires the responding officer to check boxes from a range of options, with an additional narrative section where the officer is asked to describe the incident in detail.

Descriptive Analysis

Based on the form, the authors created a database in SPSS that records 38 different variables for each case. The data are officer based, so that if two officers use their Tasers on a suspect, two separate incidents are recorded. However, if one officer uses the Taser twice on the same suspect, the case is counted only once, although there is a variable to indicate multiple uses by the same officer. This chapter presents a descriptive analysis of the Taser incidents because of the dearth of research involving the Taser and the resulting unanswered questions about its use, prevalence, and effectiveness. The descriptive analysis also provides a basic framework for the multivariate and comparative analyses. The descriptive analysis uses the structure of the department's reporting form, thus categorizing the findings into suspect, officer, and incident-related characteristics. The chapter then classifies incidents into different levels of risk based on a rough lethality measure and investigates whether low-, medium-, and high-risk incidents have different outcomes in terms of officer satisfaction with the Taser.

Multivariate Analysis

The dependent variables used in the study include three separate but related measures of effectiveness. The first two are based on the extent of suspect resistance. Specifically, the field report contains several items that measure whether suspect resistance ended after the Taser was deployed and notes how much time transpired (in seconds) before the suspect was incapacitated. In a third of the cases (33.0 percent), the suspect continued resisting the officer after the Taser was deployed. The cases involving continued resistance can be divided into two categories based on the nature and duration of the resistance. In 32 cases, the resistance continued immediately following the Taser deployment because the suspect was not restrained by the weapon; that is, at no point was the subject subdued, and he or she continued to resist ("continual resistance"). The Taser was clearly ineffective during these incidents. In the other 65 cases involving continued resistance, the subject was initially incapacitated, allowing the officer(s) to gain control temporarily; however, the suspect began resisting again at a subsequent point in time ("any resistance"). The distinction between these two different outcomes draws attention to the temporary impact of the Taser—the involuntary loss of muscle control is not long term—and shows the importance of carefully observing the suspect's actions immediately after the Taser is deployed. Because of the practical importance of this distinction in resistance, both measures are used as dependent variables in the analysis. The base rates for any subsequent resistance and continual resistance are 33.0 percent and 10.9 percent, respectively.[5]

At the end of the Taser/stun device report, the officer is instructed to indicate whether the device performed satisfactorily (yes/no). Police officers' responses to this question serve as the third measure of effectiveness. Officers reported that the Taser performed satisfactorily in 78.7 percent of the cases. Officer satisfaction is likely related to a host of factors, including the device's physiological effect on the suspect and the outcome of the deployment taken as a whole. This measure offers a different perspective on weapon effectiveness that incorporates officers' perceptions. In the analysis, logistic regression is employed because all three measures of effectiveness are dichotomous outcomes with yes/no responses.

Comparative Analysis with Media Data

Most citizens have no significant contact with the criminal justice system, and to a large extent the print media, television, and movies shape their perceptions and beliefs about crime and criminal justice (Gaines, Kaune, and Miller 2001). Unfortunately, a substantial body of literature demonstrates that the media's portrayal of crime and criminal justice is far from accurate and that this inaccurate portrayal distorts the public's understanding of these issues (Hallett 2007; Chermak 1995; Manning 1997). The police, in particular, have a unique relationship with the media. Manning argues that "the police self is shaped by mass media" and that police go to considerable lengths to control their image and how it is presented in the news media (2001, 153; see also Chermak 1995 and Ericson 1989). Police have been less effective in "controlling the media message," however, in highly publicized cases involving the use of force (Tuch and Weitzer 1997; Weitzer 2002; Lasley 1994). Media coverage of these types of events has placed additional strain on police-community relations and has also influenced police policy (Chermak 1995). The final part of this chapter examines this issue by comparing media reports of Taser incidents to the NYPD data.

The authors conducted an extensive search of news reports describing police use of the Taser through *LexisNexis* and the *New York Times* (*Timeselect*). Keyword searches identified all news reports involving the Taser from January 2002 through December 2005. Once we identified the universe of news reports, we then recorded information for 68 variables relating to the general content of the articles and the circumstances in which police used the Taser. The coding scheme for the content analysis was modeled after the NYPD's Taser report to allow for consistency in data collection and to facilitate a valid comparison. Duplicate cases were excluded to prevent certain incidents from being overrepresented in the comparative analysis. The duplicates were identified by cross-referencing the articles using the author, suspect's name, date and location of the incident, and the newspaper in which the article was published. The content analysis below is based on 353 nonduplicate *LexisNexis* (national) and *New York Times* (regional) articles on police use of the Taser published during the study period. The police and media data are first compared on a descriptive level, and then logistic regression is employed for a multivariate comparison focusing on two outcomes: repeated use of the Taser by an officer and suspect resistance (the more inclusive measure with a base rate of 33 percent).

NYPD Data: Descriptive Findings

The NYPD Taser data are remarkably consistent across officer, suspect, and incident-related characteristics.

- Most suspects were male, African American or Hispanic, and in their 30s.
- Few suspects were under the influence of alcohol or drugs, but nearly all were identified as exhibiting signs of mental illness.[6]
- Nearly all suspects engaged in violent behavior.
- Just under half of suspects were armed, the majority of whom possessed a knife or cutting instrument.
- Nearly all officers using the Taser were assigned to the ESU.
- Backup officers and supervisors were present in almost all cases.
- Most of the subjects were not arrested on criminal charges, although nearly all were transported to a hospital for physical or psychological evaluation.
- In 84 percent of the cases, a supervisor indicated that the Taser deployment was consistent with departmental policy. In the remaining 16 percent, the form was not signed, and there was no information about whether the deployment was consistent with policy.[7]

Since one objective of the Taser is to reduce the likelihood of serious injury or death to suspects and officers, we developed a preliminary violence escalation scale and classified all incidents according to this scale. The scale ranges from 0 (lowest potential for a violent outcome) to 9 (highest potential for a violent outcome) with points assigned based on:

- *Suspect possessed a weapon* (up to 3 points)
    - +3 for armed with a gun
    - +3 for armed with a knife or cutting instrument at a distance 20 feet or less from officer[8]
    - +1 for armed with other weapon or knife or cutting instrument with distance greater than 20 feet
    - +0 for unarmed
- *Suspect engaged in violent behavior* (2 points)
    - +2 for violent behavior (toward officer, self, other citizens, or multiple)
    - +0 for no violent behavior
- *Under influence of drugs or alcohol* (1 point)
    - +1 for intoxicated (drugs, alcohol, or both)
    - +0 for not intoxicated
- *Mentally ill/emotionally disturbed* (1 point)
    - +1 for exhibiting signs of mental illness
    - +0 for not exhibiting signs of mental illness
- *Number of officers present* (1 point)
    - +1 for one officer present (no backup or supervisor)
    - +0 for multiple officers present
- *Suspect weight* (1 point)
    - +1 for suspect weight greater than 210 pounds
    - +0 for suspect weight 210 pounds or less[9]

These scores were subsequently collapsed into a three-level risk escalation scale: 0–3 = low; 4–5 = moderate; and 6–8 = high. Table 4.1 shows that 37 percent of the incidents were identified as low risk for violence escalation, 36.5 percent were classified as moderate risk, and 26.0 percent were categorized as high risk. Within each risk category (see table 4.2), we then examined the extent of officer satisfaction: low risk = 77.3 percent, medium risk = 68.3 percent, and high risk = 89.1 percent.

It appears from this preliminary analysis that police satisfaction with the Taser is greatest (nearly 90 percent) in those situations where the potential for serious injury or death is highest. The explanation for this finding remains unclear, although we suggest several possibilities: high-risk situations may be qualitatively different in ways that affect officer satisfaction; the physiological impact of the Taser may be different when

Table 4.1. Violence Escalation Scale

Violence escalation score	Percent (N)
0	0.5 (1)
1	2.1 (4)
2	5.2 (10)
3	29.7 (57)
4	28.1 (54)
5	8.3 (16)
6	17.7 (34)
7	7.8 (15)
8	0.5 (1)
Total	100.0 (192)

Source: White and Ready (2007)

Table 4.2. Officer Satisfaction with the Taser According to Risk of Violence

Risk of violence escalation	Percentage satisfactory use	Percentage of total	N
Low (0–3)	77.3	37.5	72
Medium (4–5)	68.3	36.5	70
High (6–8)	89.1	26.0	50
Total	100.0	100.0	192

Source: White and Ready (2007)

certain conditions are present; police performance during and after the Taser use may be different in high-risk encounters (i.e., quicker reaction times, better handcuffing, and the like); and officers may experience a greater sense of relief when the Taser successfully incapacitates a particularly dangerous suspect—which then affects their assessment of satisfaction.

NYPD Data: Multivariate Analysis

Logistic regression models were run for each outcome measure. Table 4.3 shows that the likelihood ratio test for each of the three models was statistically significant, and Nagelkerke R^2 estimates suggest that the

Table 4.3. Logistic Regression Predicting Three Measures
of Taser Effectiveness

Predictor variables	B	S.E.	Exp(B)
Any Suspect Resistance			
Suspect weight	.612	.302	1.844*
Distance	−.667	.306	.513*
Suspect intoxicated	.954	.410	2.596*
Suspect violent toward others	.884	.373	2.421*
One or both prongs miss target	1.393	.531	4.028**
Other less-lethal weapon used	1.057	.312	2.877**
Log likelihood	285.065		
R^2 (Nagelkerke)	.227		
Chi square	46.051		
DF	6		
Significance	.000		
N	255		
Continual Resistance			
Suspect weight	.882	.416	2.415*
Suspect intoxicated	1.285	.486	3.614**
One or both prongs miss target	1.744	.569	5.717**
Log likelihood	164.691		
R^2 (Nagelkerke)	.130		
Chi square	17.634		
DF	3		
Significance	.001		
N	262		
Officer Satisfaction			
Suspect weight	−.904	.338	.405**
Distance	.928	.337	2.528**
Suspect armed with gun or knife	1.111	.422	3.037**
One or both prongs miss target	−2.193	.578	.112**
Log likelihood	229.067		
R^2 (Nagelkerke)	.213		
Chi square	37.268		
DF	4		
Significance	.000		
N	246		

Source: White and Ready (2010)

* $p < .05$.

** $p < .001$.

Notes: B indicates parameter estimates; S.E. represents standard error; Exp(B) denotes odds ratios.

models predicting any suspect resistance, continual resistance, and officer satisfaction accounted for 23 percent, 13 percent, and 21 percent of the explained variation, respectively.[10] Findings are fairly consistent across all three measures of effectiveness. Predictors include the following:

Any suspect resistance (a measure of ineffectiveness)
- Suspect body weight was over 200 pounds.
- Suspect was intoxicated.
- One or both Taser darts missed the intended target.
- Officer used another less-lethal weapon.
- Distance between the officer and the suspect was three feet or less.
- Suspect directed violence toward an officer or citizen.

Continual resistance (a measure of ineffectiveness)
- Suspect was intoxicated.
- One or both Taser darts missed the intended target.
- Suspect body weight was over 200 pounds.

Officer satisfaction (a measure of effectiveness)
- Suspect and officer were more than three feet apart.
- Both Taser darts struck the intended target.
- Suspect body weight was 200 pounds or less.
- Suspect was armed with a gun or knife.

Three findings emerge from the analysis. First, the analysis suggests that Taser effectiveness can be modeled—or predicted—using multivariate techniques. Considering the paucity of research on the use and effectiveness of the Taser, this finding alone is important. Second, a number of variables were not statistically significant in the multivariate analysis. For example, the age, race, and gender of the suspect were not associated with Taser effectiveness. Also important was that whether or not the suspect was classified as "emotionally disturbed" was unrelated to Taser effectiveness.[11] The findings concerning EDPs are particularly interesting because anecdotal evidence available through the news media and interest groups suggests that the mentally ill may be more likely to continue to resist the police and to experience serious injury or death when stunned by the Taser. We find no evidence of that here. Finally, no officer-related variables were significant according to the multivariate analyses.

The third important research finding relates to the variables that were identified as significant predictors in the multivariate analyses. Each is described below.

- *Suspect intoxication:* A relatively small proportion of the Taser incidents involved an intoxicated suspect (13 percent), but effectiveness dropped significantly for those cases. While the reason for this finding is not clear, one possible explanation relates to the effect of drugs and alcohol on the suspect's ability to reason and process information. The intoxicated suspects may be less capable of thinking rationally during the encounter with the police and therefore may be less inclined to comply with the officer's instructions after the effects of the Taser wear off. If replicated elsewhere, this finding clearly warrants attention from police researchers and practitioners, as there may be both policy and training implications.
- *Suspect body weight:* Evidence that the weapon is less effective against heavier individuals is not apparent from the CED industry reports or the growing clinical research. Depending on the degree to which body weight moderates the effects of the Taser, there are important implications for its use and for police policy and training. Police officers may benefit from preparing for a greater likelihood of resistance from larger suspects. Policy should offer guidance on subsequent responses, which may include additional Taser deployments or alternative less lethal weapons. Moreover, research should investigate the potential effect of the interaction between suspect body weight and intoxication. In this regard, 18 cases in the study data involved an intoxicated suspect who weighed more than 200 pounds—13 of these suspects (72 percent) continued to resist after being subjected to the Taser.
- *Suicide or self-harm:* Suspects who were suicidal or engaged in self-harm were less likely to continue resisting after being stunned with the Taser, compared to those who were acting violently toward an officer or another citizen.
- *Armed suspects:* The association between armed suspects and increased effectiveness reinforces research findings from the descriptive analysis (i.e., the violence escalation scale), suggesting that greater satisfaction is reported for encounters where the threat of serious injury or death is greatest.

- *Two clean contacts:* For the Taser to deliver the full current, both darts must strike the suspect, penetrate the clothing, and make contact with the skin. If this does not occur, the weapon's effectiveness may decrease substantially.
- *Multiple low-lethal weapons:* The fact that more than one weapon is used implies that one or more devices were ineffective in curtailing resistance. In about 75 percent of these cases, the Taser was used first, followed by another weapon. In the remaining cases, the Taser was used *after* another weapon (i.e., mace) failed to incapacitate the suspect.
- *Distance: TASER International* offers cartridges with maximum ranges of 15, 21, 25, and 35 feet. The study findings suggest that the Taser is less effective when used at close range—within three feet or less of the target. The Taser can also be used in a "direct contact" or dry stun mode by placing the device directly on the suspect. We controlled for direct contact incidents to ensure that the distance finding involves only the traditional dart-firing method when officer and suspect are in close proximity. The reasons for the distance finding are unclear, although use at close range may increase the likelihood that suspect movement could affect the accuracy of the weapon, the suspect could grasp or jolt the weapon at time of discharge, or the darts may not spread out sufficiently to deliver the optimal current. Police agencies may want to consult with each other to determine if this short-range problem has emerged elsewhere. Regardless, maintaining a safe distance whenever possible is of central importance, and when the officer and suspect are in close quarters and safe distance cannot be maintained, the Taser should be used in the direct contact mode.

Comparative Analysis of News Reports and NYPD Records

Table 4.4 shows that the consistency between the media reports and the NYPD data is notable for many variables. Suspects were mostly male according to national news reports (93.9 percent), regional news reports (93.8 percent), and police records (88.8 percent). A fairly small proportion of the suspects were under 18 or over 60 years old, according to the three data sources (16.3 percent, 12.6 percent, and 3.9 percent, respec-

Table 4.4. A Comparison of News Reports and Police Records Describing Police Use of the Taser, 2002–2005

Variables	National news reports[a]		Regional news reports[b]		Police records[c]	
	Percentage	N	Percentage	N	Percentage	N
Suspect Characteristics						
Male suspect	93.9	(278)	93.8	(16)	88.8	(374)
Minor or senior citizen	16.3	(233)	12.6	(16)	3.9	(332)
Emotionally disturbed or mentally ill	25.9	(282)	56.3	(16)	92.5	(375)
Under influence of drugs or alcohol	19.4	(283)	28.6	(14)	12.8	(368)
Armed with a weapon	36.2	(282)	26.7	(15)	39.6	(359)
Assaulted a police officer	38.6	(280)	50.0	(16)	53.3	(366)
Suspect arrested	59.9	(282)	56.3	(16)	24.1	(361)
Verbal or passive resistance	14.7	(264)	14.3	(14)	5.2	(366)
Incident Characteristics						
Officer used Taser more than once	33.8	(263)	50.0	(16)	19.3	(352)
Suspect continued to resist	28.7	(272)	73.3	(15)	33.0	(351)
Suspect died after Taser used	31.8	(283)	68.8	(16)	00.0	(375)
Officer missed target	5.3	(283)	6.3	(16)	7.8	(296)
Other low-lethal weapon used before Taser	24.3	(281)	20.0	(15)	4.8	(368)
Other low-lethal weapon used after Taser	33.1	(275)	13.3	(15)	12.8	(375)
Backup officer(s) present	88.5	(243)	93.3	(15)	93.5	(340)
Officer not satisfied with Taser	34.5	(284)	6.3	(16)	21.3	(347)

Source: Ready et al. (2008)

a. LexisNexis.

b. *New York Times.*

c. NYPD.

tively). Few of the suspects described in the national and regional news and police records were reported to be under the influence of drugs or alcohol (19.4 percent, 28.6 percent, and 12.8 percent, respectively). About a third of the Taser incidents involved an armed suspect, according to the national (36.2 percent) and regional (26.7 percent) news reports and police records (39.6 percent). About half (53.3 percent) of the police reports involved a situation in which the suspect assaulted an officer, compared with 38.6 percent of national news reports and 50.0 percent of regional news reports. The level of suspect resistance was surprisingly consistent across the data sources. The Taser was deployed in response to verbal or passive resistance in 14.7 percent of the national news reports, 14.3 percent of the regional news reports, and 5.2 percent of NYPD police reports.

Several variables show inconsistencies across the data sources. First, substantial differences exist among national news reports, regional reports, and police records in regard to the percentage of suspects described as emotionally disturbed or mentally ill (25.9 percent, 56.3 percent, and 92.5 percent, respectively). Large differences also exist in regard to the proportion of suspects arrested (59.9 percent, 56.3 percent, and 24.1 percent, respectively). These differences are likely the result of the restrictive NYPD policy governing deployment and use. Second, the Taser was used repeatedly by an officer during the same incident in 33.8 percent of the national news reports and 50.0 percent of the regional news reports, compared with only 19.3 percent of the police records. Third, 31.8 percent of the national news reports and 68.8 percent of the regional reports indicated that the suspect died after the Taser was deployed. In contrast, one fatality (less than 1 percent) was recorded by the NYPD during the study period. This finding is noteworthy because it underscores the extent to which the media focus on deadly or scandalous police practices that are newsworthy. Last, the suspect continued to resist after the officer used the Taser in 28.7 percent of the national news reports, 73.3 percent of the regional news reports, and 33.0 percent of the police records.

In the logistic regression analysis, we found consistency in the predictors of the two outcomes—suspect resistance and repeated deployment of the Taser by an officer.[12] Both the media and the NYPD reports show three of the same significant predictors of any suspect resistance:

- suspect under the influence of drugs or alcohol
- suspect assault on an officer
- police use of another low-lethal weapon

For the media report model, the likelihood ratio test was statistically significant and Nagelkerke R^2 estimates indicate that the model accounted for 24.9 percent of the explained variation (see table 4.4 for NYPD model results). In the models predicting repeated use of the Taser by an officer (i.e., multiple deployments), table 4.5 shows that both data sources identified continued suspect resistance as a significant predictor.[13] Again, missing the intended target is a predictor, according to the police data. Several key variables of interest did *not* emerge as significant predictors of repeated use of the weapon, including suspect age and mental illness and suspect use of a weapon. These findings suggest that the officers in the study used the Taser more than once based on events that occurred *after* the initial deployment of the weapon rather than circumstances that were evident *before* the weapon was deployed (e.g., drug or alcohol intoxication, mental illness, and possession of a weapon). This finding reflects favorably on police practices relating to use of the Taser.

Conclusion

By early 2008, more than half of all police agencies in the United States used CEDs in some form; yet basic questions about their use, effectiveness, and physiological impact remain largely unanswered. The limited empirical research is particularly troubling since much of the ongoing debate surrounding the Taser has been widely publicized in the media. In fact, the tongue-in-cheek title of this chapter—referring to the incident mentioned at the beginning of the chapter—underscores the controversy surrounding the Taser, as well as the national media attention that police use of the device garners.

Using data from two distinct sources, this chapter represents one of the few empirical assessments of the Taser specifically addressing the use and effectiveness questions. We draw a number of conclusions based on the analyses described here. First, the findings are generally positive regarding use and effectiveness, likely the result of how the NYPD issues, monitors, and controls use of the weapon. Beyond the health risks, the controversy surrounding the Taser has focused on when it should be deployed (e.g., against passive resisters), how should it be used (e.g., repeated use against a suspect), and whom it should be used against (e.g., children). The NYPD has avoided nearly all these controversies through its restrictive use and control of the weapon. These findings demonstrate the viability of the Taser as an effective less-lethal alternative, if properly monitored and controlled.

Table 4.5. Logistic Regression Models Predicting Police Use of Taser More than Once: A Comparison of News Reports and Police Records, 2002–2005

Predictor variables	News reports			Police reports		
	B	S.E.	Exp(B)	B	S.E.	Exp(B)
Suspect continued to resist	2.069	.406	7.921**	1.046	.370	2.847**
Under influence of drugs or alcohol	.312	.423	1.367	.464	.479	1.590
Assaulted a police officer	−.525	.390	.592	.319	.364	1.376
Officer missed target	1.309	.710	3.702	1.507	.543	4.512**
Other low-lethal weapon used before Taser	−.334	.421	.716	1.018	.675	2.766
Other low-lethal weapon used after Taser	−.068	.379	.934	.759	.445	2.137
Suspect armed with weapon	−.620	.375	.538	.142	.354	1.153
Age of suspect	.000	.015	1.000	−.004	.016	.996
Emotionally disturbed or mentally ill	.679	.374	1.972	.272	.717	1.312
Constant	−1.351	.572	.259	−2.480	.988	.084
Log likelihood	215.453			218.190		
R square (Nagelkerke)	.263			.194		
Chi square	42.938			32.196		
DF	9			9		
Significance	.000			.000		
N	206			239		

Source: Ready, White, and Fisher (2008)

* p < .05.

** p < .001.

Notes: B indicates parameter estimates; S.E. represents standard errors; Exp(B) denotes odds ratios.

Second, in the analyses exploring factors related to weapon effectiveness, a number of statistically significant predictors surfaced with policy and training implications for police departments, including suspect body weight, drug and alcohol use, violent behavior, and the physical distance between the responding officer and the suspect. Clearly, more research is needed to explore whether these findings persist over time and across police departments. Particularly because of the lack of empirical research on the Taser, this chapter takes an important step by identifying the circumstances in which favorable deployment outcomes are likely to occur.

Third, the comparative analysis suggests that news reports describing police use of the Taser are fairly consistent with NYPD records of Taser deployments for the typical circumstances in which the device is used and the characteristics of suspects, as well as in the identification of the predictors of suspect resistance and multiple Taser deployments. This convergence of findings across data sources—one on a local level and the other on the national level—does not support allegations of an ideological bias in media reporting of Taser incidents, particularly with regard to the use of the device against vulnerable populations, levels of suspect resistance, and weapon effectiveness. The content analysis, however, suggests that there may be a media-related bias regarding the potentially lethal effects of the Taser. There is clearly an overrepresentation of death cases in the news media, but the authors question whether this can be attributed solely to a bias myth focusing on the Taser or whether the finding reflects the tendency of news reporting to emphasize violence (i.e., "if it bleeds, it leads").

Last, more independent empirical research on the Taser is clearly needed, not only because the technology is relatively new but because police agencies are adopting the weapon to varying degrees and developing different standards and expectations for its proper use. A multisite analysis of police agencies that have incorporated the Taser into routine practice but with different deployment and use patterns would yield valuable comparative data on whether use and effectiveness (and its predictors) vary by department and by policy guidelines. Moreover, we currently have no national baseline data measuring how often the Taser has been used, against whom, under what circumstances, and with what result. In effect, what we do know about the Taser is based largely on sources with questionable objectivity (the CED industry and civil and human rights groups) and on media reporting. Objective, national data reported by police departments would allow researchers to examine the use and effectiveness questions more broadly, and it would also permit exploration of the physiological impact question. With national reporting, researchers could calculate rates of lives potentially saved and lost:

- Rate of *lives potentially saved* per 1,000 Taser uses = (number of lethal situations de-escalated / total number of Taser uses) × 1,000.
- Rate of *lives potentially lost* per, 1,000 Taser uses = (number of deaths after use / total number of Taser uses) × 1,000.

The data relating to the number of uses (currently unknown) represent the denominator in the equations to calculate lives potentially saved and lost. Although Amnesty International has initiated this important discourse by documenting lives lost following Taser use (without establishing a causal link), we currently have no estimates of lives potentially saved (the numerator in the first equation). These figures cannot be calculated until accurate data are available to researchers, and without these rates, any conclusions drawn about the use and effectiveness of the Taser—and its physiological impact—are necessarily premature.

NOTES

1. For a detailed description of this course, see chapter 8 in this book.

2. This is the term used by the NYPD to described mentally ill persons in crisis.

3. This research is described in greater detail in three published articles by Michael D. White and Justin Ready. See the reference list.

4. The *Patrol Guide* also offers a definition of an "emotionally disturbed person":

> A person who appears to be mentally ill or temporarily deranged and is conducting himself in a manner which a police officer reasonably believes is likely to result in serious injury to himself or others.

5. Given that the intent of the Taser is temporary incapacitation only, the latter suspect resistance measure—10.9 percent—is probably a fairer measure of its effectiveness. Also, the any-suspect-resistance measure includes both types of resistance (i.e., continual resistance is a subset of the more general resistance measure). Both measures are examined in the multivariate analysis.

6. These are not clinical judgments. Rather, they are conclusions drawn by the officers on-scene based on available evidence.

7. However, a review of the narrative of those cases suggests that they too conformed to department policy on use of the Taser.

8. Cases where the suspect is armed with a knife and is 20 feet or less from the officer are assigned three points because police are trained that suspects can "close the gap" from that distance before the officer can unholster and draw his or her gun. Generally speaking, deadly force is permitted under such conditions.

9. See White and Ready (2007) for the scoring rationale.

10. Nagelkerke R^2 provides an approximation of the explained variation in a logistic regression model. This measure of model strength is considered slightly more conservative than the R^2 statistic in OLS regression, but less conservative than the Cox and Snell R^2 estimate, which does not have a maximum value of 1.0.

11. Note that only 28 cases did *not* involve a suspect classified as an EDP, so caution should be used in generalizing about this subgroup.

12. The small number of *New York Times* cases prevented us from running multivariate analyses on those regional media reports.

13. Suspect resistance is used as a predictor of multiple deployments, but multiple deployments are not used as a predictor of suspect resistance. This decision was made based on the logical sequence of events.

REFERENCES

Amnesty International. 2004. *United States of America: Excessive and Lethal Force? Amnesty International's Concerns about Deaths and Ill Treatment Involving Police Use of Tasers.* London: Amnesty International.

Chermak, Steven. 1995. "Image Control: How Police Affect the Presentation of Crime News." *American Journal of Police* 14(2): 21–43.

Ericson, Richard. 1989. "Patrolling the Facts: Secrecy and Publicity in Police Work." *British Journal of Sociology* 40(2): 205–26.

Gaines, Larry K., M. Kaune, and Roger L. Miller. 2001. *Criminal Justice in Action: The Core.* Belmont, CA: Wadsworth.

Government Accountability Office. 2005. "TASER Weapons: Use of TASERs by Selected Law Enforcement Agencies." Washington, DC: Government Accountability Office. http://www.gao.gov/new.items/do5464.pdf.

Hallett, Michael A. 2007. " 'COPS' and 'CSI': Reality Television?" In *Current Issues and Controversies in Policing,* edited by Michael D. White. Boston: Allyn and Bacon.

Ho, Jeffrey D., James R. Miner, Dhanunjaya R. Lakireddy, Laura L. Bultman, and William G. Heegaard. 2006. "Cardiovascular and Physiologic Effects of Conducted Electrical Weapon Discharge in Resting Adults." *Academic Emergency Medicine* 13(6): 589–95.

Lasley, J. R. 1994. "The Impact of the Rodney King Incident on Citizen Attitudes toward Police." *Policing and Society* 3:245–55.

Maier, Andrew, Patricia Nance, Paul Price, Clifford J. Sherry, J. P. Reilly, B. J. Klauenberg, and Jonathan T. Drummond. 2005. "Human Effectiveness and Risk Characterization of the Electromuscular Incapacitation Device—A Limited Analysis of the TASER." Joint Non-Lethal Weapons Human Effects Center of Excellence.

Manning, P. 1997. "Media Loops." In *Popular Culture, Crime and Justice,* edited by Frankie Bailey and Donna Hale (25–39). Belmont, CA: Wadsworth.

———. 2001. "Policing and Reflection." In *Classical Issues in Policing,* edited by Roger Dunham and Geoffrey Alpert (149–57). Prospect Heights, IL: Waveland.

McDaniel, Wayne C., Robert A. Stratbucker, Max Nerheim, and James E. Brewer. 2005. "Cardiac Safety of Neuromuscular Incapacitating Defensive Devices." *Pacing and Clinical Electrophysiology* 28(1): 284–87.

New York Police Department. 2000. *Patrol Guide.* New York: NYPD.

Ready, Justin, Michael D. White, and Christopher Fisher. 2008. "Shock Value: A Comparative Analysis of News Reports and Official Police records on TASER Deployments." *Policing: An International Journal of Police Strategies and Management* 31:148–70.

Tuch, Steven A., and Ronald Weitzer. 1997. "The Polls-Trends: Racial Differences in Attitudes toward the Police." *Public Opinion Quarterly* 61:642–63.

Weitzer, Ronald. 2002. "Incidents of Police Misconduct and Public Opinion." *Journal of Criminal Justice* 30: 397–408.

White, Michael D., and Justin Ready. 2007. "The TASER as a Less-Lethal Force Alternative: Findings on Use and Effectiveness in a Large Metropolitan Police Agency." *Police Quarterly* 10(2): 170–91.

———. 2010. "The Impact of the TASER on Suspect Resistance: Identifying Predictors of Effectiveness." *Crime and Delinquency* 56(1): 70–102.

Wrobeleski, Henry M., and Karen M. Hess. 2003. *Police Operations: Theory and Practice.* Belmont, CA: Wadsworth.

5

Can Police Training Affect the Use of Force on the Streets?

The Metro-Dade Violence Reduction Field Experiment

David Klinger

V iolent interactions involving police officers and members of the American public have been a prominent social issue since the first modern police agencies cropped up in the United States during the middle of the 19th century (Geller and Scott 1992). Since the turbulent 1960s—when several controversial incidents in which officers used force against citizens led to rioting (Klinger and Brunson 2009)—numerous programs for reducing tensions between the police and the public have been implemented in the policing community. One of the major initiatives in this effort has been to increase the training that line officers receive on various aspects of the use of force. The logic behind the push for increased training is that it should lead police officers to use less force, which, in turn, should lead to less public discontent with police actions. While this logic makes intuitive sense, it has been subject to almost no empirical scrutiny since the initiative to increase police training was launched decades ago.

In the late 1970s and early 1980s, a series of civil disturbances wracked the Dade County area of south Florida, sparked by violent interactions between local police officers and citizens. In 1985, the Police Foundation in Washington, D.C., entered into an agreement with the Metropolitan Dade County Police Department to develop and evaluate a training program for reducing the incidence of violence between Metro-Dade officers and the citizens they police. This effort, which came to be known as the Metro-Dade Police/Citizen Violence Reduction Project (Violence Reduction Project hereafter), involved a classical experiment in which approximately half the several dozen randomly selected officers attended a three-day use-of-force training program. Before the administration of the training program to the experimental group, trained observers accompanied all the officers who participated in the study on several patrol shifts and recorded information about officers' use of force and other aspects of the their interactions with citizens. After the officers in the experimental group completed the training, the observers again accompanied all study officers on a second wave of patrol shifts and again recorded information about what transpired during their interactions with citizens (see below for a detailed description of research procedures). Because the Violence Reduction Project included a classical experimental design, it affords opportunity for a rigorous assessment of the effect of specific use-of-force training. Up to now, however, the only published analyses of data produced during the Violence Reduction Project have been limited to basic bivariate comparisons of the actions taken by experimental and control group officers (Fyfe 1987).

This chapter takes a fresh look at the utility of the Violence Reduction Project training program by using multivariate analysis to examine the effect of the program while holding constant other factors that might influence the officers' forceful actions. By doing so, the chapter sheds new light on the more general proposition that use-of-force training programs can affect officers' actions on the street and (perhaps) increase citizen satisfaction with the police. Following a brief review of the research on the use of force by police that identifies relevant control variables and discusses how scholars have measured police use of force, the chapter provides a detailed description of the Violence Reduction Project, describes the data produced during the study, presents the results of the data analysis, and then discusses the implications of the findings.

Previous Literature

Scholars who have examined nonlethal force have used data collected through a variety of methodologies, including surveys of citizens (Langan et al. 2001), police records (Alpert and Dunham 1999), specialized reporting by officers and interviews of individuals they had arrested (Garner and Maxwell 1999), and systematic observation (Terrill 2001). While each methodology has its advantages and disadvantages, data obtained through systematic observation have the unique characteristic of being collected by independent observers at the moment that force is exercised. Because data collected by field researchers are unadulterated by the interpretive colorings of either officers or citizens, they have enjoyed considerable prominence in the literature on nonlethal force. Indeed, systematic observation has been an important source of data for the study of nonlethal force since the methodology was first employed on a large scale by Al Reiss and his team of three dozen researchers who rode along with members of the Boston, Chicago, and Washington, D.C., police departments in the mid-1960s.

The first publications to use data from this seminal observational study to examine the use of force by the police (Reiss 1968, 1971) focused on the extent to which officers used force inappropriately and presented basic descriptive statistics that bore on this matter (the percentage of cases in which officers physically mistreated citizens, for example). Several years later, Friedrich (1980) extended the quantitative assessment of the data Reiss and his colleagues had collected by estimating the independent effect of several factors thought to influence whether officers used any physical force during their interactions with citizens.

The next piece of observational research on nonlethal force came in 1989 when Bayley and Garofalo used data from a study of New York City officers. The study examined the extent to which officers' tactical proficiency and selected aspects of their interactions with citizens were associated with the likelihood they would use any physical force. Six years later, Worden (1995) used data from a multicity observational study (the Police Services Study conducted in 1977) to examine whether specific features of interactions with citizens could predict whether officers used excessive force.

Each of these studies used binary measures of force, simply measuring whether officers used any form of physical force (Friedrich 1980; Bayley and Garofalo 1989) or whether they used excessive physical force (Reiss 1968, 1971; Worden 1995). Klinger took a different tack in his 1995 study that sought to improve the way social scientists conceive of and measure forceful police actions. He noted that treating police use of force as a dichotomy overlooks two important aspects of the picture of nonlethal force. First, by treating actions as different as grabbing someone's arm and striking someone in the head with a police baton as the same phenomenon, it fails to account for variability in the sorts of things officers do when they use physical force. Second, it fails to account for the fact that the law enforcement profession conceptually defines force as including verbal commands that officers issue to citizens. Klinger (1995) addressed these two aspects by differentiating among various coercive actions officers might take and rank-ordering them according to the degree of physical harm they posed to citizens (verbal commands, for example, involve less potential harm than grabbing, which involves less potential harm than hitting; see below). He then provided descriptive data on how frequently the officers in his study used various levels of force (including none) in dealing with citizens.[1]

Since the appearance of Klinger's 1995 work, it has become standard in use-of-force research to employ measures that differentiate among various sorts of coercive police actions. In the realm of observational research, this practice is most evident in the work of Terrill and his colleagues, who have used data from the Project on Policing Neighborhoods—which was conducted in Indianapolis, Indiana, and St. Petersburg, Florida—to examine a variety of issues pertaining to the determinants of police use of force (Terrill 2001; Terrill and Mastrofski 2002; Terrill and Reisig 2003). Following the logic laid out in Klinger's 1995 piece, this body of work uses ordinal force measures that rank officers' actions according to the degree of potential harm they pose. Terrill and his colleagues then used this measure to estimate several statistical models that assessed an array of hypotheses about the determinants of force. Among the key findings of their analyses were that the force officers used increased along with increasing citizen resistance, that officers tended to use greater force in their dealings with minority citizens, and that force was not related to the degree of disrespect or hostility citizens displayed toward officers.

In short, research on police use of force conducted over the past two decades has produced a good deal of information about the types of force that officers use, the relative degree of coercion they inhere, and the situations under which they are and should be employed. But the question of whether departmental training can affect the forceful actions that officers take on the streets has been surprisingly understudied. With all this as background, attention now turns to a detailed discussion of the research procedures used in the Violence Reduction Project and how the data it developed were applied in the current analysis.

Studying Force in Dade County

The first step in the Violence Reduction Project was selecting a random sample of approximately 100 officers from three patrol districts of the Metro-Dade Police Department to serve as research subjects. Trained observers then accompanied each study officer on five eight-hour patrol shifts and recorded detailed information about any forceful actions the subject officers took (see details of the force measurement scheme below), as well as numerous other aspects of the officers' interactions with citizens. Approximately half the study officers were then randomly selected to attend a three-day training program that focused on police field tactics and conflict resolution strategies designed to decrease the level of force the officers used when dealing with citizens on the streets. This 24-hour training block included lectures on how officers should approach and manage potentially violent interactions with citizens, videotapes depicting case histories of actual police-citizen interactions that led to various forceful police actions, and role-playing in which officers armed with nonfunctioning firearms handled scenarios in which professional actors took the roles of citizens. After the officers in the experimental group had completed the training regime, the observers then accompanied officers from both the experimental and the control group on a second wave of patrol shifts, a methodology designed to allow for pre- and posttraining comparisons to determine if officer performance improved. Over the course of the study, observers recorded information about officers' contacts with citizens during a total of 877 patrol shifts (see Fyfe 1987 for a thorough description of the Violence Reduction Project).

Observers carried with them separate observational instruments for four types of encounters: routine traffic stops, high-risk traffic stops, crimes in progress, and disputes. Due to certain vagaries of the Metro-Dade study, the instruments used to measure force in the crimes-in-progress and high-risk traffic stops included fewer force response categories than did the instruments used for routine traffic stops and disputes. Consequently, it is not possible to pool the various types of encounters for analysis where use of force is concerned. So that the information about force in the Metro-Dade data could be maximized, those encounters that had less information about officers' use of force (that is, those involving high-risk traffic and crimes in progress) have been eliminated from analytical consideration. Traffic stops were also eliminated from the pool of cases in the current analysis because only the dispute instrument included measures of crimes against both police officers and citizens during the time that officers were interacting with citizens. As Klinger (1994, 1996b) pointed out, multivariate models that seek to predict police action that do not include both these factors will be misspecified (see list of independent variables below). The current study will thus examine the effects of the training provided to the officers in the experimental group by analyzing the 241 disputes that Metro-Dade officers handled during the Violence Reduction Project. It does so by regressing an indicator of forceful police action on an indicator that measures the training that control officers underwent, as well as nine factors that previous research suggests might independently affect police behavior.

Measuring Force and Training

The dispute instrument allowed the observers to record whether study officers did any of the following:

- Issued voice commands
- Physically grabbed any disputants
- Applied any pain compliance holds
- Applied any neck holds
- Punched or kicked any disputants
- Struck any disputants with their batons[2]

Klinger (1995) noted that the top-to-bottom listing of these six types of police actions rank-orders them from least to most force, based on the potential they hold to harm the citizens against whom they are used. This understanding was used as the first step in crafting an ordinal-level measure of force for the current analysis. The next step was to examine how frequently officers used each type of force during the disputes in question. As shown in table 5.1, this effort showed that Metro-Dade officers typically managed to deal with the disputes they were called upon to handle without resorting to any sort of force (59.8 percent of the cases), that when they did resort to force that it usually took the form of nonphysical voice commands (used in 39.4 percent of cases), and that the use of firm grips was by far the most common form of physical force (officers grabbed citizens in 17 percent of cases, applied pain compliance holds in 7 percent, used neck holds in 2.1 percent, struck citizens with batons in 1.6 percent, and hit or kicked citizens in less than 1 percent of

Table 5.1. Frequency of Nonlethal Force Used
by Metro-Dade Officers in Disputes during
Violence Reduction Project, 1985–1986

	Number of cases	Percent
No force used	144	59.8
Voice command	95	39.4
Firm grip	41	17.0
Pain hold	17	7.0
Choke hold	5	2.1
Baton blows	4	1.6
Hit or kick	2	.8
$N = 241$		

Source: Metro-Dade Violence Reduction Project

Note: Number of cases and percentages do not sum to 241 and
100%, respectively, because officers sometimes used more than
one type of force in a single encounter.

the cases). This information was then used to create a measure that captured the highest level of force officers used in each encounter. Because officers so infrequently punched, kicked, choked, or struck citizens with their batons, the three highest types of force were collapsed into a single measurement category to yield a five-step force measure: no force used equaled 1, voice commands equaled 2, firm grip equaled 3, pain hold equaled 4, hit-kick/baton blows/neck holds equaled 5. The frequency distribution of this force measure is displayed in table 5.2.

Devising a training measure was more straightforward: a dummy variable was crafted where 1 equaled a posttraining dispute handled by an officer who attended the training, and 0 equaled other disputes.

Control Variables

Observational research on the use of force (Terrill 2001)—as well as other aspects of police behavior (for example, issuing tickets [Lundman 1994] and making arrests [Black and Reiss 1970])—has considered a variety of situational factors as possible predictors of police action. Among those most often examined are the race of citizens with whom officers deal, whether encounters occur indoors or outdoors, whether the parties

Table 5.2. Highest Level of Force Used by Metro-Dade Police during Disputes with Citizens

	Number of cases	Percent
No force used	144	59.8
Voice command	56	23.2
Firm grip	24	10.0
Pain hold	11	4.6
Choke/baton/hit or kick	6	2.5
$N = 241$		

Source: Metro-Dade Violence Reduction Project

Note: Percentages do not sum to 100 percent due to rounding.

involved in the incident prompting police intervention had a domestic relationship, whether citizens appeared to be under the influence of drugs or alcohol, the number of citizens involved in the incident, the demeanor of citizens toward the police, and criminal activity (see Riksheim and Chermak 1993 for a summary discussion of situational predictors in police research). The Metro-Dade data included information that permitted the development of the following measures of these factors:

- Citizen race: 0 = white (including Hispanic), 1 = black.
- Location: 0 = outdoors, 1 = indoors.
- Whether the dispute was domestic: 0 = no, 1 = yes.
- Whether any of the citizens involved were apparently under the influence of alcohol or drugs: 0 = no, 1 = yes.
- Number of parties to dispute: from 2 to 5, with 5+ counted as 5.
- Citizen demeanor: 1 = civil, 2 = moderate hostility, 3 = high hostility.

And three distinct aspects of criminal activity:

- The legal seriousness of the event that precipitated police response: measured with a revised Sellin-Wolfgang scale where 1 = no crime, 2 = minor property crime, 3 = minor violent and major property crime, 4 = moderate violent crime, and 5 = major violent crime.
- Attacks on citizens in the presence of responding officers: 1 = none, 2 = unarmed assault, 3 = armed assault.
- Whether any citizens attack officers: 0 = no, 1 = yes.

Analysis and Findings

Measuring force with the five-step indicator detailed above provides the opportunity to examine both the core question of whether the training program reduced the amount of force that officers used and the ancillary questions about the effects of other factors that are treated as controls in the analysis, because it permits the use of ordinary least squares (OLS) regression to examine the relationship between the use of force and the various factors hypothesized to influence it. While OLS assumes a dependent variable measured at the interval or ratio level, it is a robust technique (Berry 1993) that has been put to good use with ordinal measures similar to the force scale used here (Klinger 1996a; Terrill and Reisig 2003). Because the coefficients yielded by OLS regression indicate unit changes in dependent variables with unit changes in predictors, use of the technique provides precise information about the effect of the training conducted in the Violence Reduction Project net of the effects of the several control variables on the amount of force officers used in their encounters with citizens (as well as the independent effects of the several controls). In addition, because the summary statistic—the R^2—of an OLS model is properly interpreted as the portion of variance in the dependent variable explained by the set of included predictors, the use of OLS shows how well the various predictors taken together explain the use of force by Metro-Dade officers.

As displayed in table 5.3, the regression analysis indicates that the training program attended by officers in the experimental group led to a statistically significant (alpha set at .05) net reduction in the amount of force that Metro-Dade officers used when handling disputes between citizens. The B coefficient of −.28 indicates that after attending the Violence Reduction Project training program, officers in the experimental group on average used approximately a quarter of one level less force than they did before attending training and compared with their peers in the control group. In short, officers used significantly less force following training in the violence reduction techniques proffered.

Regarding the control variables, the analysis indicates that the manner in which Metro-Dade officers exercised their coercive powers was determined largely by the behavior of the citizens they encountered. None of the nonbehavioral factors—citizens' race, whether the encounter took place inside or outside, whether the disputants had a history of shared intimacy, the number of disputants involved, or whether any of them

Table 5.3. OLS Regression of Force
on Explanatory Variables

	B	SE	Beta
Race	.03	.12	.01
Location	−.16	.10	−.08
Domestic	−.11	.11	−.05
Drunk	−.17	.12	−.07
Number	.04	.09	.03
Demeanor	.32*	.08	.23
Prior crime	.20*	.04	.24
Encounter assault	.70*	.20	.19
Officer attacked	2.27*	.34	.35
Training	−.28*	.12	−.12
Constant	.82	.25	
R^2	.44		
R^2 adjusted	.41		
$N = 241$			

Source: Metro-Dade Violence Reduction Project

were apparently intoxicated—were significantly related to the amount of force officers used, but all the variables that measured aspects of citizens' behavior were. The amount of force officers used increased as the level of crime involved in disputes before their arrival increased, as the level of violence between disputants after they had arrived increased, as the level of violence directed against them increased, and as the level of hostility exhibited toward them increased. Overall, the model explained more than 40 percent of the variation in officers' use of force (adjusted $R^2 = .41$), a notable statistic given that police-citizen encounters are microlevel data.[3]

Discussion and Conclusion

This is the first published study to use multivariate statistical modeling of data collected through systematic observation to test the effect of a police training program on officers' use-of-force practices. The analysis is encouraging, for it shows that the training provided during the Violence Reduction Project had its intended effect of reducing the level of force officers used and that use-of-force training can affect officers' actions on the streets. We must be careful, however, to place the current finding in the context of police use-of-force training writ large. Such training comes in many forms across the nation. Among the various sorts of training are classroom lectures, video presentations, "hands-on" combative sessions in protective gear, case history discussions, and scenario-based role-playing in a variety of shapes and sizes. As noted above, the training component of the Violence Reduction Project included classroom lectures, video presentations, and scenario-based training with professional actors as role-players. Just because this specific training program—which took place in a large police agency following civil unrest springing from controversial use-of-force incidents—had its intended effect of reducing force, we cannot assume that other sorts of use-of-force training in other contexts will have whatever effect those providing the training seek. Because such training varies along many dimensions and occurs in a variety of organizational and other social contexts, the present finding does not speak to the validity of use-of-force training beyond that provided in the Violence Reduction Project when and where it occurred.

The findings are encouraging, however. First, they demonstrate that training can lead to reduced violence between police officers and citizens. This finding is important because so much time, effort, and money have been expended on use-of-force training across the United States in recent years. Second, the program in question included scenario-based role-playing, a form of training now viewed as a "best practice" in contemporary American law enforcement (Murray 2004). That the use-of-force training program subject to the most complete assessment yet undertaken included role-playing and produced the desired effect suggests that the effort to find an effective approach to training has not gone for naught. While detailed analyses of other training programs that include role-playing are needed to validate the utility of scenario-based training, the present findings suggest the methodology has merit.

Other findings from the analysis are encouraging for other reasons. The findings that the legal aspect of citizens' behavior (that is, committing crimes before officers arrived, attacking other disputants, and attacking officers) had the largest effect on officers' conduct and that the nonbehavioral variables (citizen race or location, for example) did not affect the level of force officers used suggest that the officers studied were paying heed to legitimate factors as they made decisions to use force. As the Supreme

Court ruled in *Graham v. Connor* (490 U.S. 386 [1989]), police officers *should* take into account the seriousness of the criminal conduct afoot (among other things) when deciding how much force to use in a given encounter with citizens. The officers studied in the Violence Reduction Project did this, and they did not include in their calculus illegitimate factors such as citizen race. As a consequence, the data suggest that study officers tended to exercise their coercive powers judiciously.

In conclusion, the results of the current analysis suggest that the officers studied during the Metro-Dade Police/Citizen Violence Reduction Project policed in a way consistent with their charge to use force in accord with legal standards and that those officers who attended the training program managed to do so while using slightly less force than their peers who did not participate. These twin findings suggest that police officers comport themselves appropriately and that with sound training they can do an even better job.

NOTES

1. Klinger's (1995) data source was the same Violence Reduction Project that is the focus of this chapter.

2. Batons were the only nonlethal weapon that Metro-Dade officers carried at the time of the study, and thus the list of items did not include chemical sprays, Tasers, or any other type of nonlethal weapon.

3. It is also worth noting in this connection that the 10-predictor model estimated herein explains substantially more variance than the 27-predictor model estimated by Terrill and Mastrofski (2002), an ordered probit model that yielded a pseudo *r*-square of .268.

REFERENCES

Alpert, Geoffrey P., and Roger G. Dunham. 1999. "The Force Factor: Measuring and Assessing Police Use of Force and Suspect Resistance." In *Use of Force by Police: Overview of National and Local Data,* edited by Kenneth Adams et al. (45–60). Washington, DC: National Institute of Justice.

Bayley, David H., and James Garofalo. 1989. "The Management of Violence by Police Patrol Officers." *Criminology* 27:1–23.

Berry, William D. 1993. *Understanding Regression Assumptions.* Newbury Park, CA: Sage.

Black, Donald J., and Albert J. Reiss Jr. 1970. "Police Control of Juveniles." *American Sociological Review* 35(1): 63–77.

Friedrich, Robert J. 1980. "Police Use of Force: Individuals, Situations, and Organizations." *Annals of the American Academy of Political and Social Sciences* 452:82–97.

Fyfe, James J. 1987. *The Metro-Dade Police/Citizen Violence Reduction Project: Final Report.* Washington, DC: Police Foundation.

Garner, Joel H., and Christopher D. Maxwell. 1999. "Measuring the Amount of Force Used by and against the Police in Six Jurisdictions." In *Use of Force by Police: Overview of National and Local Data,* edited by Kenneth Adams et al. (25–44). Washington, DC: National Institute of Justice.

Geller, William A., and Michael S. Scott. 1992. *Deadly Force: What We Know.* Washington, DC: Police Executive Research Forum.

Klinger, David A. 1994. "Demeanor or Crime? Why 'Hostile' Citizens Are More Likely to Be Arrested." *Criminology* 32:475–93.

———. 1995. "The Micro-Structure of Nonlethal Force: Baseline Data from an Observational Study." *Criminal Justice Review* 20:169–86.

———. 1996a. "Quantifying Law in Police-Citizen Encounters." *Journal of Quantitative Criminology* 12:391–415.

———. 1996b. "Bringing Crime Back In: Toward a Better Understanding of Police Arrest Decisions." *Journal of Research in Crime and Delinquency* 33:333–36.

Klinger, David A., and Rod K. Brunson. 2009. "Police Officers' Perceptual Distortions during Lethal Force Situations." *Criminology and Public Policy* 8:117–40.

Langan, Patrick A., Lawrence A. Greenfeld, Steven K. Smith, Matthew R. Durose, and David J. Levin. 2001. *Contacts between Police and the Public: Findings from the 1999 National Survey.* Washington, DC: Bureau of Justice Statistics.

Lundman, Richard J. 1994. "Demeanor or Crime? The Midwest City Police-Citizen Encounters Study." *Criminology* 32:631–53.

Murray, Kenneth R. 2004. *Training at the Speed of Life.* Gotha, FL: Armiger Publications.

Riksheim, Eric C., and Steven M. Chermak. 1993. "Causes of Police Behavior Revisited." *Journal of Criminal Justice* 21:353–82.

Reiss, Albert J., Jr. 1968. "Police Brutality—Answers to Key Questions." *Trans-Action* 5(8): 10–19.

———. 1971. *The Police and the Public.* New Haven, CT: Yale University Press.

Terrill, William. 2001. *Police Coercion: Application of the Force Continuum.* New York: LFB Scholarly Publishing.

Terrill, William, and Stephen D. Mastrofski. 2002. "Situational and Officer-Based Determinants of Police Coercion." *Justice Quarterly* 19:215–48.

Terrill, William, and Michael D. Reisig. 2003. "Neighborhood Context and Police Use of Force." *Journal of Research in Crime and Delinquency* 40:291–321.

Worden, Robert E. 1995. "The 'Causes' of Police Brutality: Theory and Evidence on Police Use of Force." In *And Justice for All: A National Agenda for Understanding and Controlling Police Abuse of Force,* edited by William Geller and Hans Toch (31–60). Washington, DC: Police Executive Research Forum.

PART III
Methods to Encourage Police Accountability

6

How Civil Rights Lawsuits Improve American Policing

Candace McCoy

In 1978, when the U.S. Supreme Court decided *Monell v. Department of Social Services,* only plaintiffs' lawyers and in-house counsel for government agencies realized how important it was. Even fewer considered how it might be applied to local police departments specifically. Now, over 30 years later, private lawsuits are understood to be a very powerful device for holding police departments and their individual officers accountable to the U.S. Constitution. In fact, "constitutional torts" have had as much or more influence on police policy and practice—and will continue to have such effect—than the operation of such well-known but now largely neutralized cases as *Mapp v. Ohio* or *Miranda v. Arizona.* This development is good for the public, good for government, good for the Constitution, and especially good for policing.

This chapter describes how constitutionally based private litigation against the police has developed over the past three decades and examines its impact. The goal is not to provide a doctrinally based examination of *Monell* case law (for that, see Collins 1997 or Avery and Rudovsky 1983 or any of the yearly litigation updates from Pratt and Schwartz 1993 and law review articles cited there). Legal literature is concerned with cases and their doctrinal interpretation, while empirical research determines the actual effects of the cases. Whether those effects are good or bad is a matter of opinion, of course, but at least it is empirically informed opinion—and the conclusion that private lawsuits against the police have improved policing significantly is such an opinion.

This chapter has four parts. The first is a quick overview of *Monell* case law in lawsuits against police departments, describing in very general, non-legal terms the holding in that case and the impact it was expected to have.

The second section describes litigation against the police both before and after *Monell* was decided, determining what happened when private plaintiffs sued police and their employers for particular types of alleged misconduct. A database drawn from an insurance company's records describing police litigation before *Monell* is analyzed as an illustration of pre-*Monell* circumstances. It portrays the earliest days of private litigation against the police, showing the initial impact of *Monell* and how it changed the legal landscape and opened the way for the constitutional tort regime that followed.

The third section covers the post-*Monell* landscape: how police misconduct litigation spread, deepened, affected, and ultimately improved local police practices. The primary conduit for this development was the legal requirement under section 1983 that aggrieved plaintiffs must prove that the police department engaged in an unconstitutional "custom, policy, or practice." The description of such litigation and how it spread, as well as its effects, is derived from the private files of James J. Fyfe, who, during 1982–2005, was the nation's leading expert witness in litigation alleging abuse of force (*New York Times* 2005; see also http://www.towntopics.com/nov1605/obits.html).

The fourth section explains why this litigation has been so useful and powerful as an accountability device. The most important reason is that insurance companies demanded that police improve their policies and practices in adherence to constitutional requirements and thus avoid monetary payouts to injured citizens. Another reason is that section 1983 court cases were reported in the media, which had been impossible, of course, in the days when police were immune from suit. As a result, police department policies have changed in order to meet constitutional requirements, have become more standardized nationwide, and are more carefully applied throughout police organizations through better training and supervision. These changes have all been accomplished in a way that should please adherents of free-market, nonregulatory ideology: since private plaintiffs drive the system, their lawyers act as "private attorneys general" from law firms and not government bureaucracies, the movement is completely decentralized and not directed from the federal government, and the market in insurance has provided a natural regulator and spur for increased innovation.

The Monell Case and the Legal Structure It Changed: An Overview

In 1978, the U.S. Supreme Court held that local governments were "persons" under section 1983 of the U.S. Code[1] and therefore open to lawsuits charging violations of the Constitution. Whether the Court contemplated that the private lawsuit, "prosecuted" by plaintiffs' attorneys, would become a tool of significant governmental reform is speculative.[2] The case ended the immunity from lawsuits that municipalities had previously enjoyed under the ancient prohibition against suing the government: "the king can do no wrong." People whose constitutional rights had been violated by municipal employees were now entitled to monetary compensation. But the impact of the case went deeper than merely providing compensation: deterrence of misbehavior was contemplated. When municipal immunity eroded under the weight of the U.S. Constitution, it did so only in the context of wider public policy. Specifically, liability was grounded in the requirement that plaintiffs prove that their injuries were caused by an unconstitutional municipal "custom, policy, or practice." A policy review component was added to the traditional tort lawsuit's allegations of negligence, and these cases have come to be known as "constitutional torts."

Monell interpreted an earlier case in which the Supreme Court had refused to hold the Police Department of Chicago liable for a warrantless search and ransacking of a black family's home and the illegal detention of the father. In *Monroe v. Pape*,[3] although the Chicago Police Department and the city were held to be immune from suit, the Court said that individual officers could be held liable. Revolutionary in its time (1961), *Monroe* held that individual police officers could not claim governmental immunity from suit[4] but that the municipality itself still retained such protection. Governmental immunity has traditionally protected municipal corporations from being sued because it is reasoned that any judgment paid by a city would be a judgment paid from the pockets of the taxpayers. The ancient dictum that "the king can do no wrong" derived from the idea that, if public coffers could be raided, everyone would suffer. In *Monroe v. Pape*, however, the Supreme Court began to insert modern constitutionalism into the equation. Protection from suit can arguably lead to a *carte blanche* invitation to governments to ignore the law, an untenable situation in a post-Enlightenment age when the Constitution (and its Bill of Rights) supposedly protects citizens from government intrusions.

Before *Monroe v. Pape,* a web of immunity had shielded both the city and its employees. In practice, it operated like a "Nuremberg defense" situation: a citizen alleging harm at the hands of the police would seek to sue the officers, but patrol officers would claim a good-faith defense because they were acting in their official capacities and passed the blame up the organizational hierarchy to supervisors who had trained them to engage in such acts or at least permitted them to continue. The supervisors could be held responsible only if they could be proven to have been "deliberately indifferent" or personally involved in the constitutional violation. If they were following the standard policies of the police department and city, they were not held liable. In turn, when the plaintiffs claimed that the city's policies themselves were illegal, the city had absolute governmental immunity from suit. Thus the "Nuremberg" chain of command was complete: "I was just following orders." But when blame for those orders rose to the level of the employer government, that entity was immune.

The 1961 case (*Monroe*) was an important statement of accountability to the U.S. Constitution, and it was the first blow against the idea that municipalities, like kings, can do no wrong even when they are violating the law of the land. Recognizing the fundamental principle of rule of law, 17 years after *Monroe,* the Supreme Court delivered a second, knock-out blow when it expanded *Monroe*'s reasoning in the *Monell* case. The legal basis for this action was a Reconstruction-era statute, the Civil Rights Act, particularly its Section 1983. That section is called the "Ku Klux Klan Act" because it was passed to control vigilantes who claimed they were "acting under color of state law." This act had been passed over a century before the Supreme Court discovered it and used it to provide a remedy for monetary damages against municipalities that violate constitutional rights "under color of state law" by operation of unconstitutional "custom, policy, or practice." It may seem odd that the act was hardly enforced at the time it was passed in 1871, only to be resurrected in 1978 in *Monell.* However, from the perspective of legal doctrinal development, this was quite consistent with the "rights revolution" begun in the 1960s under the Warren Court. Section 1983 had been enacted at roughly the same time as the Fourteenth, Fifteenth, and Sixteenth Amendments to the U.S. Constitution. Not until the 1960s, when the Warren Court used the Fourteenth Amendment to apply the Bill of Rights to state action, was this amendment implemented in legal practice to apply to police actions. Seen in this light, a monetary remedy for damages caused by unconstitutional acts of municipalities was the logical extension of earlier cases, such as *Mapp* and *Miranda*. Those cases provided the "remedy" of exclusionary rules for violation of suspects' constitutional rights, and a decade later, the Supreme Court provided another remedy: money damages from civil lawsuits.

Monell took the important step of eliminating governmental immunity not only of individual employees but also of the city government itself.[5] The requirement that governments be held accountable to the law overrode the old rationale for immunity as protection of the public purse: surely the suffering of citizens when municipal employees violated their constitutional rights is greater than their suffering if the public purse were somewhat reduced through lawsuits. And, over time—though the Court did not explicitly say so—the impact of removing immunity would be that risk-averse and money-saving municipalities would demand that their employees learn to follow the Constitution so that money would not have to be paid to injured plaintiffs. In the long run, the municipalities would be expected to change the behavior of their employees to follow the law, thus protecting citizens, the Constitution, *and* the public purse.

These two cases arose under the legal structure of tort liability, that is, private plaintiffs suing for monetary compensation for their injuries. Because the Ku Klux Klan Act permitted plaintiffs to sue for violation of constitutional rights, rather than for common-law "civil wrongs," the "constitutional tort" was born. Tort litigation is intended to achieve monetary compensation for plaintiffs—medical expenses reimbursed, lost wages returned, crashed automobiles replaced, pain and suffering recompensed, and so forth—and whether the defendant changes his behavior in the future is left up to the defendant himself (although his insurance company is likely to have something to say about the matter). Constitutional torts follow the same pattern, and the Supreme Court worked under compensatory assumptions in deciding *Monroe* and *Monell*. The possibility of deterrence of future unconstitutional behavior, not merely compensation of victims, was an underlying though only implicit purpose. But deterrence achieved over time cannot be ignored, even though demands for compensation are more immediate and observable.

It is the requirement that plaintiffs prove a violation of "custom, policy, or practice" that would achieve deterrence over time.[6] *Monell* opened the door to inspection of police department operations (indeed, to *any* municipal department operations), and if those operations produce systematic violations of constitutional rights and thus monetary liability under *Monell,* the municipality would be acting in its own pecuniary self-interest to change the offending practices. Matching the observed policies to the requirements of the U.S. Constitution is a very useful exercise that would not necessarily be conducted without the threat of "constitutional tort lawsuits."

Contrast this device with the more heavily debated exclusionary rule remedy for violations of the Fourth or Fifth Amendments. *Mapp*[7] and *Miranda*[8] are studied by every undergraduate criminal justice major and every American law student, and any viewer of the many popular television police dramas can recite *Miranda* warnings by heart. Their exclusionary rules are commonly expected to be deterrents of police misconduct. After all, every case adjudicated in any of the various incarnations of *Law and Order* revolves around developing evidence and getting it admitted at trial—and all the television cases go to trial. By regulating the evidence that gets admitted into all criminal prosecutions, thereby inserting an element of constitutional accountability into every single arrest and prosecution, deterrence of police illegality is assumed. But in an age in which 95 percent of felony cases end in guilty pleas (although, presumably, some do so after a motion to suppress illegal evidence is made) and in which judges will extremely rarely grant such a motion, we may question the depth of the deterrent effect of the Fourth and Fifth Amendment exclusionary rules. Furthermore, although the reasoning behind the exclusionary rule assumes that police care deeply about the eventual conviction of the people they arrest, some arrests are made not necessarily with an eye toward court-ordered punishment but with an eye toward immediate street-level impact—an action that may be illegal under the Constitution. In addition, a rule that may or may not operate to exclude evidence from a case in some remote future cannot be expected to have a fully deterrent effect, especially under the conditions currently prevailing in Supreme Court case law, in which police officers who show that their illegal actions were taken "in good faith" will not suffer the sanction of having evidence excluded.[9] Over time, the exclusionary rule case law has moved accountability back to the standard that prevailed before *Monell:* essentially, a Nuremberg-style structure. By contrast, the constitutional tort case law is vigorous in holding police accountable to constitutional standards, although, as discussed below, it is generally used in types of situations different from those in which the exclusionary rule is used.

Neither remedy for unconstitutional police actions—neither the exclusionary rule nor the constitutional tort—can achieve full deterrence of illegal acts. In a comparison of the two, however, it is possible that a remedy that directly reforms police department rules and procedures governing arrest or interrogation—and enforced within the department's disciplinary system—would arguably achieve more deterrence and accountability than a prosecution-based rule.[10] That its impact has been overlooked by police scholars and legal commentators is somewhat surprising. Perhaps all the debate about the exclusionary rule—and how law developed in ways that emasculate it under political and legal pressures—diverted attention from a quiet revolution that was occurring in the private law offices of civil rights attorneys and federal civil courts (and not criminal courts) throughout the country. The point of noting the impact of the exclusionary rule and referring to the political debate it inspired is not that it is a bad idea or that constitutional torts constitute a perfect accountability device, but simply that the section 1983 lawsuit has been scarcely noticed as the powerful tool for accountability that it is and that legal and justice scholars should explore its influence much more carefully.[11]

The impact of section 1983 litigation on deterring police illegality can now be assessed because *Monell* has been law for 30 years. We can describe the load of litigation that ensued after the case was decided and determine what kinds of constitutional violations were alleged and how many such allegations the courts supported and with what monetary awards. This information, however, does not settle the question of what impact this litigation has had. Nor does it address the issue of whether that impact is achieved in cost-effective or policy-preferable ways. Nevertheless, an empirical description of what actually happens in constitutional litigation is a good starting point for unpacking the arguments around these questions.

Monell's Impact as Shown through an Insurance Company's Records

If for no other reason than that *Monell* opened the deep pockets of municipal liability to injured plaintiffs, we would expect a surge of section 1983 lawsuits to be filed in federal courts beginning around 1979 (the year following the *Monell* decision). It is clear that few cases were filed before, when *Monroe v. Pape* was the controlling law, because *Monroe* permitted lawsuits only against individual police officers whose pockets were quite shallow. In the federal district court for the Central District of California (Los Angeles) in 1975 and 1976, for instance:

> Of the 276 nonprisoner cases, 117 alleged unlawful arrest, assault or battery by the police, and/or unlawful search and seizure. . . . The 117 police misconduct cases generated 33 settlements or trials and 19 dismissals by stipulation. (Eisenstein 1982, 522)

For this entire federal district, which covers the city and county of Los Angeles over a two-year span, this is hardly a flood of litigation. Under *Monroe,* the cases would have been against individual police officers or supervisory personnel. Juries would be sympathetic to the police officers, officers' pockets were shallow, and the costs of the litigation outweighed the amount likely to be recovered. This explanation was confirmed in another study from that time. In an article titled "Project: Suing the Police in Federal Court" that appeared in the *Yale Law Journal,* student editors examined 149 misconduct cases from 1970 to 1977 in a different federal district; the students also interviewed many attorneys, judges, and police officials (Davis et al. 1979). The research results indicated that plaintiffs won very few cases, mostly because juries were unsympathetic to plaintiffs who, although victims of police abuse, were often nevertheless involved in criminal lifestyles that had drawn the attention of the police in the first place. The Yale authors inferred that there would be little deterrent effect from the litigation, and they bolstered this argument by noting that "both the individual [officer] defendants and the police departments were insulated from the financial burden consequent to a [successful] section 1983 suit" (Davis et al. 1979, 814). And in those few cases in which plaintiffs won, not many officers personally paid their adverse judgments; insurance companies or self-insured municipalities indemnified them.

It is quite difficult to assess the overall impact of lawsuits against the police both before and after 1978, when *Monell* was decided, without such statistics. What these two studies show is that, before *Monell* was decided, police misconduct litigation was quite limited in scope and seldom attempted,[12] and when it was pursued, would likely not have affected police officers' behavior much. (Police behavior was especially unlikely to be affected if the departments and their insurers simply reimbursed individual officers for judgments against them, although surely the officers would want to avoid the humiliation of trial.) We would expect this situation to change after *Monell,* for reasons outlined above and for reasons having to do with the insurance industry's response to police misconduct.

Note that these statistics on litigation before *Monell* were drawn from court records in only two federal district courts and thus might not have been representative of the country in general and that they did not include lawsuits filed in state courts. (There would be very few cases filed in state courts under section 1983 because it is a federal law designed to punish violation of the U.S. Constitution; however, police officers could be sued in state court for common law torts such as wrongful death or illegal arrest.) Furthermore, although these studies of two federal district courts present only a sketchy picture of how many cases were filed and their final outcomes, they do not capture the full range of allegations threatened and not filed or filed but dropped. A more comprehensive data source, describing the full range of police litigation in both state and federal courts and extending through the years both before and after *Monell* was decided, would give a fuller picture and also afford a more accurate assessment of the litigation's impact. One study (Kappeler, Kappeler, and del Carmen 2001) examined federal cases from official opinions published in the *Federal Reporter 3d* from 1978 to 1990, concluding that the volume of cases had increased significantly and that *Monell* as a 1978 case was probably responsible. The study covered only cases actually litigated to verdict, however, missing the whole range of settlements that constitute the bulk of litigation.

An obvious source of litigation data covering the entire nation at many points in time and capturing all complaint behavior whether resulting in trial verdict or not is records of insurance companies that indemnify police departments. Every case in which a police officer or police department asked for legal help, no matter what actually happened with the case, would be included. Unfortunately, insurance company records are private and seldom released to researchers. However, one small database from an insurance source, covering the years 1974 to 1984 and thus before and after *Monell,* was compiled and analyzed in 1987 (McCoy 1987a). This insurance company had been the primary insurer[13] for the National Sheriffs' Association (NSA), an organization that has members all over the nation ranging from the most populous jurisdictions (Cook County, Los Angeles County, Dade County) to completely rural counties. The NSA offered this insurance to county sheriffs, deputy sheriffs, and their employer counties. Sheriffs, of course, are the local police for counties, and they also have primary responsibility for running local jails. Therefore, litigation against them would be expected to include allegations not only of unconstitutional police actions under the Fourth, Fifth, Sixth, and Fourteenth Amendments, but under the Eighth Amendment (alleging cruel and unusual punishment, such as from operating county jails).

The database drawn from this insurer's records of litigation over the decade 1974–84 has considerable strengths:

- All types of county jurisdictions nationwide are covered.
- All types of lawsuits filed against sheriffs or counties, whether filed in federal or state court or even threatened but not filed, are described here.
- The statistics describe the types of cases, their dispositions, the amounts of the monetary judgments, and the costs incurred in providing defenses against the charges.
- The time period 1974–1984 affords a look at the volume and types of litigation before and after *Monell,* which was decided in 1978.

A major weakness of the database is that county governments were immune from suit under the Eleventh Amendment. *Monell,* which dissolved *municipal* immunity, would not have applied unless the county waived its immunity, so it might be difficult to discern any changes in patterns of litigation before and after *Monell* was decided in 1978. Somewhat surprisingly, however, most of the large populous counties insured under this company's policies had waived their immunities from suit when allegations of municipal employee misbehavior were made, even before *Monell,* when *Monroe* was the controlling standard. Perhaps such waivers were common because municipal union contracts demanded that individual employees be reimbursed if plaintiffs were to prove successfully that those employees had acted unconstitutionally. An examination of the records of this insurance company revealed the patterns of litigation brought against sheriffs, their deputies, and the county itself over time.

There were 998 cases, and in 90 percent, the sheriff's department, not individual sheriff's personnel alone, was sued. Note at the outset how few the cases were; a mere thousand cases over the course of a decade, covering sheriffs' departments throughout the entire nation, is minuscule compared to caseloads of the late 1980s up to the present. (Perhaps this is partly due to the fact that sheriffs in populous jurisdictions often declined to buy insurance; these counties "self-insured," that is, paid court judgments themselves.) About 3 percent of these cases were brought by employees of the department alleging unconstitutional actions in personnel matters, often charges of racial or gender discrimination in promotion or salary matters. In 74 percent of the cases, an individual deputy sheriff (police officer) was sued, usually along with multiple defendants including the sheriff or the county. The sheriff of the county (the chief) was sued alone in 255 cases, or 25.6 percent of the total.

Plaintiffs all demanded compensatory damages, and many asked for punitive damages. Extremely few asked for injunctive relief even though the "policy defendants" such as the sheriff or the county could presumably make changes that would have an impact on future police behavior. The notion that lawsuits could deter police misconduct was scarcely evident in the data describing litigation against sheriffs, either before or after *Monell* was decided. Individual plaintiffs wanted compensation, but, over time, the logic of *Monell* was that police executives would change unconstitutional practices and policies that had led to compensatory awards. We have no way of telling from these particular data whether that actually occurred, although other evidence such as that from the Fyfe files, analyzed in the next section, can be used to examine the question.

What were the reasons that plaintiffs sued? The data described about 28 typical legal "causes of action." They fell into three main categories: lawsuits stemming from normal policing operations, lawsuits by jail inmates, and lawsuits by employees of the sheriff's department. (The latter category had only 3 percent of the cases.) In addition, seven other causes of action were occasionally mentioned but did not fit easily into these categories.

Jail complaints were the most common reasons for lawsuits. Most were concerned with conditions of confinement, and of these, the great majority were allegations of constitutional torts that did not also request injunctive relief. Many were of the type usually described by exasperated federal judges as nuisances: failure to permit an inmate to visit the law library, dietary restrictions, and the like. However, 156 of the cases (or 16 percent of the total) alleged denial of medical care and resulting physical ailments and pain and suffering. Other jail cases, although few, were even more serious. There were eight suicides and five rapes that plaintiffs alleged should have been prevented by good jail management, and 25 jail inmates sued because they had been assaulted by other inmates.

Most interesting for the inquiry into whether lawsuits can enforce the Fourth Amendment's prohibition against unreasonable searches and seizures, a large number of the cases alleged false arrest or illegal search. The false arrest cases, however, were seldom purely Fourth Amendment situations, since they generally also alleged assaults by sheriffs' personnel. There were only 50 cases over this 10-year period solely alleging illegal search without any other associated allegations.[14] Fifty cases out of 989 (only 5 percent) is not a large number and would not likely exert a significant influence over deputies' behavior.

A few cases could have affected police policy. Forty, for example, cited poor training and supervision as the underlying cause of alleged misconduct. These are the policy cases aimed at supervisory personnel, and the fact that only 4 percent of the total number of cases were concerned with organizational dynamics and policies shows how different the legal landscape looked before *Monell*. Furthermore, very little deterrent impact would be expected if these few plaintiffs did not, in fact, prevail in court.

Of these cases, 10.4 percent were not even filed in court. In this group, plaintiffs' lawyers had contacted the insurance company's lawyers and told them of the cases, threatened to sue, and invited investigation. In most, the insurer agreed that its insured had been at fault and immediately paid compensation as demanded. These prefiling settlements were seldom for large amounts of money and would probably have been described by the sheriffs' lawyers as "nuisances" and the plaintiffs' lawyers as "face-savers." For the parties involved, they probably reflected claimants' deeply felt injustices or perhaps personal animosities directed at individual officers who had arrested or detained them.

The other 89.6 percent of the cases were filed in court. Table 6.1 shows their dispositions. In other words, 38.3 percent of the lawsuits were decided in favor of plaintiffs who had alleged police misconduct,[15] leaving about two-thirds of the cases decided in favor of the defendant police officers or supervisors. No one expected this situation to change much after *Monell*—although the number of cases filed rather than their outcomes might be expected to increase significantly because the case permitted plaintiffs to sue the deep-pocketed cities and thus more litigation might be contemplated over police practices as they existed before *Monell*. If anything, the 1:2 ratio of plaintiff wins to defendant police wins suggests that police need not fear litigation as a potential bank breaker, while the fact that plaintiffs prevailed in a third of the cases indicates that police should take steps to improve their practices.

To determine *Monell*'s impact, we should see what monetary damages were like in police litigation before and after the case was decided. In the

Table 6.1. Disposition of Lawsuits Filed against Sheriffs, 1974–84

Disposition	Frequency	Percentage
Dismissed	159	19.3
Settled	244	29.6
Default judgment (unclear for whom)	92	11.2
Summary judgment for defense	231	28.0
Summary judgment for plaintiff	2	0.2
Trial verdict for defense	26	3.2
Trial verdict for plaintiff	69	8.4
Settled during trial	1	0.1

N = 824 cases filed in court

Source: Insurer for members of the National Sheriffs' Association, 1974–84, summaries of claims made and their dispositions. Data on file with author.

database from the sheriffs' insurer, 23.8 percent of all cases (both filed and not filed) produced compensatory monetary damages for plaintiffs. This number included settlements and also the hotly debated item of plaintiffs' attorneys' fees paid by the losing defendants. Some 8 percent resulted in punitive damages, a number that might give us pause when we consider how egregious the misconduct must have been for a court to have ordered such damages. Only 1.2 percent of the cases produced some form of injunctive or declaratory relief ordering changes within the sheriffs' department. These patterns did not vary much in comparisons of money damages before and after *Monell* was decided.

How much money did plaintiffs actually receive? The total of compensatory damages, attorneys' fees, and punitive damages paid out to plaintiffs over a decade was $2,221,821. The lowest award was $1; the highest was $165,000. A total sum well over $2 million (at a time when a dollar was worth a lot more than it is today) might seem sufficiently important for the insurer to have prevailed on sheriffs' departments to take serious steps to prevent litigation. But the sum represents all money paid to plaintiffs from lawsuits in the counties all over the nation for an entire decade. Compared with many jury awards in police misconduct cases since 1990, many of which involve multimillion-dollar sums in individual lawsuits alone, this amount seems minuscule. And, contrary to concerns at the time about runaway jury awards, only 0.3 percent of these plaintiffs received over $100,000.

In summary, the number of cases, what they alleged, and how much was paid in compensation indicate that litigation against sheriffs was not a major concern to sheriff departments over the decade 1974–84, even though in very unusual, egregious cases, it could have been quite important.

For an assessment of the impact of *Monell*, however, the research question is whether these patterns changed after that case was decided in 1978. The data indicate that indeed there was a change—not in numbers of cases brought or in their outcomes, but in the type of allegations made. Specifically, cases alleging illegal shootings became more frequent. Other types of alleged police misconduct stayed about the same in frequency and outcome. Throughout the pre-*Monell* period from 1974 to 1978 and a lag period from 1979 to 1980 in which the implications of the case were being absorbed by plaintiffs' litigators, the number of lawsuits alleging wrongful use of deadly force stayed steady, but after 1980, they climbed.

This change was not due to any increase in the raw number of police shootings nationwide, since at the time several states were changing their laws to limit police shootings.[16] Probably, this climb indicates that civil rights attorneys had discovered the potential power of *Monell* and were filing suits with the type of allegations lawyers would say were worth pursuing: situations in which large amounts of money are at issue. Families suing for the wrongful death of breadwinners or for disabling plaintiffs who would need hospital or medical care over the course of a lifetime (even worse from the compensatory point of view) would all go to court: before *Monell*, there would have been little remedy. And even though the new case permitted compensatory lawsuits in cases alleging other types of police misconduct (searches, seizures, racial discrimination, jail conditions, and so forth), the potential monetary recoveries would still not favor bringing suit, given the costs. In sum, from these insurance company data, it appears that the first impact of *Monell v. Department of Social Services* was that people who had been shot or beaten by the police were more likely to sue.

As a quick aside, note that this trend toward more litigation was fostered not necessarily by an increased litigiousness on the part of the population but by changes in the law itself. At the time (the early 1980s), there was a vehement political debate in the media and in policymaking circles about "the litigation explosion." Critics associated with the Reagan administration[17] claimed that civil litigation had expanded so much that it hurt the economy, unjustly enriched whining gold-digging plaintiffs, and generally encouraged a culture of complaint. This claim occurred in an atmosphere in which courts had begun to impose strict liability for injuries caused by defective manufactured products, "mass tort class actions" had become possible under new rules of civil procedure, and unfettered jury discretion had produced several spectacularly high awards to plaintiffs. Defenders of these developments (not surprisingly, often plaintiffs' trial lawyers) claimed that the critics were funded by big private firms vulnerable to these claims with a vested interest in attacking the system that produced them and that the so-called tort crisis was a twisted media campaign mounted by the insurance industry, not a crisis at all. The lawyers claimed that shortsighted insurance planners had lowered their premiums in the early 1980s to attract new customers and that they had invested the premiums at the high interest rates then prevailing in the market. Later, when interest rates fell and the insurance companies could not make the profits they had before, they suddenly blamed courts for ordering payouts that the insurers should have known would be forthcoming from the larger pool of policyholders.

As a result, many states responded to the pressure and passed laws to cap jury awards, limit "pain and suffering" damages, or modify strict liability standards. In the specific area of municipal liability, much of it obtained through "constitutional tort" litigation, insurance coverage was the major issue. The U.S. Conference of Mayors conducted a survey of 145 cities and found that *Monell* had caused a huge boom in litigation and jury awards. That boom coincided with increasing insurance premiums due to "mismanagement of the insurance industry" and "a prevailing attitude among the citizenry that someone is at fault for all accidents, the 'sue syndrome' " (U.S. Conference of Mayors 1986, 3; see also ICMA 1986 for a similar study on the personal liability of city managers). Stories of sky-high jury awards against police departments became typical; the awards were higher, and the attendant insurance crisis more urgent than when it was first noted in 1978 (Krajick 1978).

In short, by 1986, eight years after *Monell* had been decided, the legal landscape was shifting significantly. Police use-of-force cases were pursued because their potential money damages were large enough to pay the considerable costs of preparing a lawsuit. The constitutional tort lawsuit was spreading to other types of police behavior that caused enough damage to merit money awards in court, such as car crashes and "failure to respond" to plaintiffs in danger. A crisis in liability insurance, whether manufactured or real, caused police and city managers to turn their attention to what it would take to insure against this burgeoning litigation threat. Finally, local civil rights attorneys drove the change in constitutional litigation as much as any public desire for police reform did. The crusading civil rights bar had discovered in the section 1983 lawsuit a mouth-watering combination of motives: doing good and getting paid well for it. Meanwhile, they would be developing and using a new type of organizational, court-based device for upholding the U.S. Constitution.

Police "Custom, Policy, or Practice" in Court

After *Monell,* police misconduct litigation spread and deepened, to affect and ultimately improve local police practices. The primary spur for this improvement was the legal requirement under section 1983 that aggrieved plaintiffs prove that the police departments engaged in unconstitutional "custom, policy, or practice" in order to win the cases and receive compensation for injuries. Lawsuits alleging illegal use of deadly force by police constituted the most important type of police litigation under *Monell,* not only because these cases involved deaths and high money damages but because the method of policy review encouraged by the litigation structure became clear and entrenched as the 1980s progressed. That method was first developed in deadly force cases litigated under *Monell* in the new litigious atmosphere. The Supreme Court case of *Tennessee v. Garner,* decided in 1985, provided the template.

After *Monell* opened the door in 1978 to lawsuits alleging police illegality, police chiefs and city managers responded by reviewing their "customs, policies, and practices" to bring them into compliance with the Constitution. But at the time, police departments nationwide operated under a patchwork of different policies covering a wide range of police actions, highly dependent on local and state customs and laws. The unstandardized and widely varied police practices were doubly vulnerable to lawsuits under *Monell*'s injunction because liability was possible even if a policy was unwritten but the illegal actions were so common that a court could determine the police were acting under a "custom." After *Monell* was decided, police chiefs and their legal advisers began to scan the professional literature and reach out to professional and legal organizations to find model policies that they could apply to the practices of their home departments. Seeking to inoculate themselves from lawsuits, they adopted more standardized written policies that had been reviewed by attorneys, who in turn were also influenced by professional networks and training seminars offering model policies. (See further discussion of these seminars and their link to insurance in the next section.)

Of course, existing case law said that inadequate supervision or training in otherwise valid policies could trigger liability as surely as a lawsuit over invalid policies could. Police managers and their advisers began to develop a "cognitive model of the legal environment" (Epp 2010), which was that legal liability could be avoided if a department had a good policy, trained officers well to follow it, and constantly supervised them to ensure compliance. (This is not to say that just because a policy changes, behavior does. But behavioral change is more likely, especially if the policy is enforced carefully in this way.) This developing cognitive model was reinforced when the Supreme Court decided *Garner* in 1985.

Garner was the landmark case that overturned the fleeing felon rule, a common law rule that went back as far as medieval England. Under that rule, police were permitted to use deadly force to apprehend a person suspected of having committed a felony. Of course, when the rule had first developed, both the police and the force were radically different. Medieval police were "night watch," not a professional full-time force, and they were unarmed because guns had not yet been invented. Using deadly force at that time meant catching the person and beating him into submission. Later, in England, where the rule developed and in which professional police forces were first constituted, officers did not carry guns even after they had been invented. By contrast, in the United States, by the 20th century all cities had full-time police forces, and they were all armed with guns. A "Wild West" mentality prevailed; policies governing the circumstances allowing police to shoot, with what training and accuracy and for what results, varied drastically across the country. Legislatures in many states—concerned that police were able to shoot people who later turned out to have been innocent or guilty of minor or noncapital crimes, and concerned that police shootings often sparked civil unrest—forbade police to shoot at suspects running from alleged crime scenes.[18]

When *Garner* was argued before the Supreme Court in 1984, a bare majority of states forbade shooting at fleeing felons. By deciding that case on constitutional grounds (stating that shooting someone without proof of criminality was an illegal seizure under the Fourth Amendment), the Supreme Court declared one uniform policy for the circumstances under which American police would be permitted to shoot: an officer may shoot to kill a fleeing felon only when that officer reasonably fears for his own life or that of others. When this defense-of-life policy is linked to *Monell's* requirement that police departments be liable for injuries sustained as the result of an unconstitutional policy, it was clear that *Garner*'s impact would be great: after all, the policy had been stated by an authority no less than the Supreme Court, so that police departments that deviated could expect to be liable in civil lawsuits. The powerful one-two punch of *Monell* followed by *Garner* caused police departments nationwide, at all levels of government, to bring their policies, training, and supervision into compliance with the Constitution under a shoot-only-in-defense-of-life policy.

This story shows why the "shared cognitive model" that Epp describes first developed. The approach became evident in the late 1980s.[19] A method of policy review developed inside police departments and soon was applied to operations other than use of deadly force. Eventually, police policies, training, and supervision in a variety of areas became more standardized and transparent. This process occurred nationwide, at all levels of policing, and took about 25 years to develop fully as a technology of policy review and implementation. It was litigation—and also, quite importantly, the insurance necessary to lower its risk—that sparked that process.

Of course, identifying the exact characteristics of historical trends and their causes is always chancy. Perhaps other factors were at work, and perhaps the causative model described here—that is, that Supreme Court decisions and the structure of tort liability combined to foster significantly improved police policy review and practices and in so doing reformed the American police in ways that no other accountability regime had been able to do—is somewhat speculative. But the data described above, and the experiences of so many people who worked in the field at the time, support that explanation. No person was more deeply involved in these developments than James Fyfe. A look at Fyfe's papers and records from 1980 to 2005 provides ample evidence of the argument made here.

Before providing an overview of Fyfe's papers and records,[20] I must slip into the first person and acknowledge my bias. As Jim's wife, I observed these legal developments and was involved in supporting the expert witnessing work described here. As an attorney, I had been involved in *Monell* litigation before I met Jim, and together we were committed to this model of police accountability. Given the situation, it could be said that I am biased toward overestimating the strength of litigation in forcing police departments to adopt better operational policies and improve their training and supervision. I will leave it to the reader to determine whether this is so but urge keeping an open mind when considering the evidence of the litigation's impact from "what was in Jim's basement."

The big basement was filled to overflowing with research papers, newspaper clippings, files of notes and bibliographies, and miscellaneous information organized by police-related subject matter; a collection of procedure manuals from police departments around the United States (and some other nations); boxes of police department files on personnel discipline, shooting incidents, dog bites (from police dogs), consent searches, and data on the race of people searched and deaths by positional asphyxia; reports from various commissions and police reform groups; proceedings of the Commission on Accreditation of Law Enforcement Agencies; background material preparing for congressional hearings on the exclusionary rule; law review articles; and a complete set of *Spring 3100* dating back to 1957.[21] There was a scholar's library covering a $10' \times 20'$ wall, heavy on police administration texts, one of which was the update of O. W. Wilson's classic *Police Administration* (Fyfe et al. 1996). All this covered about a quarter of the basement space. The remainder was filled with boxes containing files as well as photos, videotapes, and audiotapes, all of it related to individual lawsuits brought against police departments during the years 1980–2003.

Fyfe served as an expert witness in all that litigation, and these case files come from over 600 lawsuits. Because he started this work soon after the Supreme Court decided *Monell v. Social Services* in 1978, his career as an expert witness maps the development of section 1983 litigation. This trove of material expands the evidence of litigation trends evident in the National Sheriffs' Association insurance company files and described in the previous section and shows how policy developed in American policing over those decades.

Of course, it would seem that the best place to start in finding information about constitutional tort lawsuits would be the attorneys who litigated them. The civil rights plaintiffs' lawyers are "children of *Monell*," but the difference between the attorneys[22] and Fyfe was that, as an expert witness, he had a specific and limited role to play in the larger narrative of each case. Individual attorneys can fully litigate a comparatively small number of cases in any given year, and the attorneys who specialize in lawsuits against the police tend to work in small firms (if they are plaintiffs' attorneys) or regularly handle a few police cases among the broader pool of litigation against the municipality (if they are defense attorneys). By contrast, Fyfe could specialize in his expert witness work and provide this service in many cases, spread out all over the country. As a retired police lieutenant from the New York Police Department as well as holder of a doctoral degree in criminal justice and a professor and writer, he had credibility as a neutral referee. When he agreed to serve as an expert in a case, he did so because under *Monell* he could match the alleged misconduct with a policy, rule, or operating standard of the department that was alleged to have violated the U.S. Constitution (or in some cases, state administrative or common law). Through his work, he was convinced that he could eventually help improve American policing.

Expert witnesses, like umpires, are required to "call 'em like you see 'em," which inevitably displeases one side. Fyfe's record as an expert shows that he favored neither side, although that in itself can be criticized as evidence not of neutrality but of sleaze, that is, being willing to say anything for a fee. The role of the expert witness is rather odd; and, in fact, Fyfe wrote some articles on the topic (Fyfe 1987, 1998). He turned down more cases than he took, often telling hopeful lawyers that the other side was in the right and that they should settle the case immediately before spending more money preparing it.[23] He stood up in court for police departments and their officers when he determined they had followed the rules, and he savaged them when they did not. As an ex-cop, he might have been expected to side with police when they were sued—not from some sort of misguided blind loyalty but because we all tend to see things through the lenses of our own professional experiences. Perhaps it was his professional experience as a scholar that convinced him to see things in a different way, to believe in the possibility of evenhanded (if not blind) justice, and to insist that everyone, including the police, follow the law. As he testified,[24] by the end of his career the breakdown of his expert services on behalf of plaintiffs and defendants in the civil cases was about 60/40 (that is, 60 percent for plaintiffs, 40 percent for police).

The high volume of cases in which Fyfe served as an expert, and the fact that they were well distributed between police and plaintiffs and drawn from jurisdictions across the country, demonstrates that any conclusions made from reviewing these case files are likely to be generalizable to what was happening in police litigation at the time. For the historical question of whether police litigation sparked serious reform of police procedures and, eventually, significant changes in police behavior, a look at the *types* of cases Fyfe handled over the time period 1982–2003 is useful. This collection of cases picks up the story where the insurance data described in the previous section left off.

In the years 1982–90, almost all the cases involved use of force, usually deadly force. A few were auto pursuit cases, which came to be regarded as a particular type of deadly force and which increased in number through the 1990s (Alpert and Fridell 1992). Documentation of cases by reviewing electronic materials from that time is difficult because the reports and court pleadings were stored on 5¼ inch floppy disks unreadable by contemporary computers; the researcher has to find electronic files that Fyfe transferred to other media or read the voluminous papers in the Fyfe archives. In my view, however, Fyfe's involvement in the *Garner* case— in which the Supreme Court's majority opinion cited his doctoral dissertation (Fyfe 1978) and in which he had assisted in writing an *amicus curiae* brief for the Police Foundation, quoted in *Garner*,[25] combined with his professional background as both a retired NYPD lieutenant and an academic who wrote his dissertation on police use of deadly force— rendered him the most desirable expert for cases alleging violations of the defense-of-life standard. Lawyers working on these cases nicknamed him "Dr. Deadly Force," and he did many investigations and wrote many expert reports in cases alleging illegal police shootings.

Only a few of these cases went to trial. Considering that the policy the Supreme Court had enunciated in *Garner* was quite clear and obviously firmly rooted in the Constitution and that states were bound to obey it, the question of whether officers had followed the policy was usually a question of fact and not of expert opinion about what the "custom, policy, or practice" of the police was supposed to be. The issue was whether the law had been violated and, if so, whether such violation was part of a pattern of ignoring *Garner*'s requirements. Fyfe's reports usually ended up recounting the facts as brought out in depositions and official reports, restating *Garner*'s policy, investigating whether police officers had been appropriately trained and supervised to follow the policy, and then leaving the facts to juries as to whose story to believe. He did testify in some trials, giving his expert opinion on what a police officer would be thinking under the conditions proven by the facts of the case, and then he would match that opinion to the *Garner* defense-of-life policy.

At first, some police attorneys were willing to take these cases to trial on the assumption that local juries would be sympathetic to police actions even if not comporting carefully with *Garner*'s standard. Fyfe testified in some cases around the nation from 1985 to 1990 in which local attorneys would try to discredit his testimony by mocking his New York accent and background as out of touch with local conditions. To my recollection (and I leave it to others to go through more boxes of written files), this tactic never worked. Whether juries disliked New Yorkers or not, plaintiffs' attorneys had *Tennessee v. Garner* on their side, and they hammered at the question of whether police had truly and objectively thought their lives were in danger when they shot. This clear standard and the police policy, training, and supervision that obviously resulted from it convinced juries around the nation to find for plaintiffs.

By 1990, Fyfe's expert witness practice was ballooning, and cases alleging misuse of force were becoming more varied. He had testified as an expert on the bizarre MOVE bombing in Philadelphia, in which Philadelphia police stormed a house and then bombed a city block from helicopters to subdue a troublesome radical political commune.[26] He gave expert opinions in a series of cases involving brutal beatings, not shootings, in which suspects had died or were maimed. The reasoning of *Garner* expanded to include such cases: not only deadly force through use of firearms, but the wider continuum of coercive force in general—an example of case law development but also the story of how a new policy review technology was evolving as a result of Supreme Court cases and litigation based on them.

In the early 1990s, Fyfe began to examine the issue of whether and how police officers should be required to remove themselves from situations in which they would be forced to defend themselves by shooting. When considering a batch of cases sent to him by lawyers for families of mentally disturbed people shot dead, Fyfe began to question whether the "shoot–don't shoot" mentality of *Garner*'s defense-of-life policy was too simplistic in addressing the wider circumstances of police shootings. Police who approached what they knew to be possibly dangerous people should know not to exacerbate the potentially violent situation by setting up scenarios in which they would be attacked and thus legally justified in killing the assailant, Fyfe believed. Many such cases were coming to his expert witness practice, and he used the insights he had gained from his research in the Miami Metro-Dade Violence Reduction Project to show how police policies on dealing with the emotionally disturbed could produce outcomes in which everybody lived.[27]

Here is an example of such a case taken at random from the files in the basement. It was a plaintiff's case against the Camden, New Jersey, Police Department and seven individual police officers. All the officers were sued personally, and the chief and city were sued as "policy defendants." The facts were these: an emotionally disturbed man ("EDP," or emotionally disturbed person in police jargon) was "acting crazy" in the street, yelling and waving a knife at passersby. He was upset about a family matter, and by the time the police were called, he was in the street. Two police officers arrived on the scene and tried to talk to him, but he just became more agitated. Because he had a knife, they determined he was a threat to the people on the street, and they called for backup. Backup arrived and blocked off the sidewalks so that nobody would be endangered by going too near the EDP with the knife. The officers kept trying to talk him into putting the knife down. More backup arrived, and by that time, seven police personnel were involved—six patrol officers and their sergeant. Rather than calming the man, the situation agitated him more, and he backed off from the officers. The officers formed a ring, each officer about fifteen feet away from him (as they had been trained to do), leaving the man and his knife at the center of the circle.

Notice how these facts would match to a *Garner* defense-of-life policy. Certainly, the man was a potential threat to the officers and people on the street, but by escalating the situation and provoking him, the officers had set up a situation in which they were all put in danger and thus "permitted" to shoot if the threat became immediate. The officers said the man lunged and swiped at an officer with the knife. (Because all passersby had been blocked away from the scene, there were no nonpolice witnesses to what happened.) When the man attacked, their deposition testimony said, the officers surrounding him shot and killed him.

The incident can be viewed from several perspectives. Social workers, for example, might think, "Oh, not another mentally ill person off his meds!" Civil libertarians might think, "Oh, not another person dead at the hands of the police!" And police might think, "My God! These guys were in a *circle* all facing the EDP? And the only person shot was the EDP? Whew! Lucky break!" Of course, all those reactions are correct. The man's family won the case and was awarded the comparatively small sum of $50,000 because his earning potential was low; the money was for punitive and not compensatory damages.

Fyfe began to testify in several such cases, and he claimed that the police were under an obligation to think ahead and plan how to approach an incendiary situation so that nobody would end up dead, including the police themselves. Did cases like this actually work to change police policies and procedures and spark training that educated police officers on how to deescalate potentially violent situations? It is difficult to prove, but multiplying this case by the dozen or so actions filed against the

Camden police every year, and multiplying that number again by the hundreds filed in the state each year, and multiplying that number by 50 states suggests that the cumulative effect of those lawsuits probably had more impact than monetary compensation for injured claimants alone might indicate. And that impact would be very *supportive* of the police themselves as policies and training developed, helping them learn to "police smarter, not harder," as Fyfe used to say.

Certainly, litigation was not the only reason that police policies changed and improved during those years. It is difficult to disentangle the various threads of causation, and the variables cannot be reduced to quantitative measures amenable to multiple regression. Perhaps it does not matter which cause was most significant, as long as the improvement happened. A prime example of such improvement is litigation concerning the duty of police to respond and intervene when a person's life is in danger. Most of Fyfe's cases before 1990 had to do with improper use of force, but litigation evolved and began to challenge other police actions, such as the *failure* to use force when appropriate. Two high-profile cases on this matter came to Fyfe's desk, one very early: 1984, the year Tracey Thurman sued the City of Torrington, Connecticut, and 24 of its police officers for failing to arrest her estranged husband after he stabbed her. Thurman had called the Torrington police before when her husband violated a restraining order; he had previously assaulted and threatened to kill her, and the police knew this.

The incident that produced the lawsuit—and eventually a $2 million trial verdict and a made-for-TV movie—occurred when the estranged husband came to her house again and Thurman called the police. He assaulted her, but no police protection arrived. Eventually, half an hour later, an officer came by but did not arrest the ex-husband even after observing him kick Thurman in the head. Eventually, he stabbed and maimed her. Her case prompted many police departments all over the nation to review their policies on response to domestic violence, although it could be said that the political environment at the time provided fertile ground for such "triggering events" to which reformers could refer in arguing for change. At the same time, the Minneapolis Domestic Violence Experiment (Sherman 1992) moved scholarly inquiry on this topic forward, and together these factors produced a definite change in public and police opinion about intervening on behalf of domestic violence victims.[28] Cynics also said that the police were willing to change their policies because they came to see domestic violence not as a family matter in which men could be allowed to dominate but rather as an opportunity for arresting people!

This story of improving police policies, however, is not as seamless as *Garner's.* Not all police departments changed their policies, and training on intervention in domestic violence incidents remained conflicted. There was no U.S. Supreme Court case setting out the policy here, only a decision from one federal district court that was adopted in most other federal courts but not all. The constitutional basis underlying the policy was also shaky. Thurman had claimed that the Torrington police department's custom of nonintervention violated the Fourteenth Amendment, specifically that the practice would deprive victims of the right to life and that it denied them equal protection of the laws because they were women. Victims of domestic violence, she argued and the district court agreed, are denied these rights when police refuse to protect life because domestic fights are a "family matter." Other courts would not accept this argument, stating that not all victims of domestic violence are women and that it is not clear that the custom of nonintervention was the result of the police department's intention to disregard the rights of women. The shaky status of this area of law is illustrated by the later U.S. Supreme Court case of *Town of Castle Rock v. Gonzales,* 545 U.S. 748 (2005), a case in which a frantic mother begged local police to stop her ex-husband from committing violence against their children, all three of whom he killed. The state of Colorado had passed a statute requiring all its police to respond immediately to calls alleging domestic violence, but the officer in this case went to dinner instead. This case was not one of lack of proper police policy and procedures but lack of action in following them. The U.S. Supreme Court said that "even if the statute could be said to have made enforcement of restraining orders 'mandatory' because of the domestic-violence context of the underlying statute, that would not necessarily mean that state law gave respondents an entitlement to *enforcement* of the mandate." This casuistic "reasoning" stopped the movement toward improved police protections for victims of domestic violence. There was no mention of the Fourteenth Amendment equal protection argument.

In sum, by 2005, this area of law had evolved through a period of policy development and police training, but because the U.S. Supreme Court refused to provide a federal constitutional imperative for it, its status currently rests on state and local law. *Monell* cases (which the *Gonzales* case was) must allege a violation of the federal Constitution, although claimants can still sue under state or local law. Nevertheless, the main point here—that is, that *Monell* litigation caused reform of police policies and procedures—still stands: the policies were put into place but will now be supported by local and state law when the federal law fails. In this case, a method of policy development and application had evolved in other types of cases and was available to apply to new situations.

As the 1990s wore on, police litigation became more varied as it expanded into those new situations. Civil rights attorneys became more adept at mounting these cases, and the Supreme Court continued to decide section 1983 cases, developing a strong body of law that both limited the scope of lawsuits while supporting the section 1983 device in principle.[29] Although the volume of litigation rose, and the type of allegations of misconduct subject to lawsuits expanded, almost all the cases involved some sort of use of deadly force by police. Increasingly, that force was not necessarily exerted at gunpoint.

By the 1990s, a great number of cases involved improper car chases in which police were pursuing people suspected of minor crimes, putting innocent lives of passersby (and, of course, those of the officers themselves and the fleeing suspects as well) in great danger. The logic of *Garner* applied to these cases: why should police engage in activity that could kill a suspect simply because he is fleeing, when he is not presenting a danger to himself or others? Better to call for backup and have him blocked by responding vehicles, or simply to take his license number and find him later. Several experts nationwide developed specific expertise in aiding attorneys in bringing lawsuits resulting from the tragic results of such pursuits, and Fyfe's basement contains records of many such cases. This development did not represent a new type of case but was simply an extension of the existing *Garner* defense-of-life paradigm. Moreover, because the injuries caused in car crashes following these chases were often severe, the monetary logic of constitutional tort litigation mirrored that of the shooting cases: compensatory damages would be high enough to justify the costs of litigating.

Almost all the cases involved serious physical injury to plaintiffs, even when guns were not involved. Fyfe served as an expert witness in a series of cases in which police dogs, trained to kill and maim, were used instead of firearms for apprehending fleeing suspects. The federal district court for the Central District of Los Angeles held that *Garner* applied because the dogs constituted deadly force. In one of the more egregious series of cases, a police assassination squad targeted suspected robbers, watched and waited until they were about to commit a crime, and shot them dead when they appeared. The Los Angeles Police Department claimed that this operation did not violate *Garner* because the suspects were *preparing* to put lives in danger. L.A. Police Chief Daryl Gates was held personally liable, along with the city, for several million dollars.[30]

At the end of his career, from 2000 to 2003, Fyfe was engaged in many cases that challenged police shootings or beatings by off-duty officers. In 1976, he had first noticed the fact that many shooting incidents occurred when officers were out of uniform and off duty; 20 percent of the shots fired that he studied for his dissertation were from officers not engaged in police duties, many of them inebriated (Fyfe 1978). He studied and wrote about the phenomenon (Fyfe 1980), inspired his students to do so (White 2000), and believed that this type of police behavior should be changed through section 1983 litigation. In 1998, Fyfe wrote a lengthy exposé of one case, *Maryanski v. City of Philadelphia,* which involved a terrible beating of two teenagers by off-duty Philadelphia police officers. He showed how the use of force, the fact that the officers claimed to be taking police action while they were drunk and off duty, and a grossly inadequate disciplinary system that did virtually nothing to punish such actions combined to present a picture of police thuggery that the federal court could not ignore. The article is a step-by-step depiction of how the case developed in which Fyfe warns other departments to learn from the case and examine the agency's professional standards, disciplinary systems, and actual officer behavior (Fyfe 1998).[31]

A variant of the off-duty problem involved officers who were undercover, in plain clothes, taking police action but not recognized as such by other officers who happened onto the scene and would attempt to arrest the plainclothes officers. (Of course, this was a more common problem when *on*-duty officers saw what they believed to be criminal activity that would turn out to be covert actions taken by plainclothes officers, but the scenario in which both officers are out of uniform is also possible.) As a police academy instructor and developer of procedures for the NYPD in the 1970s, Fyfe and others had initiated a training protocol whereby an arresting officer, whether on or off duty, must shout, "Police, Don't Move," at which time plainclothes officers mistakenly suspected of being criminals were instructed to raise their hands and declare, "I'm on the job." This situation was harder to enforce when the arresting officer was off duty, because the arrestee plainclothes officer could not be sure of the other's police status. In the most extreme case, two people in plainclothes could both be claiming to be police officers, and each would be skeptical of the police status of the other. Obviously, a clear police protocol for dealing with this situation is necessary, and officers must be trained carefully to follow it.

Young v. City of Providence bounced between the federal district court and appellate court in a campaign of procedural warfare.[32] It had gone to trial years before, and Fyfe had testified at that time when he was still a university professor and not deputy commissioner for training with the NYPD. (When he became commissioner in 2002, he took on no new work as an expert but continued to fulfill his contractual obligations in cases that were dragging on from before that time. Thus, the data from which this story is constructed end in 2005, with his death.) The Court of Appeals for the First Circuit returned the case for retrial, and attorney Barry Scheck once more took it to a jury. In a two-day videotaped trial testimony on behalf of a mother whose on-the-job plainclothes officer son had been shot and killed by a fellow officer off duty at the time, Fyfe gave the last sworn testimony of his career. The dead officer was black and the shooter was white, and the case had difficult racial overtones. Dying of cancer, and told that testifying would dangerously weaken him, Fyfe said, "But that poor bastard is already dead. Somebody's got to stand up for him." Fyfe died two weeks later, and his testimony was shown posthumously in the trial.[33]

Police policies governing off-duty officers carrying guns, and the actions they may take while off duty, are still developing. Although the popular press (*Boston Globe* 2005) and many police department policies and training protocols declare that significant changes are being made in the area, no scholarship or major cases yet demonstrate that this is so. Fyfe and other scholars (Kean 1999) saw the area as ripe for policy development and the next topic for extension of *Garner* reasoning.[34]

Outrageous though the police actions in all these types of cases might have been, they did not strain the basic outline of section 1983 litigation: use of force and compensation for wrongful death were still at issue, and the constitutional tort remedy did not spread to other types of police conduct. The fact that section 1983 litigation was almost exclusively concerned with use of force, failure to use force, and the situations in which force could be used, could indicate that the main conclusion of this chapter (i.e., that litigation is responsible for significantly improving police policies and thus police practices) is too sweeping. Comparatively few cases alleged violations of other constitutional provisions, and nowhere is this more obvious than in an area of police activity that has been the focus of reformers' concerns for decades: searches and seizures under the Fourth Amendment.

The "files in Fyfe's basement" contain some cases alleging illegal searches and seizures, but all involve police actions that resulted in physical harm to plaintiffs. Even then, police usually won these cases, perhaps because juries regarded the plaintiffs as whiners (in situations where the plaintiffs were not seriously injured) or lowlifes (in situations in which plaintiffs, though injured, had indeed been involved in criminal activity). The Fyfe files also include boxes of materials on the exclusionary rule, research on how it operates (see Fyfe 1983; Davies 1983), legislative materials involving his testimony before Congress on the issue, and news clippings quoting people from all sides in the debates over the rule's future. None of these materials mentions the private action for compensatory damages as a possible alternative to the exclusionary rule as a method for enforcing the Fourth Amendment.

Warren Burger's pet policy prescription for illegal police activity, which has come to be known as "the *Bivens* action" (see note 9), has never gained traction. Procedurally, section 1983 actions could be used to sue police for illegal searches and seizures just as surely as it has been to sue for illegal use of force, but it very seldom has been. The main reason is not difficult to imagine: compensatory structures would only work for police misbehavior that has ended with someone's death or injury. How much is a constitutional right worth? Unless the plaintiff can put a provable price on it, nothing. A family that has lost a breadwinner because of an unconstitutional shooting can prove it lost money. A person who has been wrongfully beaten, incurring huge hospital bills, can prove he lost money. A person who is the subject of an illegal search can seldom demonstrate monetary loss sufficient to make a lawsuit worthwhile. And even if he can show such a loss, if he was involved in a crime at the time his rights were violated, juries would be reluctant to compensate him.

None of these conditions precludes using the section 1983 lawsuit as a means of affecting search and arrest policies. But plaintiffs would presumably have to do so not primarily for money but for declaratory and injunctive relief. This path is the direct route to policy change through constitutional tort litigation (as opposed to a more mediated, indirect route as described here in changing police agencies through monetary liability), and it has been used often as a reform device for a different criminal justice agency: prisons. There are similarities between prison reform and police reform insofar as 42 U.S.C. section 1983 lawsuits are used in both.

But there are many differences. In prison litigation, section 1983 was used primarily as a device for achieving injunctions and consent decrees, not compensation for individual prisoner plaintiffs. The consequences of these injunctions and consent decrees were often not what reformers hoped, and the judicial activism involved in obtaining and implementing them created troublesome constitutional concerns (Feeley and Rubin 2000). While achieving reform through the compensatory lawsuit creates none of these problems, it requires that there be a compensable injury in the first instance.

In short, the constitutional tort regime was not applied to uphold the Fourth Amendment because there is just no money in it. From an accountability standpoint, that might be just as well, because the exclusionary rule is supposedly sufficient to deter misconduct in that area of police activity. Skeptics have charged, however, that the exclusionary rule's good-faith defense against allegations of illegal searches or seizures "rewards cops for being stupid," as Fyfe used to say. Transcripts of his testimony before Congress during hearings on the good-faith exception are in library archives, and basically they boil down to that observation. Of course, he and all the other people who fought enactment of the good-faith exception lost that battle. Most police officers today will tell you that the exclusionary rule does not bother them, that they have learned to work under its threat, and that it is not much of a threat in everyday police practice anyway.

Supporters of the exclusionary rule claim that the rule has become so entrenched in law enforcement training that it now exerts considerable control over police behavior. Over time, police managers have been educated on search and seizure, and all officers are trained to comply with Fourth Amendment requirements. The fact that judges only very rarely throw evidence out of court shows that the exclusionary rule is indeed working to deter unconstitutional actions, supporters claim. This accountability device may have worked, and if there have been very few lawsuits over Fourth Amendment violations, it may be because police are acting well within the law.

Or perhaps not. But resolving the debate about whether the exclusionary rule exerts a meaningful deterrent effect on police misconduct is not the issue here. The question here is, has the constitutional tort litigation regime been useful in enforcing the Fourth Amendment, thus adding more confirming evidence to the assertion that litigation has been a major cause of police reform over the past three decades?[35]

Using the cases Fyfe worked on as examples, the answer to this question is yes and no. Yes, there were section 1983 cases alleging illegal searches and seizures, and yes, they have been useful; but no, they were not a major cause of police reform in this area. The Fyfe files contain records of a few private lawsuits alleging illegal search and seizure, involving people with money who had a lot to lose if they were convicted and the resources to fight back against the police after the criminal proceedings concluded.[36]

Another such file is from a *criminal* case, the very unusual situation of a "class action motion to suppress" (see note 19), not a private civil lawsuit. More powerful are cases of which there were no examples in the Fyfe basement: cases in which a group of people who have been subjected to illegal searches band together to sue the police over a specific arrest policy. These cases can have powerful political effects in forcing police departments to explain their policies in court and in the media (Kappeler 2006), but they are rare and seldom result in large compensatory judgments. They are usually aimed at specific statutes or extensive police programs, and their immediate objective is political reform, not compensation. Litigation over the federal drug interdiction program called Operation Pipeline, with its specific orders to local police to arrest interstate highway drivers who looked Jamaican, is an example. The racial profiling scandals of the late 1990s, which at base are about unconstitutional stop and arrest procedures, began when arrestees defended themselves against criminal charges, not by civil rights lawsuits. (Fyfe was a witness in the *Soto* case and all the subsequent political fallout over racial profiling on the New Jersey Turnpike. For a state-by-state overview of policies in reaction to it, designed to stop racial profiling, see *Law Enforcement News* 2000.) The fact that the constitutional tort accountability device is available to challenge search-and-seizure policies, even though it is rarely used, is probably a background concern to police officials in setting up police operations of search and seizure, but it is not likely to be a pressing consideration. Overall, arrest practices in run-of-the-mill police work not involving a special program are even less often challenged with section 1983, but of course they are seldom successfully challenged with the exclusionary rule, either.

Another constitutional provision that could be vindicated through constitutional tort lawsuits is the Fourteenth Amendment's equal protection provision. Allegations of racist actions on the part of the police were common in 1978, when *Monell* was decided, and they are common now. Fyfe wrote a law review article claiming that the "forgotten issue" of

Garner was the fact that Garner was black while the police officer was white and that a racist pattern of shootings was statistically discernible in Memphis but not necessarily in other cities (Fyfe 1982 and 1986). Why, then, have there been few section 1983 lawsuits claiming denial of equal protection of the laws, compared to lawsuits alleging misuse of force generally? Perhaps the same difficulty in monetizing rights that kept the number of Fourth Amendment allegations low is also at work here. Furthermore, courts are often reluctant to venture into the statistical proofs necessary for proving group discrimination, although they do so in employment cases (a type of case that is indeed brought against police departments but has been declining over the past decade as police agencies have become increasingly gender and race diverse). If groups of citizens aggrieved by police actions could prove that the actions were sparked by racial motives, they could band together in a section 1983 lawsuit demanding both money and policy change—but proving such intent is very difficult.

The fact that there are only a few examples of Fourth and Fourteenth Amendment violations being challenged under section 1983 seems to indicate that the major impact of police litigation has mostly been in cases challenging use of force. If this is so, the major thesis of this article—the impact of section 1983 litigation has been that it encourages administrative rule making and enforcement within police departments as a means of avoiding lawsuits—would apply only to police policies on use of force. If so, the conclusion would be that section 1983 litigation has been extremely useful in controlling police use of force but has not been and will not likely be a powerful accountability device in other areas of police activity.[37] This conclusion would be wrong, because it ignores another important development that occurred in the early 1990s as a response to *Monell* and *Garner:* insurance underwriting of law enforcement agencies, model rules and policies developed alongside it, and a self-replicating oversight methodology that could be, was, and is applied to many areas of law enforcement endeavor.

The Final Piece of the Puzzle: Insurance, Model Policies, and Standardization

This chapter has recounted the history of constitutional tort litigation against the police over the period 1978–2005, using records of a defunct insurance company and archives of a leading expert witness on use of force. It looked at numbers and types of cases filed and their results in court and hypothesized that these results caused police chiefs and city managers to develop a "cognitive model" in response to this litigation that assumed that better policies, supervision, and training would improve police behavior on the street and thus prevent litigation. Charles Epp's research (2010) has traced the genesis of that cognitive model to section 1983 litigation, and this chapter adds a piece to that puzzle: the effects of insurance.

Before *Monell* and *Garner,* few cities insured their police departments. There was no reason to do so if courts would hold them immune from suit. Recall the insurance company data described in the second section of this chapter: that insurance company was the preferred provider for sheriffs' departments nationwide; yet so few agencies obtained insurance that there were only $2.2 million worth of claims paid out in the years 1974 to 1984. Once the courtroom doors opened to plaintiffs alleging constitutional violations for compensatory damages and cities began to feel the impact, law enforcement officials began to take notice and search for ways to shield their departments from liability. City attorneys could advise them about the state of the law and warn them of the implications of *Monell* and *Garner,* and in fact Epp's three-pronged cognitive model maps precisely the state of the law on personal and municipal liability at the time. The new and potentially revolutionary twist that *Monell* added was the chance that the city would be liable if the police department's "custom, policy, or practice" was unconstitutional.

Where would an alarmed police official turn to find out whether his department's policies complied with the U.S. Constitution? Like any other executive, he would rely on his legal counsel to tell him of applicable case law, he would scan the professional literature to find model policies that had survived court challenges, and he would turn to his colleagues in professional organizations to compare notes and develop common strategies for preventing problems. Moreover, because the problems involved monetary liability, he would shop for insurance to cover his risks.

In the late 1980s, after *Monell* and *Garner* had time to produce the first multimillion-dollar jury verdicts against police departments in many federal district courts, the implications of these cases were beginning to sink into the law enforcement psyche. Police executives began to attend seminars on avoiding liability. Several police organizations offered seminars on vigorously defending against the legal complaints and on reviewing and improving police procedures to show they were not unconstitutional customs, practices, or policies. (See especially a long series of seminars sponsored by Americans for Effective Law Enforcement of Chicago or workshops offered by the Legal Officers Section of the International Association of Chiefs of Police, or IACP, at the annual conferences.) A literature emerged "for law enforcement executives in the development of extensive training programs, explicit written directives, and the preparation of supervisors . . . [to control] the personnel assigned to them" (Di Grazia 1987, 13, reviewing Silver's 1986 book marketed to law enforcement officials with the statement that it would "show you preventive measures that will minimize your risk of being charged with police misconduct").

The obvious questions asked in such seminars were, What policies will withstand legal challenge? And where do I find them? Soon projects analyzing, formulating, and disseminating model policies emerged. Following its widely distributed publication of model policy on deadly force (Matulia 1982, 1985), the IACP instituted an in-house model policy project and published a detailed set of policy manuals (IACP 1988). The Commission on Accreditation of Law Enforcement Agencies, which was formed in 1979 to foster professionalism in policing through accreditation review, produced a book of standards and policies that was circulated widely and is well established as a major reference work today[38] (CALEA 1982). Most important to the argument about whether section 1983 litigation sparked reform in areas other than police use of force, these model policies covered a wide range of police operations.

Simultaneously, law enforcement officials sought to reduce their exposure to lawsuits by obtaining insurance. But insurance companies would not offer attractively priced policies if police agencies could not demonstrate they had done everything possible to reduce the risk of lawsuits. Stung by the 1985–86 "liability crisis" and a crisis in their own underwriting and payouts, the insurance industry restructured itself.[39] Now allowed to offer insurance to groups of municipalities that could pool their risks and resources, insurers moved to organize risk management protocols for police departments. By 1985, two trade organizations had published manuals to help police departments reduce their legal liability through risk management (Wasserman and Phelus 1985; Wennerholm 1985), and by 1990 the first major books and articles prescribing liability avoidance through risk management associated with insurability were published (Gallagher 1990a, 1990b, 1992). Experts such as Patrick Gallagher and, again, James Fyfe[40] addressed insurance groups on what to look for and what policy changes are required of police agencies seeking insurance against legal liability risks.

Soon it became common knowledge in the law enforcement profession that the way to obtain insurance was to review departmental policies and bring them into line with national standards, which covered a wide range of police operations, not only use of force. Demonstrating compliance with accreditation standards, for instance, could help a police agency get insurance whether the agency actually sought accreditation or not. The Commission on Accreditation of Law Enforcement Agencies (CALEA) web site today offers testimonials from satisfied police executives of agencies that have been accredited by going through an exhaustive process of policy and practice review. Here is one from 1996:

> Thanks for your help in providing me with a list of Law Enforcement Liability Providers who offer discounts for accredited agencies. I presented your list to our Risk Manager. She contacted our insurance broker who subsequently agreed to a reduction in our premiums of $19,000 annually. This equates to a 16.7 percent decrease.[41]

Charles Epp, in his writings on the effect of litigation on municipal policy improvements, acknowledges the role of insurance. He quotes an article from the *Police Chief* (the magazine of the IACP) reporting that the primary insurer of police agencies stopped offering coverage in 1988. He says that

> a North Carolina governmental commission had found that insurance company's police liability loss record "was very good" but that the high degree of unpredictability of liability suits had contributed to the insurance crisis. Later, the same writer attributed the growing liability threat directly to several key Supreme Court decisions, particularly *Monroe v. Pape* (1961), *Monell v. Department of Social Services* (1978), and *Owen v. City of Independence* (1980), and to growing pressure from plaintiffs' attorneys in the wake of those decisions. (Epp 2010, summarizing Thomas 1979, 1982)

Eventually insurers returned to the police market, especially when municipalities themselves developed strategies for obtaining insurance, but they did so only if the agencies could demonstrate that they were not vulnerable to lawsuits. Patrick V. Gallagher, who often consulted with insurers and sometimes served as an expert witness on behalf of police agencies, developed a protocol for reviewing police policies, procedures, and practices for reducing the risk of liability and marketed it to police agencies (Gallagher 1992). As a result of such efforts shared among police departments, their legal advisers, and insurance companies, police operations improved significantly over the course of the 1990s.

Whether for traditional torts or constitutional torts, legal liability and insurance are inextricably linked. That this link has largely been over-looked in recognizing the depth of the reform that has occurred in law enforcement agencies over the past three decades is perhaps due to the fact that reformers do not think of compensatory lawsuits as a meaningful accountability device. Even scholars who study risk management in police agencies seem to have only dimly perceived the broad effect of linking litigation, accreditation, policy standardization, and insurance and instead are sidetracked by asking why police departments seldom employ risk managers (Archbold 2005). The answer is that cities themselves employ risk managers; only police chiefs in huge city departments can afford their own. In most jurisdictions, police chiefs rely on the city's expertise and the standards available to them through their professional channels, such as the IACP and CALEA, and all departments can rely on the advice of risk-avoiding lawyers, whether they can afford to employ in-house counsel, rely on the help of city attorneys, or are part of a city's contractual arrangement with private general counsel to provide legal advice.

Why has the section 1983 lawsuit, along with the broad methodology of policy review and implementation that it spawned, been overlooked in debates about police accountability? Two reasons spring to mind, although there are probably many others. First, the effects of this litigation are difficult to discern empirically. No national lawsuit database exists, and there is no centralized source of information. The data used for this chapter—that is, insurance company records and an overview of an expert witness's personal files—are one of the few reports of data on this issue, and the cases described in these data are a compendium of lawsuits from all over the nation, not from a centralized reporting system. (Actu-ally, it is this very decentralization that has rendered the section 1983 constitutional tort lawsuit so effective, as discussed below.) Second, other accountability devices, such as consent decrees or the exclusionary rule or citizen review boards, are "sexier" because they rely on regula-tion, and experts can have a part in designing such regulations. Lawsuits, although often covered in screaming detail in newspapers and broad-casts, are not usually subjects of scholarly inquiry. Social scientists leave this to the lawyers, and the lawyers do not think empirically.

While other accountability devices have been much more interesting to scholars, that does not mean they prove to be the most effective in influencing police officer behavior. The exclusionary rule debate—with its intersecting pressures of Congress, the courts, police resistance, and political gamesmanship—has provided fodder for a small industry of criminal justice publishing, but the actual effect of the rule on search and seizure practices is still contested (McCoy 1996).

Consent decrees, which are detailed injunctive orders to which plaintiffs and police departments agree in order to settle section 1983 lawsuits for injunctive relief (if brought by private plaintiffs) or orders for compliance monitoring (if brought by the federal Justice Department) have received some scholarly attention (Walker 2003, 2005) and even more discussion in professional police circles. The public consent decree device is established statutorily by the Violent Crime Control and Law Enforcement Act of 1994 and set into law as 42 U.S.C. § 14141. It permits the U.S. Department of Justice to sue local police departments for violations of accepted police "custom, policy, and practice"—a verbatim quotation of the historic section 1983 language. Walker goes so far as to call the consent decree a "new paradigm," but he carefully explains that it is made possible because the "specific reforms mandated in those agreements were not developed by the Justice Department itself but were drawn from recognized 'best practices' related to accountability already in place in other more progressive police departments" (Walker 2003, 6).[42] As this chapter has described, those "best practices" standards came to be developed in the 1980s and 1990s, and it is private litigation rather than consent decrees pursued by the federal Justice Department that first sparked the movement and that continues to do so today.

Walker argues that the section 14141 consent decree offers great hope as an accountability device, and on paper this is surely so. (See the report explaining how it works, published by the Vera Institute of Justice in 1998, showing that obtaining a "pattern-and-practice consent decree will reform police departments better than criminal prosecution of individual officers will.") Walker said in 2003 that "to date, there have been a total of eight such settlements, with the most highly publicized ones involving the Pittsburgh Police Bureau, the New Jersey State Police, the Los Angeles Police Department, and the Metropolitan Police Department of the District of Columbia." Examining these eight consent decree cases, we see clearly that all were initiated only after the departments in question were involved in scandalous misconduct that attracted national news coverage (in Cincinnati's case, a race riot). All of them were initiated before 2002, under the Clinton administration, and no other lawsuits under section 14141 on their scale have produced consent decrees since. The Bush administration's Department of Justice did prosecute a smaller-scale case under section 14141, against Washington, D.C., suburban Prince George's County Police Department for its use of dogs as coercive force. Cynically, it can be observed that in Washington, D.C., where many federal civil servants live in the Maryland suburbs, this story would have been quite a scandal, and there may have been internal pressure on the Justice Department to do something about it.

Although it can be said that the civil rights division of the Department of Justice under the Bush administration simply did not regard section 14141 as a priority, no political administration is immune from selective prosecution practices. The success of the section 14141 remedy depends on how the Justice Department answers such questions as:

> How difficult a task will the attorney general face in proving a pattern or practice of rights deprivations under 14141? Will the Department of Justice obtain and employ the resources necessary to vigorously enforce the law? Will federal courts prove willing and able to invest the energy, time, and ingenuity needed to fashion effective equitable relief? If implementation of the law results in extensive intervention into the administration of local police departments, would Congress accept such a result? (Miller 1998, 151)

Section 14141 was an important provision of the 1994 Crime Act that was arguably Clinton's greatest legislative achievement, and Clinton's civil rights division was developing a strategy for using section 14141 aggressively. One of its first consent decrees was obtained against the police department of Steubenville, Ohio. There is a Fyfe file on this, since Fyfe was engaged as an expert to help prepare the litigation. For various reasons, including the fact that the Department of Justice attorneys did not need many of his services, Fyfe did not do extensive work on the case. Perhaps it was because he had invested little of his time or energy in it, but he was skeptical of the federal consent decree device because he worried it would be used only against those agencies that the federal Justice Department wanted to embarrass. Clinton administration attorneys sought consent decrees primarily against jurisdictions with Republican executives,[43] and presumably Bush administration attorneys would seek to embarrass Democratic mayors if its Justice Department were to wield the consent decree device energetically. Since 2002, however, there have been extremely few consent decrees against local police departments prosecuted by the Department of Justice.

The consent decree device has been in use since the 1970s, before passage of the 1994 statute, in cases where civil rights organizations brought class actions on behalf of prisoners demanding changes in prison conditions. Fashioned as section 1983 cases demanding monetary compensation, these cases sought instead an injunctive decree for court-ordered monitoring of reform. The outcome has not been deep and lasting reform of American prisons. Instead, the lawsuits can be said to have stretched the expertise of judges beyond that which a legal structure can handle and have subjected the bench to great criticism for being too activist (Feeley and Rubin 2000; Cohen 2004; Rosenberg 1991). The success of various consent decrees against state prisons was also dependent on the personal management styles of the court-appointed monitors (Chilton 1991).

This flaw in the consent decree device perfectly illustrates why the private lawsuit for compensatory damages has, by contrast, been very successful. A lawsuit simply demands money, and if it gets it, the loser is left on its own to determine how to avoid payouts in the future. By providing high incentives for defendants to change their illegal behavior on their own terms, the device fosters the deepest behavioral change. (We are more likely to change more thoroughly if we do it ourselves than if someone tells us how to.) It does not rely on politically driven enforcement, and it is not administered by a centralized government bureaucracy. American policing is radically decentralized—local schools and local police are almost completely locally controlled—and imposing federal constitutional standards on them is a Sisyphean task when attempted from Washington.

This is not to say that consent decrees are useless or have no place in a system of police accountability that relies on interlocking remedies, of which consent decrees can be one. It is simply to say that consent decrees are best aimed at a particular outrageous problem—racial profiling on the New Jersey Turnpike, for example—and are unlikely to affect police policies nationwide at the deepest policy levels. The strength of the private constitutional tort is that attorneys in any locality in America, pursuing the monetary interest of both themselves and their individual clients, can permeate every location in the nation without relying on an unwieldy and often politically driven bureaucracy, and all applying the same law: that of the U.S. Constitution.

Perhaps paradoxically, accountability to the Constitution may be best accomplished when it is driven locally (see generally Dowdle 2006, especially Rubin's chapter). The "private attorneys general" (Meltzer 1988), that is, local attorneys seeking to do good by doing well for themselves and their clients, have fashioned a revolution in police departments all over the nation. Though not unnoticed, section 1983 litigation and the policy development and implementation that developed because of it, coupled with the professional risk management skills and oversight of the private insurance industry, have not been given the credit they deserve. This accountability device has probably been the source of the most far-reaching yet deep reforms in American policing over the past three decades. It is through these low-level and constantly challenging events, and the political system's responses to them, that people learn how to follow the law.

NOTES

1. *Monell v. Department of Social Services of the City of New York*, 436 U.S. 658, 56 L.Ed. 2d 611, 98 S.Ct. 2018 (1978), interpreting U.S. Code, Title 42, section 1983, which states: "Every person who under color of any statute, ordinance, regulation, custom, or usage, of any State or Territory or the District of Columbia, subjects, or causes to be subjected, any citizen of the United States or other person within the jurisdiction thereof to the deprivation of any rights, privileges, or immunities secured by the Constitution and laws, shall be liable to the party injured in an action at law. . . ."

2. Transcripts of oral arguments before the Supreme Court in the *Monell* case indicate that the Justices—and, indeed, the lawyers—regarded it primarily as a sex discrimination case that would affect the law of equal protection under the Fourteenth Amendment. *Monell* involved a pregnant city worker who lost her job with the city of New York because she was pregnant. In holding that the city could not deny constitutional rights under a municipal "custom, policy, or practice," the court stated that Ms. Monell could sue the city for lost wages and damages because she was the victim of the city's policy of such gender discrimination. It is doubtful that the Justices imagined they were opening the way to private lawsuits against all municipal agencies, including police, where it was possible to prove a link to an unconstitutional (often unwritten) policy. However, according to Professor Charles Epp, who has studied the transcripts, Justice Marshall probably understood the revolutionary nature of the holding (personal discussion with Charles Epp, July 28, 2007).

3. 365 U.S. 167 (1961).

4. The *Monroe* plaintiffs eventually recovered $11,000 from the 13 individual officers who had conducted the raid. In 1961, that sum went a lot farther than it does today, and the fact that it could be obtained at all was groundbreaking.

5. *Monell* thus prevented a constitutional tort lawsuit against the police from vanishing if police personnel could make a cognizable claim that their unconstitutional actions were simply conforming to municipal custom. The liability web was completed in *Owen v. City of Independence*, 445 U.S. 622 (1980), which held that municipalities could not claim good faith defenses to constitutional violations.

6. Traditional tort lawsuits against individual police officers in the *Monroe v. Pape* mode, in which plaintiffs allege negligence or even intentional misconduct in taking police action, might exert some deterrent effect. Data on numbers and types of lawsuits filed before 1978 (when *Monell* was decided) indicate that "most of the suits filed in 1967 through 1971 (40.6 percent) were for false arrest or imprisonment. Another quarter (27.2 percent) were for brutality" (Sherman 1979, 169, citing "Survey of Police Mis-

conduct Litigation 1967–1971" by Americans for Effective Law Enforcement). These were cases against individual officers alleging common law torts and were brought mostly in state court. These types of cases continued to be filed after *Monell*, of course, but the difference was that plaintiffs would also strive to prove that the wrongful actions were taken as part of the custom, policy, or practice of the department and thus its municipality. It is this added dimension of litigation that contributed to significant improvement in police procedures and training and thus improved American policing over time. Common law tort lawsuits against individual officers occurred both before and after *Monell*, but their deterrent effect would be less because they did not have a policy review component built into the controlling case law.

7. *Mapp v. Ohio*, 367 U.S. 643 (1961).

8. *Miranda v. Arizona*, 384 U.S. 436 (1966).

9. *United States v. Leon*, 468 U.S. 897 (1984). Compare this case to *Owen v. City of Independence*, cited above, in which the Supreme Court held that there is no good-faith defense available to municipal officers who claim their actions, although illegal, were done in good faith. This may be one reason that the constitutional tort lawsuit has had significant impact on police procedures over the past three decades, while that of the exclusionary rule is fading.

10. In fact, Chief Justice Warren Burger opposed the exclusionary rule because he thought deterrence of police misbehavior could be achieved better through private lawsuits and an administrative structure in which aggrieved citizens would make monetary claims against officers. See Burger's dissenting opinion in *Bivens v. Six Unknown Named Agents*, 403 U.S. 388 (1971).

11. Professor Christopher Slobogin (2007) reaches a similar conclusion in his hard-hitting article "The Liberal Assault on the Fourth Amendment." He states that "the obsession with exclusion as a remedy" has led liberal groups to force the exclusionary rule into the faces of judges "who cannot stomach dismissal of criminal charges against guilty people" and respond with decisions that weaken both the Fourth Amendment and the exclusionary rule as its remedy. Instead, if a different method of deterring Fourth Amendment violations could be found, these judges would be willing to use it. Slobogin proposes a private damages scheme to supplement the exclusionary rule. See pages 617–19 of that article. Note that such a scheme need not be a full-blown tort lawsuits regime such as that described here.

12. The private organization Americans for Effective Law Enforcement conducted an ongoing survey of litigation from 1967 through 1976 and found that police lawsuits had increased over 500 percent in that time, and this was before *Monell*. A survey by the International Association of Chiefs of Police confirmed this. Although these trade organizations were understandably alarmed at the trend—and it was occurring mostly in state courts nationwide, not in federal courts—the concurrent baby boom growth in population at the time and the civil unrest of the 1960s and 1970s are probable explanations for it, and the rate of lawsuits per capita was still quite small compared to later filing volume. These lawsuits were against individual police officers, and in this light, it is possible to say that *Monell* in 1978 relieved the pressure on individual officers by shifting monetary liability onto their departments and cities. For an overview of data and surveys about police litigation, see Worrall (2001, 11–13).

13. The company, anonymous here, is now defunct. That was the reason I was able to obtain its records. Its former general counsel assured me that the company was in no

way atypical and that the business problems that caused it to dissolve its incorporation in 1984 flowed from areas of insurance unrelated to its police line of coverage. Neither was the advent of *Monell* claims in 1983 the reason the company stopped offering insurance, the lawyer said.

14. These would be Fourth Amendment cases and are the type of cases that form an alternative model of deterrence of illegal searches and seizures, contrasted to the exclusionary rule. Of course, money losses are alleged here; the search or seizure had to have produced some serious monetary loss to the plaintiff. Moreover, given juries' reluctance to award money to guilty criminals, these cases probably involved innocent plaintiffs. This is not a strong model for an alternative to the exclusionary rule, but the point is that individual claiming against police actions is possible and its structure—not necessarily this one—should be examined creatively.

15. That is, the combination of settlements, summary judgments for plaintiffs, trial verdicts for plaintiffs, and perhaps a few more if there had been default judgments for plaintiffs, though if so, these would have been insignificant cases in which the police defendants did not bother to show up for a court date.

16. Slowly over that decade, many states were changing their state laws to forbid police to shoot fleeing felons, and many municipal police departments had adopted policies that were more restrictive than their state laws allowed. Eventually, when the U.S. Supreme Court was asked to rule on the practice in 1985, a slim majority of states forbade such police shootings; 23 states retained the old "fleeing felon rule"; 22 forbade shooting at fleeing suspects unless the officer was endangered or the runner was suspected of a serious crime of violence; and in five states, the standard was unclear. See *Tennessee v. Garner*, 471 U.S. 1 (1985), p. 12. The Supreme Court noted that shooting and crime rates were uncorrelated with whatever standard a state used.

17. Indeed, the Reagan administration itself had a tort reform working group inside the Justice Department, and in March 1986, it released its recommendations, which aimed to restrict monetary awards in tort cases. Subsequently, various bills were proposed in Congress, but since tort liability is fundamentally a matter for state courts, little could be done. However, in one area, section 1983 constitutional torts, the federal government controlled. Senator Orrin Hatch introduced legislation (Senate Bill 584) that would have limited the types of claims that could be made under section 1983 and also would have instituted a good-faith defense similar to that of the exclusionary rule cases. For whatever reasons, the bill did not gain traction and did not pass. However, agitation for reform of laws governing liability insurance proceeded in the House, and in March 1986, the Subcommittee on Monopolies and Commercial Law held hearings to consider whether to increase regulation of the insurance industry. One major reform approved was that local governments would be allowed to join together and obtain insurance policies covering the wide pool of governments. Availability of insurance was a major concern for municipalities around the country, especially since they were being hit with rapidly escalating costs for their insurance, and many cities "went bare" because they could no longer afford the premiums. Congress responded by helping restructure the insurance industry through changes in federal regulation so that localities could more easily obtain insurance. Scholars have noted that the insurance industry has "cycles" in which its profitability goes up or down depending on a variety of factors, few of them related to the actual risks insured against (Baker 2005).

18. More than 20 years later, young police recruits are often surprised to learn that it was only recently, in living memory, that the old medieval rule allowing police to shoot

fleeing suspects was abolished. Tactical intelligence and restraint of force are taught today at police academies, and contemporary officers are often surprised to hear about how vehement the opposition to limiting police shooting was at the time. In the 1985 case of *Garner,* the Supreme Court quoted the arguments of the Memphis Police Department: "Effectiveness in making arrests requires the resort to deadly force, or at least the meaningful threat thereof. 'Being able to arrest such individuals is a condition precedent to the state's entire system of law enforcement.' Brief for Petitioners 14" *Garner,* page 10. Imagine how less genteel the words were in public policy debates at the time. Many police predicted huge crime waves if police were forbidden to shoot fleeing suspects.

19. Two research organizations conducted surveys in 1986, after *Monell* had had time to sink in and one year after *Garner* was decided. Both surveyed chiefs of cities, not rural jurisdictions. The Police Foundation surveyed 100 chiefs of police of the largest cities in the nation, asking them to rank the types of cases that were of most concern to them, and also to indicate whether they had legal advisers to handle such litigation, what the insurance implications were, and how they perceived the "litigation crisis" (McCoy 1987b). The Police Executive Research Forum also surveyed police chiefs, adding other supervisory or professional personnel as well. This internal PERF report covered the most common types of litigation and whether there had been significant organizational responses to them (Nowicki et al. 1987).

These surveys provided some evidence on the deterrent effect litigation has on police organizations. Perhaps because they surveyed somewhat different populations, the responses differed slightly. In the Police Foundation survey, all chiefs were well aware of the dangers of litigation and listed use of force, auto pursuits, arrests and searches, and employment-related matters as the areas of greatest concern, in that order. The chiefs' consensus was that liability, though a bother, was a fact of life. The police chiefs believed their legal liability could be reduced by good training and management practices. They therefore did not perceive a "litigation crisis." Some mentioned that they believed the crisis mentality emanated from insurance companies, not from the police themselves.

If good management and training were perceived as the appropriate way to prevent lawsuits, this is evidence that deterrence, although diffuse, might be at work. The PERF survey underscored the fact that police personnel in many different job categories were aware of litigation risks and were more concerned about it than the police chiefs surveyed by the Police Foundation apparently were. The PERF survey discerned a notable lack of communication between police chiefs and legal counsel for their departments. Although 71 percent of the departments reported that they had lost a lawsuit in the past two years, only about half the police chiefs reported that their attorneys even informed them of the issues raised in the civil action or provided them with a statement specifying why the case was won or lost. Most discouraging from a deterrence standpoint, fewer than half received an assessment of what department procedures could be redesigned to reduce future liability. The authors of the PERF study were sounding the alarm: by 1987, it was time to realize that the legal landscape had changed and that chiefs should begin to review the "customs, policies, and practices" of their departments to avoid litigation.

20. Fyfe's papers are archived in the library of his undergraduate alma mater, the City University of New York, John Jay College. References to those papers made in this article can be checked in that archive. The materials of most general interest are the background research and investigation papers from such cases as *Garner, Lawson v. Kolender,* MOVE, Ruby Ridge, Jeffrey Dahmer/*Sinthasomphone, Thurman v. Torrington,* and of course *Diallo,* among other cases that were high profile in the news of the day. But there are records of over 600 more typical cases that were news stories only in their local areas, and that is where the real impact of this litigation can be discerned.

21. *Spring 3100* is a monthly magazine published internally for the New York City Police Department, basically a newsletter covering personnel actions, program successes, and personalities in that huge department. These issues are now archived at the Police Museum of the City of New York.

22. The names of the attorneys who brought these cases, often in the face of intense political and media pressures and sometimes outright harassment from the police, could produce a roll call of people whose stories deserve books of their own. Since the point of this chapter is to describe the effects of the litigation and not the people who developed it, no names are mentioned. This omission should not be regarded in any way as detracting from the hard and in many cases courageous work these people did.

23. Almost all Fyfe's cases were civil lawsuits, but there were a few criminal prosecutions, and two of those were some of the most high-profile cases of his career. He testified against the police in one and for the police in the other. He served as expert on traffic stops on behalf of a group of minority citizens who had filed a "class action" motion to suppress evidence due to illegal racial profiling on the New Jersey Turnpike. The case, *New Jersey v. Soto,* defended by public defender Fred Last of a small rural county, was the first to spark a high public outcry against racial profiling through the federal program Operation Pipeline. By contrast, Fyfe testified on behalf of the police in the criminal case against four NYPD officers who had killed Amadou Diallo. The trial was broadcast live on Court TV. After Fyfe's testimony on behalf of the officers, Court TV commentators stated that the prosecution's cross-examination "right after our commercial break" was sure to be scathing. But the prosecutor stood and declared that he had no questions for the witness, stunning the courtroom. The reason was that the prosecution had been the first to engage Fyfe as an expert witness in the case, but Fyfe gave his expert opinion that the four officers were not guilty of manslaughter beyond a reasonable doubt. Obviously the prosecution would not use him as a witness. Subsequently, the defense found him and engaged his services. In the trial, if the prosecutors had questioned him after his direct testimony for the defense, they could not have impeached his credibility because on redirect examination the defense would have brought out the fact that they themselves had first hired him. Thus, the prosecutors wisely said nothing.

24. From a deposition in an Ohio case, 2001: The attorney asked how much time he worked as a university professor, as an expert, and how often as an expert for or against police. Fyfe answered: "I'm allowed to work [on outside contracts] one day a week, and during the summer, I probably work three. So, overall, it's probably about 30 percent of my time." Attorney: "I noticed in your list of cases you have been involved in the past four years, it looked like probably about 75 percent or 80 percent of those would be plaintiff oriented." Opposing attorney: "Objection. I don't think that's a list of all cases, but a list of cases in which he has actually testified." Attorney: "Okay. I'll clarify that, then. The cases that you have actually testified either by trial or deposition?" Fyfe: "That's correct, yes. That's probably about 75 or 80 percent for plaintiffs. I do a lot of work for defendants. That is not reflected here because usually it results in summary judgments or nuisance settlements." Attorney: "Overall, how would your percentage breakdown then be, including all cases that you review and actually issue a report?" Fyfe: "I would say it's something like 60/40, plaintiffs to defendants."

25. Notes and drafts of the preparation for that case, collaborating with attorneys Steven Winter and Martha Fleetwood, are archived in the John Jay College library. The National Bar Association, an association of African-American lawyers, filed an *amicus curiae* brief in the case, as did the Police Foundation, which is a research group for which Fyfe worked at the time.

26. Theses cases are detailed in Skolnick and Fyfe's *Above the Law: Police and the Use of Force.*

27. See the chapter by David Klinger in this volume.

28. The other failure-to-intervene case was *Sinthasomphone v. City of Milwaukee,* the Jeffrey Dahmer case. Dahmer was a serial killer whose gruesome crimes came to light in 1991. Sinthasomphone was a Laotian immigrant teenager whom Dahmer had lured to his apartment and was preparing to kill. The boy escaped and ran, nude, out to the street where he found police and asked for help. Dahmer convinced the police that this was a "lovers' quarrel" and that they should not intervene. The police returned the boy to Dahmer, who killed and cannibalized him. In all the horror that arose when Dahmer was caught and his crimes revealed, the fact that the teenager's family sued the Milwaukee police was one minor part of the news frenzy. Fyfe's deposition in the case emphasized that "the primary role of the police is to protect life." The family won the case, the officers were fired but reinstated years later, and eventually one was elected head of the police union in the city.

29. This is not a law review article, so the cases will not be recounted here. However, an excellent overview of cases as they developed and the effect of these cases on police standards is Victor Kappeler's *Police Civil Liability: Supreme Court Cases and Materials.*

30. In terms of pure volume of paper, files of lawsuits from Los Angeles and Philadelphia took up the most space in the Fyfe basement. This does not prove that these two cities had the most brutal police departments, only that plaintiffs' lawyers from those cities were very active and effective, that the cities had continuing problems with police misconduct, and that the size of the cities meant that the number of cases was large, too. Midsize New Orleans took the prize for the most appalling although not the highest number of incidents (cases amounting to premeditated murder by police) and many cities in Texas were sued by an effective crusading plaintiffs' lawyer from Nacogdoches. Bunches of cases from small cities in Colorado, Maryland, Massachusetts, and Ohio are found together; again, it would be incorrect to assume these indicated worse problems of police illegality in those states than in others, and instead it might be regarded as evidence of more active civil rights bars there. There are no files from New York City, not because the NYPD is perfect, but because Fyfe would not testify against his former employer.

31. Fyfe testified quite successfully in many cases against the Philadelphia police, prompting Philadelphia attorney Alan Yatvin to say in his eulogy at Fyfe's funeral that "I paid for a wing of that house in Princeton!"

32. The federal appeals court overturned the results of the first trial, citing errors in interpreting the proper standard of liability of supervisors and the municipality. The appellate case details the procedural saga; see *Young v. City of Providence, Rhode Island,* at http://www.ca1.uscourts.gov/cgi-bin/getopn.pl?OPINION=04-1374.01A.

33. Mrs. Young lost her case in the second trial. Jurors later stated that they had discounted Fyfe's testimony because he was under the influence of chemotherapy and painkillers when he gave it.

34. Few people remember how vitriolic the atmosphere in police policy circles was before the decision in *Garner* in 1985. Young officers are often amazed to hear that police were allowed to shoot and, indeed, encouraged to do so as a supposed crime deterrent. While 1985 is not so long ago, a sea change in understanding of the police role has occurred. Fyfe believed that such a sea change would also be possible in the off-duty shootings field, especially in relation to off-duty shootings when police officers had been drinking or

using drugs off duty. The policy atmosphere that exists when changes are first proposed can change drastically in only a few decades, as it did in the case of shooting fleeing felons. In 2009, the state of New York convened an independent commission to study the problem of off-duty officers' shootings and recommend model policies for police departments in that state.

35. If there has been no reform in the Fourth Amendment arena, it would probably not be from lack of litigation, but because the U.S. Supreme Court over the past three decades has systematically weakened Fourth Amendment law. There is no equivalent of a *Garner* defense-of-life bright line in Fourth Amendment case law.

36. A Supreme Court case on this is *Malley v. Briggs,* 475 U.S. 335 (1986), in which state police arrested a town councilman and his wife for smoking marijuana, although there was very scant evidence linking them personally to any illegal behavior. The state police had heard on a wiretap that there was a party at their home in which marijuana was smoked. The grand jury refused to indict, and after the criminal case was dropped, the Briggses sued, alleging defamation and illegal search and seizure. The U.S. Supreme Court held that the officers who had obtained warrants were not immune from suit. Important as that standard may be, this lawsuit was commenced by people with money who are not the usual victims of illegal police searches and are unlikely to exert much influence on police behavior in search and seizure situations (McCoy 1986). Fyfe's files contain a case in which a millionaire sued the local sheriff and county council in a case heavy with political overtones. The plaintiff had inherited a large tract of land that, he claimed, the county wanted for a park. He was a constant user of marijuana, which was common knowledge in the county, and he grew it for his own use on the land. Sheriffs' deputies came to his house and arrested him for using, producing, and dealing drugs. He claimed there was no probable cause to arrest for producing or dealing, a point that was extremely important because if he were found guilty, the county could seize his land under forfeiture law. The county prosecutor (Ventura County, California) declined to prosecute the case, and forfeiture was prevented. Subsequently, the rich stoner brought a damages action against the police, alleging Fourth Amendment violations. While these cases are somewhat stunning, they are scarcely typical of the types of cases in which searches and seizures usually occur.

37. Auto pursuit policies also would apply here, since they are covered by Fourth Amendment law on seizures in the same way as deadly force through use of guns is. On the effect of pursuit litigation, see Crew, Kessler, and Fridell (1994).

38. CALEA's web site reports that its

> accreditation program provides law enforcement agencies an opportunity to voluntarily demonstrate that they meet an established set of professional standards which: (1) require an agency to develop a comprehensive, well thought out, uniform set of written directives; (2) provide the necessary reports and analyses a CEO needs to make fact-based, informed management decisions . . . (5) strengthen an agency's accountability, both within the agency and the community, through a continuum of standards that clearly define authority, performance, and responsibilities; (6) *can limit an agency's liability and risk exposure because it demonstrates that internationally recognized standards for law enforcement have been met, as verified by a team of independent outside CALEA-trained assessors;* and (7) facilitates an agency's pursuit of professional excellence. [italics added]

See http://www.calea.org.

39. See discussion of the "liability crisis" and insurers above.

40. See Fyfe's outline for a speech he made in 1992 at a conference of insurers, available in the Fyfe Archives, Sealy Library, John Jay College, City University of New York.

41. Excerpt from a letter mailed to CALEA in September 1996 and reprinted with permission from Assistant Chief Kenneth Findley, Tyler (Texas) Police Department.

42. Walker cites as a source of these professional standards the U.S. Department of Justice's Principles for Promoting Police Integrity (2001), which he says is "the best summary of these best practices." This report was developed through a series of Justice Department–sponsored conferences and workshops in the preceding years. See also U.S. Department of Justice (1999). Walker served as a consultant to the Justice Department in compiling these standards.

43. In the case of the New Jersey racial profiling scandal, Republican Christine Todd Whitman was governor of the state of New Jersey, and the consent decree covered practices that had been encouraged in the first instance by the federal government itself, in its War on Drugs under the first Bush administration.

REFERENCES

Alpert, Geoffrey, and Lori Fridell. 1992. *Police Vehicles and Firearms: Instruments of Deadly Force.* Prospect Heights, IL: Waveland Press.

Archbold, Carol A. 2005. "Managing the Bottom Line: Risk Management in Policing." *Policing* 28:30–49.

Avery, Michael, and David Rudovsky. 1983. *Police Misconduct Law and Litigation,* 2nd ed. New York: Clark Boardman Co.

Baker, Tom. 2005. *The Medical Malpractice Myth.* Chicago: University of Chicago Press.

Boston Globe. 2005. "Police Scaling Back 'Always Armed' Policies." November 26.

Chilton, Bradley Stewart. 1991. *Prisons under the Gavel: The Federal Takeover of Georgia Prisons.* Columbus: Ohio State University Press.

Cohen, Fred. 2004. "The Limits of the Judicial Reform of Prisons: What Works; What Does Not." *Criminal Law Bulletin* (Sept.–Oct.).

Collins, Michael G. 1997. *Section 1983 Litigation in a Nutshell.* St. Paul: West Publishing.

Commission on Accreditation of Law Enforcement Agencies. 1982. *Standards for Law Enforcement Agencies.* Fairfax, VA: CALEA.

Crew, R. Jr., D. Kessler, and L. Fridell. 1994. "Changing Hot Pursuit Policy: An Empirical Assessment of the Impact on Pursuit Behavior." *Evaluation Review* 18:513–19.

Davies, Thomas Y. 1983. "A Hard Look at What We Know (and Still Need to Learn) about the 'Costs' of the Exclusionary Rule: The NIJ Study and Other Studies of 'Lost' Arrests." *American Bar Foundation Research Journal* 8(3): 611–90.

Davis, Lant B., J. H. Small, and D. J. Wohlberg. 1979. "Project: Suing the Police in Federal Court." *Yale Law Journal* 88(2): 781–95.

Di Grazia, Robert J. 1987. "New Liability Book: Grab It and Start Reading." *Law Enforcement News.* January 13.

Dowdle, Michael, ed. 2006. *Public Accountability: Designs, Dilemmas, and Experiences.* Cambridge, U.K.: Cambridge University Press.

Eisenstein, James. 1982. "Section 1983: Doctrinal Foundation and an Empirical Study." *Cornell Law Review* 67:482–556.

Epp, Charles. 2010. *Making Rights Real: Activists, Bureaucrats, and the Creation of the Legalistic State.* Chicago: University of Chicago Press.

Law Enforcement News. 2000. "Facing Up to an Unflattering Profile" and "New Jersey: Ground Zero in Racial Profiling Uproar." December 15, 10–11.

Feeley, Malcolm M., and Edward L. Rubin. 2000. *Judicial Policy Making and the Modern State: How the Courts Reformed America's Prisons.* London: Cambridge University Press.

Foote, Caleb. 1954. "Tort Remedies for Police Violations of Individual Rights." *Minnesota Law Review* 39:493–516.

Fyfe, James J. 1978. "Shots Fired: An Analysis of New York City Police Firearms Discharges." Ph.D. diss., State University of New York, Albany, New York.

———. 1980. "Always Prepared: Police Off-Duty Guns." *Annals of the American Academy of Political and Social Science* 452:72–81

———. 1982. "Blind Justice: Police Shootings in Memphis." *Journal of Criminal Law and Criminology* 73:702–22.

———. 1983. "Enforcement Workshop: The NIJ Study of the Exclusionary Rule." *Criminal Law Bulletin* 19:253–60.

———. 1986. "Tennessee v. Garner: The Issue Not Addressed." *New York University Review of Law and Social Change* 14(3): 721–31.

———. 1987. "Police Expert Witnesses." In *Expert Witnesses: Criminologists in the Courtroom,* edited by Patrick Anderson and L. Thomas Winfree, Jr. (chapter 7). Albany: State University of New York Press.

———. 1998. "Good Judgment: Defending Police against Civil Suits." *Police Quarterly* 1(1): 91.

Fyfe, James J., Jack R. Greene, William F. Walsh, O. W. Wilson, and Roy McLaren. 1996. *Police Administration,* 5th ed. Columbus, Ohio: McGraw-Hill.

Fyfe, James J., and Robert Kane. 2000. "Police Use of Force." In *Encyclopedia of Violence in the United States,* edited by Ronald Gottesman and Richard Maxwell Brown (546–51). New York: Scribner and Sons.

Gallagher, G. Patrick. 1990a. "The Six-Layered Liability Protection System for Police." *Police Chief.* June.

———. 1990b. "Risk Management for Police Administrators." *Police Chief.* June.

———. 1992. *Risk Management behind the Blue Curtain: A Primer on Law Enforcement Liability.* Arlington, VA: Public Risk Management Association.

Geller, William, and M. Scott. 1992. *Deadly Force: What We Know: A Practitioner's Desk Reference on Police-Involved Shootings.* Washington, DC: Police Executive Research Forum.

International Association of Chiefs of Police (IACP). 1988. *Model Policies for Law Enforcement.* Arlington, VA: IACP.

International City Management Association (ICMA). 1986. *Public Officials Liability Insurance: Understanding the Market.* Washington, DC: ICMA and the Wyatt Company.

Kappeler, Victor. 2001. *Police Civil Liability: Supreme Court Cases and Materials.* Long Grove, IL: Waveland Press.

———. 2006. *Critical Issues in Police Civil Liability,* 4th ed. Long Grove, IL: Waveland Press.

Kappeler, Victor E., Stephen F. Kappeler, and Rolando del Carmen. 2001. "A Content Analysis of Police Civil Liability Cases: Decisions of the Federal District Courts: 1978–1990." In *Critical Issues in Police Civil Liability,* 3rd ed., edited by Victor E. Kappeler (18–19). Prospect Heights, IL: Waveland Press.

Kean, Seth M. 1999. "Note: Municipal Liability for Off-Duty Police Misconduct under Section 1983: The 'Under Color of Law' Requirement." *Boston University Law Review* 79:195–231.

Krajick, Kevin. 1978. "The Liability Crisis: Who Will Insure the Police?" *Police Magazine* (March): 33–40.

Matulia, Kenneth J. 1982; 2nd. ed. 1985. *A Balance of Forces: Model Deadly Force Policy and Procedure.* Gaithersburg, MD: International Association of Chiefs of Police.

McCoy, Candace. 1986. "Civil Liability for Fourth Amendment Violations: Rhetoric and Reality." *Criminal Law Bulletin* 22:461–70.

———. 1987a. "Constitutional Tort Litigation: Controlling the Police?" Paper presented at annual meeting of the American Political Science Association, Chicago, September 3–6.

———. 1987b. "Police Legal Liability Is 'Not a Crisis,' 99 Chiefs Say." *Criminal Justice Digest* 6(1): 1.

———. 1996. "Congress Is (Not) Repealing the Exclusionary Rule! Symbolic Politics and Criminal Justice (Non)Reform." *Criminal Justice Review* 21(2): 181–91.

Meltzer, Daniel J. 1988. "Deterring Constitutional Violations by Law Enforcement Officials: Plaintiffs and Defendants as Private Attorneys General." *Columbia Law Review* 88 (March): 247–329.

Miller, Marshall. 1998. "Note: Police Brutality." *Yale Law and Policy Review* 17:149–58.

New York Times. 2005. "James Fyfe, 63, Criminologist and Police Training Director, Is Dead." November 15.

Nowicki, Dennis, et al. 1987. "The Impact of Concern for Liability on Police Agency Self-Improvement." Paper presented at annual meeting of the Police Executive Research Forum, Washington, D.C., May 19.

Pratt, George C., and Martin A. Schwartz. 1983. *Section 1983 Civil Rights Litigation and Attorneys' Fees: Current Developments.* Serial volumes beginning in 1983 prepared as materials for yearly seminars. New York: Practicing Law Institute.

Rosenberg, Gerald N. 1991. *The Hollow Hope: Can Courts Bring About Social Change?* Chicago: University of Chicago Press.

Sherman, Lawrence W. 1979. "Enforcement Workshops: Suing the Police." *Criminal Law Bulletin* 15(2):168–73.

———. 1992. *Policing Domestic Violence: Experiments and Dilemmas.* New York: Free Press.

Silver, Isidore. 1986. *Police Civil Liability.* New York: Matthew Bender Publishers.

Skolnick, Jerome H., and James J. Fyfe. 1993. *Above the Law: Police and the Excessive Use of Force.* New York: Free Press.

Slobogin, Christopher. 2007. "The Liberal Assault on the Fourth Amendment." *Ohio State Journal of Criminal Law* 4:603–18.

Thomas, Robert F. Jr. 1979. "Insurance for Police Agencies." *Police Chief.* January 16.

———. 1982. "Remarks." *Police Chief.*

U.S. Conference of Mayors. 1986. *Municipal Liability Concerns: A 145 City Survey.* Washington, DC: U.S. Conference of Mayors.

U.S. Department of Justice. 1999. "Attorney General's Conference: Strengthening Police Community Relationships, Summary Report." Washington, DC: U.S. Department of Justice.

———. 2001. "Principles for Promoting Police Integrity: Examples of Promising Police Practices and Policies." Washington, DC: U.S. Department of Justice. http://www.ncjrs.gov/pdffiles1/ojp/186189.pdf.

Walker, Samuel. 2003. "The New Paradigm of Police Accountability: The U.S. Justice Department 'Pattern or Practice' Suits in Context." *Saint Louis University Public Law Review* 22.

———. 2005. *The New World of Police Accountability.* Thousand Oaks, CA: Sage Publications.

Wasserman, Natalie, and Dean C. Phelus, eds. 1985. *Risk Management Today: A How-To Guide for Local Government.* Alexandria, VA: Public Risk and Insurance Management Association.

Wennerholm, R. W. 1985. *Guide for Local Government.* Washington, DC: Public Risk and Insurance Management Association and International City Management Association.

White, Michael D. 2000. "Assessing the Impact of Administrative Policy on Use of Deadly Force by On- and Off-Duty Police." *Evaluation Review* 24(3): 295–318.

Worrall, John L. 2001. *Civil Lawsuits, Citizen Complaints, and Policing Innovations.* New York: LFB Scholarly Publishing.

Vera Institute of Justice. 1998. *Prosecuting Police Misconduct: Reflections on the Role of the U.S. Civil Rights Division.* New York: Vera Institute of Justice.

7

The Effects of Officer Fatigue on Accountability and the Exercise of Police Discretion

Bryan Vila

Police fatigue and long work hours undermine accountability and threaten justice—on the streets and in the workplace. Accountability measures work through deterrence by providing negative consequences for police officers who misuse their substantial discretionary powers. But effective deterrence requires that an officer think about the consequences of improper behavior before acting, and that he or she rationally weigh the potential rewards of improper behavior against potential consequences. For example, as McCoy explained it, an officer contemplating an apartment search "will be deterred from conducting the search in an unconstitutional manner partly because his thought processes are rational; he is planning purposive action and will therefore take into account the unpleasant consequences his illegal actions could engender should he be held accountable for them in court" (1985, 55–56).

However, the peculiar structure of police shift assignments, overtime policies, and the requirement that they be always on duty, 24/7—a tradition against which James J. Fyfe argued vociferously (1980)—can produce levels of sleep deprivation and disruption that impair officers' abilities to think clearly about the consequences of their actions, solve problems, and manage emotions such as anger. This problem is pervasive; many officers work while they are seriously impaired by lack of sleep. A substantial body of scientific evidence demonstrates that work-hour and scheduling practices, such as those that are usual and accepted for police in the United States, tend to interfere with a person's ability to make rational decisions. Fundamental neurophysiological changes happen in the body when people routinely have their sleep disrupted, work more than 12 hours a day, and suffer from sleep disorders, as roughly 40 percent of cops in the United States do (Vila and Samuels forthcoming). Those changes substantially impair the functioning of the parts of the brain required for planning, weighing consequences, and applying moral principles. Worse still, people who are fatigued consistently underestimate their own impairment. Thus, inappropriate police shift work and deployment patterns undermine officers' capacity to follow department policies and regulations—and even to follow the law itself.

Police Accountability, Discretion, and Deterrence

For more than 40 years, we have acknowledged that police discretion is a fundamental necessity for justice and that police officers exercise substantial discretion about how and when they use their unique occupational powers. The rub, of course, is that the abuse of discretion is a major source of injustice. Police are faced with a nearly infinite variety of situations that require them to exercise their discretionary authority in order to solve problems effectively. The proper use of discretion

> is essential if the police are to achieve a system of law enforcement that is not only efficient, but also fair and effective. The degree to which the police succeed in meeting these latter objectives will determine, in the long run, the strength of the law enforcement function in our democratic society. (Goldstein 1967a, 1124)

To ensure the just use of discretion, we develop policies, screen new employees, and then train, educate, and develop officers so that they understand how to use discretion properly. We also make sure that they know they will be held accountable for misusing their powers. Then we watch what they do, correcting where possible and punishing when necessary (Goldstein 1967b, 161). Our assumption is that the right combination of moral fiber, ethical standards, training, supervision, and deterrence will do a satisfactory job of keeping cops in line.

Police officers are given great power as we delegate to them many tasks that are intrusive or unpleasant as well as dangerous. They are allowed substantial discretion in the use of that power as they confront, detain, ticket, and arrest people; mediate disputes; direct traffic; and assist people in crisis. Officers decide when and how to drive emergency vehicles, confront disturbed and violent individuals, make arrests, and use deadly force. Many of their most difficult and complex decisions are made in fluid, ambiguous, and emotionally charged situations where lives, property, and liberty can be lost in a split second. Even the less dramatic decisions that officers make can carry grave consequences for individuals, families, communities, and the officers themselves. Errors made in the gray area between black-letter law and the hard concrete of the streets put their lives and their careers at risk and endanger the citizens they are sworn to protect.

Discretion is a necessary component of effective policing in part because it promotes flexibility and common sense in enforcement situations. Officers often respond to calls for service with limited or generic information. They are trained and expected to assess a situation quickly and divine a route to its successful resolution. Discretion provides officers with the flexibility and autonomy necessary to tailor their response to each unique situation. Police administrators use policy and procedure manuals and standard operating procedures to help guide officers in the proper use of authority. Eliminating discretion would require the improbable task of creating a set of policies and procedures to address every potential situation officers could encounter.

Even such an encyclopedic set of policies and procedures, however, would not eliminate the need to use common sense to determine the most appropriate and effective type of enforcement for a particular situation. Policing rarely presents a simple, all-or-nothing, clear-cut scenario. In the real world, officers face difficult and ambiguous situations that require creative problem solving and common sense. They cannot—and should not—make an arrest each time a law is violated. Instead, officers must select the appropriate mode and level of enforcement. Allowing for such flexibility, however, increases the need for appropriate guidelines and policies—and for enforcing them.

Accountability refers to the means and methods by which officers are held responsible for following those guidelines and policies. Consequences flow to police officers when they act improperly or exceed their authority without good reason. Accountability plays an important role in reducing the abuse of discretionary powers by providing consequences for improper actions. When applied properly, those consequences can discourage and minimize abuse of authority, assuming of course that officers weigh them when choosing a course of action.

Accountability systems can be located inside or outside an organization. Internal systems include self-reporting, reporting on peers, supervision, retraining, internal affairs investigations, and disciplinary processes. External accountability mechanisms include citizen complaints, review boards, and the news media, as well as civil litigation and criminal prosecution. All these elements work to deter police misconduct by using either the threat of punishment or actual punishment.

According to classic deterrence theory (e.g., Beccaria 1777; Bentham 1830), accountability systems will work only if the subjects perceive that the certainty, severity, and swiftness of the consequences they will suffer in response to their abuse of discretionary powers outweigh the value they place on abusive acts or the benefits they expect from wrongful acts. Thus, for deterrence to be effective, police officers must have clear knowledge and understanding of departmental expectations. They also must think that violations of those expectations will be detected and punished within a meaningful time frame—and that the probability (certainty) of detection and punishment is high enough that the risks outweigh perceived benefits. All this assumes that officers planning a course of action consider the consequences and conduct some sort of cost-benefit analysis. At a minimum, to be deterred, they must think about consequences before they act.

Of course, the fact that accountability has general deterrence goals as well as specific deterrence goals is the rationale for holding officers accountable even for unintentional mistakes. In particular, officers who engage in permitted but risky activities, such as vehicle pursuits or use of deadly force, need to know that their actions will be very carefully reviewed to determine if they were legal, within policy, and necessary. Note, however, that the goal here is to encourage officers to act prudently and properly, not to refrain from risky activities. After all, that is their job.

For example, police officers are sometimes required to make life-or-death decisions in ambiguous, fast-paced, and highly emotional confrontations. We rightly expect them as professionals to do so with skill and appropriate restraint. Also rightly, we carefully review their performance in such incidents. But do we always have realistic—or even rational—expectations for their behavior?

One fundamental criterion for determining whether a norm, rule, or law is reasonable is whether the people it affects are *capable* of fulfilling the obligation it places on them. As Harvard ethicist Kwame Anthony Appiah put it, "If you say somebody *ought* to do something, you must be supposing that it is something they *can* do" (2008, 22). What if the routine conditions of work *inevitably and foreseeably* make out-of-policy or even illegal mistakes likely? Ample evidence, we believe, suggests that this is the case.

Fatigue and Police Performance

Unfortunately, everything done to ensure proper use of police discretion depends on the ability of well-intentioned officers to make the best possible decisions. This link between intent and action can be seriously degraded by officer fatigue—especially in the kinds of complex, rapidly evolving situations that most challenge discretionary decisionmaking. A large body of hard scientific research makes it clear that shift work and the kinds of long, erratic hours that many officers routinely work tend to interfere with precisely those parts of the brain that are most important for making morally charged decisions in dynamic, stressful situations. Sleep loss impairs rational decisionmaking.

As we lay out in more detail below, many laboratory studies confirm that sleep loss affects a broad range of skills associated with decision-making, including insight, risk assessment, innovation, communication, and mood control (Harrison and Horne 2000). In fact, brain imaging studies demonstrate that lack of sleep has a disproportionate effect on the prefrontal cortex—the "executive" region of the brain where problems are solved and prioritized according to moral and situational criteria and where consequences are considered and responses are planned and coordinated.[1] Thus, even though tired cops still may be able to perceive a great deal about a situation because some parts of their brains are functioning well, they will be less likely to make sound decisions about what to do. Recent studies indicate that they will also be more likely to make hasty moral decisions and engage in riskier behavior (Killgore et al. 2005; Killgore et al. 2007).

Stanford University professor William C. Dement, who pioneered modern sleep research and recently chaired a congressional panel on the impact of sleep on society, summarizes the issue of police fatigue:

> Police work is the one profession in which we would want all practitioners to have adequate and healthful sleep to perform their duties at peak alertness levels. Not only is fatigue associated with individual misery, but it can also lead to counterproductive behavior. It is well known that impulsiveness, aggression, irritability and angry outbursts are associated with sleep deprivation. (Vila 2000, xiv)

Shift work and police work-hour practices interact to rob officers of sleep. Like those of other animals, human bodies require sleep, and they have rhythms that keep them in sync with natural cycles of day and night. The effects of sleep deprivation are especially insidious because they tend to be both unavoidable and opaque to self-detection. Research by the National Aeronautic and Space Administration's Fatigue Countermeasures Program shows that fatigue cannot "be willed away or overcome through motivation or discipline" because it is rooted in physiological mechanisms related to sleep, sleep loss, and circadian rhythms (NASA 1999). Worse still, research also shows that people tend to underestimate substantially their own level of sleep impairment.

Night shift work that requires sleep during the day is an important source of fatigue for officers because natural circadian rhythms enhance alertness during daylight hours and encourage sleep at night. People tend to be most alert during the morning and in the late afternoon or early evening hours. During those times, energy levels are elevated, eyes focus more easily, and physical abilities and coordination peak. When circadian rhythms dip as evening wears on, waves of sleepiness wash over us; appetites diminish, recollection dulls, reaction times slow, and we fall asleep (see Dement and Vaughn 1999; Monk and Folkard 1992). As a result, officers on night shifts must struggle to stay awake when their bodies want to sleep and then later try to fall asleep when they are naturally primed to be most alert. Even officers who try to adapt to a night-shift schedule and minimize schedule disruption tend to get poorer quality sleep during daylight hours because their internal clocks are receiving conflicting time cues from the environment (Folkard and Monk 1985; Rosekind et al. 1996a).

As though shift work were not challenge enough, police officers in the United States often work large amounts of overtime (Vila 2000, 2006; Vila et al. 2000; Vila, Morrison, and Kenney 2002). Overtime causes fatigue by increasing the number of consecutive hours officers are awake, by depriving them of adequate time for recuperation, by disrupting sleep patterns established in normal work schedules, and by disrupting sleep when it finally comes. The same dynamic occurs with off-duty employment (moonlighting), which is also pervasive in many police departments. Overtime and moonlighting practices vary from department to department and among officers within each department. Although the extent and distribution of overtime work and off-duty employment are not well understood, several things are clear from discussion of this issue with thousands of officers from across the United States during the past 30 years:

- Almost every policing agency uses overtime to meet demands for service.
- Few agencies limit or track hours worked per officer per day, week, or month.
- It is common for officers to work 16 or more hours in a single day and a large proportion of officers have worked 24 or more hours in a row at some time.
- Overtime is unevenly distributed, with a relatively small proportion of officers in most agencies working much more overtime than the department average.[2]

Almost no police agencies have comprehensive policies and procedures in place to manage fatigue.

Extreme examples collected from jurisdictions scattered across the United States identify officers working more than 3,000 hours of *overtime* a year (Armstrong 1996; Cassidy and Armstrong 1999; Grad and Schoch 1995; Marisco 2003; Miller and Delfiner 2003). In August 2005, the Boston Police Department began enforcing a long-standing rule that limited total work time (i.e., both departmental work and private "details") to 96 hours per week. Within six months, 85 officers had been disciplined for exceeding that already generous limit (Estes and Slack 2006; Slack and Cramer 2006).

Over the course of a career in policing, long and erratic work hours and shift work often lead to a host of serious chronic health problems, many of which interfere with sleep. As a consequence, *nearly half* of all American police officers appear to have serious sleep disorders (Liberman et al. 2002; Rajaratnam et al. 2007; Vila et al. 2002). Among these disorders, sleep apnea is especially problematic because of its deadly long-term health consequences (Luenda et al. 2007) and because people with mild to moderate sleep apnea have demonstrated impairment equivalent to that exhibited by healthy people with blood alcohol levels of .06 percent—a level that many nations consider sufficient to establish drunken driving (Powell et al. 1999).

Research shows that excessive work hours, circadian disruption, and inadequate sleep significantly impair human performance. Regardless of whether those humans are physicians (Barger et al. 2005; Landrigan et al.

2004; Lockley et al. 2004), pilots (Mann 1999; Rosekind et al. 1996a, b; Van Dongen, Caldwell, and Caldwell 2006), astronauts (Dijk et al. 2001), commandos (Wesensten, Belenky, and Balkin 2005), cops (Vila 2006; Vila et al. 2002), or just average people, they are more likely to make bad decisions, crash cars, and be cranky when tired (e.g., Belenky, Wesensten, and Thorne 2003; Bonnett 1985; Thayer 1989).

Fairly modest amounts of sleep deprivation impair cognitive performance, hand-eye coordination, and a host of other skills central to police fieldwork as much as several doses of alcohol would. Independent experiments by two research teams testing the relative impact of sleep loss vs. alcohol consumption on hand-eye coordination, motor speed, task accuracy, and alertness found that being awake for 17 hours tends to impair people to the same extent as a blood alcohol of .05 percent. Being awake for 24 hours causes impairment equivalent to a blood alcohol concentration of .10 percent; this number is 20 percent above the current U.S. standard for drunk driving (Dawson and Reid 1997; Williamson and Feyer 2000).[3] Reaction time on some of the tests in Williamson and Feyer's more extensive study was 50 percent worse in the sleep-deprived condition than in the alcohol condition. As a matter of public safety, it seems appropriate to ask whether fatigue-impaired officers should tackle the tough job of policing, particularly because they may at times be as impaired as the drunken drivers they arrest.

The consequences of causing, permitting, and enabling police officers to work while impaired by fatigue can be dire. Even though their conduct is governed by a large, complex body of laws, regulations, and policies, situational imperatives and the limits of human decisionmaking can neutralize the effectiveness of formal restraints on behavior. Officers whose frontal lobes are out of service even though they themselves are on duty are less likely to think about consequences or to be able to analyze a situation correctly and apply complex rules to their behavior. They are also less able to manage the anger and frustration that often accompany confrontations in the field. These decrements to performance are especially likely to have tragic consequences when decisions must be made in rapidly evolving, complex, emotionally charged, and threatening situations.

Clearly, fatigue-impaired officers can present threats to public safety and expose the communities they serve to substantial liability. The conclusion is inescapable: law enforcement agencies must manage police fatigue if they are to manage the use of discretion. Furthermore, the emotional and personal pain these officers suffer in the aftermath of bad decisions made while sleep-deprived should be a major concern for any humane police administrator.

Managing Fatigue to Manage Discretion

Sometimes long and erratic work hours are an unavoidable part of police work. Catastrophes occur, children go missing, and hometown teams win or lose the World Series. Other times, the long and erratic hours that officers work result from archaic rules, poorly thought-out procedures, greed, politics, or simply a failure to distribute overtime more evenly across all staff. In many departments, we suspect that the concentration of high overtime and moonlighting work hours is the greatest threat to the safety of both officers and the public. This threat often arises because a few officers actively seek more work or are extraordinarily productive and thus spend far more time in court and processing late arrests. It also seems to be more common in police assignments such as homicide, narcotics, and special units that are called back to duty outside usual working hours. Clearly, no matter the cause, we need to manage officer fatigue, just as we manage other risks.

As former police officers who have studied this problem extensively, we know that some police readers will be thinking things such as:

- "They can't take away our overtime; that's what pays for private school for my kids (a home in a decent part of town, the groceries, a nice vacation each year . . .)."
- "I can't run a police department without the flexibility overtime provides."
- "We're so understaffed that mandatory overtime has become a normal part of doing business."
- "Court time is the biggest source of overtime, and judges couldn't care less about tired cops."

These commonly heard complaints miss the point: fatigue management does not require fatigue eradication, which is simply not possible in organizations where emergencies create unpredictable and sometimes enormous staffing demands. Nor does it require doing away with overtime. What fatigue management *does* require is that we minimize fatigue risks with the same diligence we apply to improving tactical safety, rooting out corruption, and recruiting, training, and developing suitable people to serve as police officers.

Both managers and individual officers must take responsibility for fatigue management—and many of them want to. Since *Tired Cops: The Importance of Managing Police Fatigue* (Vila 2000) was published, pleas for help in managing police fatigue have come from large—and roughly equal—numbers of police executives, union leaders, and individual cops. In many instances, calls and e-mails have come from people frustrated because they could not get either labor or management to listen to reason. For every department whose police chief or sheriff cannot get a collective bargaining unit to discuss changing work shifts to manage fatigue or putting reasonable limits on hours worked per day, week, or month, there seems to be a police bargaining unit leader, sergeant, or line officer who cannot get his or her chief or sheriff to discuss the same things.

Successful fatigue management requires labor and management to work together to build a common ground for cooperation by focusing on well-supported, fact-based arguments that neither can ignore. That common ground emerges when police executives are presented with such arguments that focus on risk management and human capital management—arguably their two biggest priorities—and when police officers, line supervisors, and collective bargaining officials are presented such arguments that focus on safety and health—*their* two biggest priorities. For example, if the union will not talk to the police chief about developing policies for managing fatigue, it must be firmly reminded of the primacy of officer safety and health issues. (Pay is important, but safety comes first.) If the chief will not talk to line officers or union leaders about these issues, he or she must be firmly reminded that fatigue increases risks and erodes human capital. These two approaches do not solve the problem, but they establish a basis for developing a workable and effective compromise.

Some examples may help illuminate how officer fatigue is relevant for policymakers and managers as well as for employees and their families. With regard to risk management, as Fyfe has said, "The best way to protect a jurisdiction's pocketbook against lawsuits is to assure that the professional law enforcement standard of care is reflected in its policies, training, and practices" (1997, 9). Managers must balance the costs and benefits of compressed work shifts, flexible schedules, overtime, and officer performance against demands for service, officer safety, legal liability, and the hazards of burnout or early retirement. Officers and their families need to know how to manage shift work, long work hours, and job-related stress as well as how to maximize alertness. They also need to understand the likely consequences of overwork, second jobs, and inadequate sleep: coming to work with a sleep-deprived brain makes officers more likely to put themselves in harm's way by using poor or reckless tactics. Good police work requires that officers come to work fit for duty to avoid poor judgment, which leads to "unnecessarily putting themselves into vulnerable situations in which they will have no choice but to shoot if anything appears threatening" (Fyfe 1997, 6; see also Fyfe 2000).

Both officers and managers also need to question some long-standing assumptions about work hours. Managers tend to assume that it costs less to have an existing officer work overtime at a bonus rate than to recruit, hire, and train a new officer and pay fringe benefits. This assumption holds true up to a point (see Vila 1996, 69–74), but managers need to appreciate that risk costs increase as work hours are extended. Once an officer has been awake for 17 or more hours, the odds of something going wrong start to make overtime a bad bet. Each additional hour on duty beyond 8 hours increases the probability of accidents, injuries, and bad decisions (U.S. DOT/FRA 2006). Officers' assumptions about fatigue also tend to be flawed. Cops, like many other occupational groups that pride themselves on toughness, are reluctant to admit that they are tired, and they are likely to regard such an admission as a sign of weakness. They also often view overtime pay as a boon without considering its personal, professional, and familial costs. Taken together, the misperceptions of officers and their managers—as well as the elected officials who control police hiring—can make it difficult to gain leverage on sleep- and fatigue-related problems. Fortunately, police culture is beginning to change.

Today, our understanding of how to cope with fatigue in policing is in its early stages—much as efforts to improve officer survival skills and physical fitness were 30 years ago. But we have a good sense of the problem. The major administratively controllable culprits responsible for police fatigue are biologically insensitive shift rotation schemes, excessive mandatory or elective overtime assignments, frequent off-duty court appearances, and the use of extra and double shifts to cope with personnel shortages. Of course, officers' personal choices, obligations, and activities can also cause fatigue, but even these can be influenced by proper training on the importance of managing fatigue and alertness. Another important set of tools are policies that "nudge" officers and managers toward doing the right thing.

Organizational Change Using "the Nudge"

Often, those who want to make the kinds of fundamental change required to manage police fatigue are discouraged when it is not possible to revamp all their organization's policies, practices, and customs to bring them in line with good fatigue management. Sometimes, the fact that everything cannot be fixed at once is offered as an excuse for not doing what *is* possible. Incremental change—what management gurus are beginning to call the "nudge"—offers a practical alternative when dramatic change is not possible (see Sunstein and Thaler 2008). The nudge is a very flexible and practical approach to social change. It starts by giving good people a push in the right direction: provide them with solid information about a problem, why it has to be corrected, and how they can solve it and then set up barriers to discourage bad choices.

An example given by *New York Times* columnist David Leonhardt has to do with hospital emergency rooms—hardly an unfamiliar place to any street cop. Researchers have known for quite some time that it is important to elevate the heads of patients on ventilators to avoid pneumonia. ER staff are taught to prop up patients instead of leaving them lying down, so that gravity will make it harder for stomach bacteria to migrate into the breathing tube and thence into the lungs where they can cause pneumonia. Translating this science into practice has been hard, despite good training, because overworked hospital staff often need to put patients on their backs to work with them. Then they tend to forget to raise them again. When the director of critical care at the University of California San Francisco Medical Center changed the rules so that a patient could be lying down only if there were a written order to that effect, ventilator-associated pneumonia fell more than 40 percent (Leonhardt 2007). This was not a huge change—simply a focused directive that nudged people into compliance with established policy. A typical nudge for a police agency begins with something simple, such as a training session where officers are introduced to the key ideas about police fatigue during a one- or two-hour session. That is the push in the right direction where they receive good information about how to avoid common pitfalls, deal better with shift work, work safer, and live healthier. Then management institutes a barrier that encourages officers to take advantage of their new knowledge. In a department where conditions of work are established in hard-fought contract negotiations, the barrier can be something fairly flimsy. For example, many chiefs and unions like to start with data collection. Just having shift sergeants or watch commanders keep track of how many hours officers work on and off the job during each 24-hour period will start them thinking about fatigue issues. Similarly, something as minor as instructing officers to note the number of hours they had been on duty before vehicle crashes or critical incidents will help keep the fatigue issue on their minds.

This sort of barrier helps guide people in the right direction, and it also provides everyone in the department with information they need to decide about future fatigue-management practices. The goal here is to help channel people toward doing the right thing—just as flimsy yellow plastic tape is used to protect a crime scene.

Where conditions of work can be changed more easily, executives can try out a minimal measure like limiting total consecutive hours on duty to 16 and requiring at least 8 hours of time off between shifts. Of course, this sort of policy must provide exceptions for extraordinary incidents. And of course a wise executive develops such a policy with as much input as possible from the rank and file. Policies governing work hours affect almost every aspect of an officer's life—on and off duty. Officers who have a stake in a policy will be more likely to help make it work and suggest ways to refine and improve it.

A participative management style is important, perhaps imperative, for dealing with fatigue issues because those problems require action both on and off duty. A chief may be able to mandate an hours-on-duty policy that reduces the risk of fatigue-related accidents, injuries, and incidents, but convincing officers to get the rest they need to come to work fit for duty without first winning their personal support is almost impossible. Of course, positive encouragement toward good behavior is more effective when accompanied by barriers to bad behavior. This brings us back to the accountability issue with which this chapter began.

Managers' and Officers' Responsibilities in Managing Police Fatigue

Both police managers and police employees must be accountable for managing fatigue because each has control over different parts of the problem, although their roles are inextricably intertwined. Managers oversee scheduling and staffing, which limit time off available for sleep and recuperation. Officers make choices about what portion of their time off to devote to sleep. There are no excuses for not dealing rationally with police fatigue other than, perhaps, sudden catastrophic events. Even during unexpectedly long shifts, there are ways to manage fatigue using careful caffeine dosing, short naps, and environmental change (Caldwell and Caldwell 2003; Committee on Military Nutrition Research 2001; Mitler, Dinges, and Dement 1994; Moore-Ede 1993; Naitoh, Kelly, and Babkoff 1990).

Even though fatigue is sometimes caused by things beyond an officer's control such as a sick child or competing family responsibilities, once an officer has been properly trained on fatigue management he or she must stand up like a professional and say, "I've been awake for 20 hours straight and I'm not ready to work the streets." This is the essence of personal accountability for fatigue. Similarly, even when understaffing and demand for services make overtime the only option, managers can distribute that overtime reasonably evenly. They also can decline to send sleep-impaired officers on nonemergency calls even though handling routine calls for service is a pressing concern. A full discussion of techniques for managing police fatigue is beyond the scope of this chapter, but the causes and consequences of police fatigue are quite well understood, as are techniques for managing fatigue and promoting healthy sleep practices (e.g., see Caldwell and Caldwell 2003; Vila 2000; Vila et al. 2002; and the National Sleep Foundation web site: http://www.sleepfoundation.com).

Managing sleep deprivation is one example of a police management practice designed to uphold the fundamental mission of law enforcement. An officer's primary responsibility is to protect life (Fyfe 2000, 10). Going on duty without sufficient rest puts this sacred responsibility at risk. But fatigue management inevitably conflicts with the common practice of requiring officers to carry firearms while off duty—or what is known as "being on duty 24/7" (see Fyfe 1980). An important task for contemporary police managers is to examine the policy that requires officers to be on call and have their firearms available at all times. This policy may directly conflict with the police obligation to protect life, insofar as it may cause stress and sleep deprivation that then lead to suboptimal use of weapons. It is unclear whether any advantages in crime reduction produced by this policy are worth the costs associated with outside-of-policy off-duty shootings, family violence involving police firearms, and the denial of any respite from job-related stressors.

Legal Liability

Until recently, police officers and managers could claim that their unsafe work-hour practices were usual and accepted within American law enforcement. But the substantial body of research cited in this chapter makes it clear that these practices are no longer reasonable or prudent. That change in understanding exposes police officers and the jurisdictions for which they work to new and potentially serious legal liabilities. Although case law in this area is still not yet fully formed, fatigue is being raised more and more frequently in civil suits regarding industrial and traffic accidents. In general, employers are being held responsible for the actions of overly fatigued employees under the theory that an employer has a duty to intervene if an employee has worked so many hours without rest that his or her impairment constitutes an unreasonable and foreseeable risk to others (Coburn 1996; Moore-Ede 1995).[4]

Because officer fatigue is likely to lead to police actions that may be construed as violating a plaintiff's constitutional rights, it seems reasonable to expect cases such as *Monell v. New York City Department of Social Services* to be brought to bear on incidents in which fatigue was a factor. Under *Monell,* officers in departments that have not formulated meaningful guidance about fatigue and work-hour management may be able to protect themselves from legal liability if they can show that they have not been trained to manage fatigue. This possibility, of course, leaves management vulnerable to the lawsuits, because court decisions subsequent to that landmark case regarded the absence of official rules or policies to guide officers' decisions as "deficient supervision" in circumstances as varied as vehicle pursuits, deadly force, domestic violence, or encounters with emotionally disturbed individuals (see Fyfe 2000, 9). It should be obvious to the reader by now how fatigue can increase the probability of an adverse outcome in each of these circumstances. It also should be obvious that effective fatigue management is in the best interest of all police officers, regardless of rank, as well as the jurisdictions and communities they serve.

Fatigue and Police Accountability: Example Situations

Fyfe called protection of life "the primary police responsibility" (2000, 10). Recognizing that police fatigue has the potential to undermine protection of life highlights particular situations in which fatigue can put lives in danger and thus raises the question of how to hold officers and managers accountable to the fundamental police mission in the face of fatigue. Examples presented below include requiring officers to have their firearms immediately available while off duty, preventing domestic violence in police households, reducing drowsy driving, and improving police performance and decisionmaking in situations that may require use of deadly force.

Carrying Firearms Off Duty

The policy of requiring police officers to carry firearms while off duty is common in police agencies throughout the United States. Armed off-duty officers are never able to get away from their work because they are constantly at risk of serious injury or death. As Fyfe wrote, "Even while off-duty, American police are expected to be armed and to actively intervene in situations threatening to life, property, or order" (Fyfe 1982, 282). In fact, more than 7 percent of officers killed in the line of duty nationwide between 1980 and 2004 were killed while off duty (U.S. DOJ, annual). Cops who are already facing long work weeks have to manage what is essentially a never-ending 24/7 work schedule, at least in the sense that the potential for switching into "policing mode" is never absent, even in leisure hours. Anecdotally, at least, it also seems likely that off-duty shootings constitute a large proportion of officer-involved shootings that law enforcement agencies ultimately rule to be "out of policy." Many of these incidents occur in places where alcohol is served or when officers have been drinking. Fatigue is likely to play a major role in these incidents, especially because officers often gather at the end of shifts to have a drink. After-duty drinking occurs when officers have already been awake for substantially longer than their 8, 10, or 12 hour shift. This means that the effect of any alcohol they consume will tend to be magnified. For example, research studies have shown that subjects who drank a dose of alcohol equivalent to one beer after having their sleep limited to only four hours the previous night had a level of impairment similar to that of a well-rested person who drank a six-pack (Roehrs et al. 1994; also see Horne, Reyner, and Barrett 2003; Krull et al. 1993).[5] Thus, the combination of fatigue and even modest alcohol consumption while armed can be expected to increase the likelihood of tragedy.

Domestic Violence

Officer-involved domestic violence is another issue likely to be aggravated by poor fatigue management. More than 7 percent of police officer families experience domestic violence (Gershon et al. 2005)—and the actual proportion may be as high as 20–40 percent (U.S. DOJ 2000). Many of the fatigue-induced impairments that decrease job performance and increase risk to officers can also increase the likelihood that they will fail to manage conflict appropriately in their personal lives. We can assume that sending highly stressed, overly fatigued, emotionally volatile officers home to their families will increase the likelihood of inappropriate or abusive behavior. Reducing the impact of fatigue-related job stressors on home life is essential for improving the overall health and well-being of officers and their families.

Automobile Accidents

Automobile accidents are a constant danger for police officers, especially while responding to an emergency call at high speed or being involved in a pursuit. Although few officers would be reckless enough to drive in a high-speed pursuit while intoxicated, they routinely get into a patrol car while similarly impaired from 24 or more hours of sustained wakefulness or many consecutive days with fewer than 5 hours of sleep. One missed day of sleep due to a court appearance, taking sick kids to a doctor, and the like could cause the officer to report to work impaired. The drive home after work is also potentially risky. Officers in many departments are cautioned to call a taxi instead of driving after drinking, but few would consider calling a cab after a 24-hour shift. Police and police administrators must confront the fact that their work-hours and scheduling practices often contribute to impaired driving on and off duty.

Incidents of Deadly Force

Deadly force incidents are especially likely to be affected by fatigue. Even though policing agencies spend large portions of their training budgets to teach officers how to be more effective in high-threat situations and use deadly force appropriately, very few agencies teach officers to take fatigue into account when responding to those situations. This failure may increase the risk of undesirable outcomes because deadly force incidents challenge higher cognitive functions that are especially vulnerable to fatigue induced by insufficient sleep. Consider, for example, decisiveness, just one of the critical officer survival skills that depends heavily on the brain's frontal lobes. Indecisive officers may have difficulty formulating a plan or implementing it effectively before they or their fellow officers enter a danger zone. Another key ability in deadly force encounters is impulse control. Fatigue increases impulsiveness and thus increases the likelihood that officers will overreact or put themselves and their fellow officers into dangerous situations that could have been avoided. Where deadly force is concerned, the consequences of fatigue can be disastrous.

Conclusions and a Look to the Future

A number of key findings emerge from the research to date on police work hours, fatigue, performance, health, and safety. Since 2003, four federal agencies—the National Institute of Justice, the National Institute for Occupational Safety and Health, the National Institute of Mental Health, and the Centers for Disease Control—have funded a set of research projects designed to help understand how long work hours, inadequate sleep, and stress interact to interfere with officer performance, health, and safety and to help police and other first responders better manage the long and often erratic hours they work. Ultimately, many products from this initiative are expected to have practical utility. These include work-hour guidelines, training programs, and technologies adapted for use by police agencies and by police officers and their families.

A number of basic research questions are also being explored by using the police as research subjects. These range from the causal links between work hours, shift work, and sleep and common sources of morbidity and mortality for shift workers to interactions among preemployment characteristics, work hours, and exposure to critical incidents with regard to developing posttraumatic stress disorders. Somewhere between the domains of applied and basic research lies the development, refinement, and testing of more sensitive instruments for assessing sleep disorders among vulnerable populations before they become symptomatic and lead to cardiovascular, metabolic, and other disorders (see Vila 2006 for a review of these efforts).

In addition to past and current research related to police officers' long work hours, a great deal needs to be learned about their impact on officer decisionmaking and performance, especially in challenging situations, such as high-speed driving, potentially threatening confrontations, and problem solving. Another high priority for policing is identifying optimal shift length. Police departments across the United States are rapidly adopting compressed shifts (mostly 12-hour variants), and both police executives and officers need hard information about the risks and benefits of this choice. Also needed are studies comparing police and other shift workers, who also happen to have higher levels of physical, emotional, and family dysfunction. Finally, because many police officers work extended hours in challenging environments throughout their 20–30 year careers, this occupational group presents a good opportunity for studying interindividual variability in the need for sleep, vulnerability to fatigue and sleep restriction, and whether people who are chronically sleep deprived may adapt in much the same way as chronic alcohol abusers do to function day to day.

What we *do* know from studies done to date is that police agencies can do a better job of meeting both demands for service and the needs of officers and their families if they employ flexible approaches to staffing and scheduling that take circadian rhythms into account. Sleep plays an important role in mediating links between stress arising from traumatic, life-threatening experiences and physical symptoms. Those sorts of critical incidents add to the burden of long work hours by disrupting sleep, although routine job stressors detract even more from the quality of officers' sleep. Finally, in addition to safety issues associated with the immediate threats officers encounter throughout their careers from dealing with dangerous people and hazardous situations, a 40-year study of a cohort of police officers indicates that we should also be very concerned about the long-term health consequences of employment in policing, consequences that arise at least in part from daily exposure to a complex combination of environmental, physical, and emotional insults (Violanti, Vena, and Petralia 1998).

In short, the inextricable link between fatigue management and police accountability goes like this. Police exercise substantial discretion during the performance of their duties. They have unique occupational powers that allow them the autonomy to decide on many occasions who will and will not be arrested. Discretion allows officers the flexibility necessary for nuanced law enforcement that facilitates justice. Since unfettered discretion can easily lead to injustice, law enforcement agencies use internal and external accountability measures to deter the abuse of discretionary powers. Effective deterrence, however, requires that an officer think about the consequences of improper behavior before acting and that he or she rationally weigh the potential rewards of improper behavior against potential consequences. Research shows that many officers work while impaired by lack of sleep associated with long work hours, shift work, and sleep disorders as well as personal choices. Officers who are impaired by fatigue are less likely to consider the consequences of their actions, less able to engage in thoughtful consideration of costs and benefits, and less able to manage the storm of emotions that accompany human confrontation.

It also is clear that current police work-hour practices are unjust for officers and their families. Whatever the limits of our knowledge about the complex causes of fatigue and about precisely how much it affects officer performance, health, and safety, many different types of research conducted by different scientists in different parts of the country all point to substantially higher levels of sleep disorders, morbidity, and mortality among police officers than among the general population. In fact, officers often work hours that exceed established standards for less challenging occupations where the potential consequences of misjudgment or ill temper are much more constrained (Vila 2000, 45–47). Justice demands that any on-duty police officer be *capable* of making sound decisions and that impairment arising from work-hour practices not reduce that capability.

Police executives, supervisors, and officers need to work together to develop policies, procedures, and a workplace culture that encourages sane fatigue-management practices. If they do, the rewards will be improved performance, safety, and health. Once such practices are in place, officers who voluntarily report for duty when they are too tired to perform properly must be held accountable—just as if they showed up drunk. Managers also must be held accountable if they fail to formulate meaningful guidance about fatigue, scheduling, and work-hour management, fail to train officers adequately about sleep deprivation and fatigue countermeasures, or are deficient in their supervision. Once accountability for fatigue is established in an organization, other, more general accountability measures will have a chance to work as intended: according to the logic of deterrence.

COURT CASES

Court of Appeals of Oregon v. McDonald's Restaurants of Oregon, Inc. 892 P. 2d 703 (133 Or.App. 514892 P. 2d 703).

United States v. Sandhu. 462 F. Supp. 2d 663 (E.D. PA, 2006).

Darling v. J. B. Expedited Services. 2006 WL 2238913 (U.S.D.C. M.D. Tenn).

Monell v. New York City Department of Social Services. (236 U.S. 658).

NOTES

1. Durmer and Dinges (2005) provide an excellent review of the impact of sleep deprivation on cognition.

2. Some officers refer to them as "overtime hogs"; others drop the *g*. This same phenomenon is found in other industries as well (Coleman 1995).

3. Williamson and Feyer also tested cognitive performance.

4. See, in addition, *Court of Appeals of Oregon v. McDonald's Restaurants of Oregon, Inc.* 892 P. 2d 703 (133 Or.App. 514892 P. 2d 703); *United States v. Sandhu.* 462 F. Supp. 2d 663 (E.D. PA, 2006); and *Darling v. J. B. Expedited Services.* 2006 WL 2238913 (U.S.D.C. M.D. Tenn).

5. Note that alcohol consumption also degrades sleep quality so that officers who drink before going to sleep will tend to be less rested the next day (Roehrs and Roth 2008).

REFERENCES

Appiah, K. Anthony. 2008. *Experiments in Ethics.* Cambridge, MA: Harvard University Press.

Armstrong, D. 1996. "Troopers' Extra Hours Spur Worry: Overtime, Details on Pike Pile up Despite Regulations." *Boston Globe.* September 3.

Barger, L. K., B. E. Cade, N. T. Ayas, J. W. Cronin, B. Rosner, F. E. Speizer, and C. A. Czeisler. 2005. "Extended Work Shifts and the Risk of Motor Vehicle Crashes among Interns." *New England Journal of Medicine* 352(2): 125–34.

Beccaria, Cesare. 1777. *An Essay on Crimes and Punishments,* 5th ed. Dublin: John Exshaw.

Belenky, G., N. J. Wesensten, and D. R. Thorne. 2003. "Patterns of Performance Degradation and Restoration during Sleep Restriction and Subsequent Recovery: A Sleep Dose-Response Study." *Journal of Sleep Research* 12:1–12.

Bentham, Jeremy. 1830. *The Rationale of Punishment.* London: Robert Heward.

Bonnet, M. H. 1985. "The Effect of Sleep Disruption on Performance, Sleep, and Mood." *Sleep* 8:11–19.

Caldwell, John A., and J. Lynn Caldwell. 2003. *Fatigue in Aviation: A Guide to Staying Awake at the Stick.* Burlington, VT: Ashgate.

Cassidy, T., and D. Armstrong. 1999. "State Police Overtime Soaring." *Boston Globe.* September 12.

Coburn, E. 1996. "Managing the Costs of Worker Fatigue." *Risk Management News*, July 29, 3–4.

Coleman, Richard, M. 1995. *The Twenty-Four Hour Business: Maximizing Productivity through Round-the-Clock Operations*. New York: American Management Association.

Committee on Military Nutrition Research, Food, and Nutrition Board. 2001. *Caffeine for the Sustainment of Mental Task Performance: Formulations for Military Operations*. Washington, DC: National Academy Press.

Dawson, D., and K. Reid. 1997. "Fatigue, Alcohol and Performance Impairment." *Nature* 388:235.

Dement, W. C., and C. Vaughan. 1999. *The Promise of Sleep: A Pioneer in Sleep Medicine Explores the Vital Connection between Health, Happiness, and a Good Night's Sleep*. New York: Delcorte.

Dijk, D.-J., D. F. Neri, J. K. Wyatt, J. M. Ronda, E. Riel, A. Ritz de Cecco, R. J. Hughes, A. R. Elliott, G. K. Prisk, J. B. West, and C. A. Czeisler. 2001. "Sleep, Performance, Circadian Rhythms, and Light-Dark Cycles during Two Space Shuttle Flights." *American Journal of Physiology—Regulatory, Integrative Comparative and Physiology* 281: R1647–64.

Durmer, J. S., and D. F. Dinges. 2005. "Neurocognitive Consequences of Sleep Deprivation." *Seminars in Neurology* 25:117–29.

Estes A., and D. Slack. 2006. "Boston Reports a Wage Drop: Payroll Decreases by $13m since '04." *Boston Globe*. March 3.

Folkard, Simon, and Timothy Monk, eds. 1985. *Hours of Work: Temporal Factors in Work Scheduling*. Chichester: John Wiley & Sons Ltd.

Fyfe, James J. 1980. "Always Prepared: Police Off-Duty Guns." *Annals of the American Academy of Political and Social Science* 452 (November): 72–81.

———. 1982. *Readings on Police Use of Deadly Force*. Washington, DC: Police Foundation.

———. 1997. "Police Liability: What Leading Law Enforcement Executives Need to Know." *CALEA Update* 65 (September): 6–13.

———. 2000. "Urban Policing in Australia and the United States." *Policing Issues* 1 (September): 1–12.

Gershon, Robyn R. M., Michael Tiburzi, Susan Lin, and Melissa J. Erwin. 2005. "Reports of Intimate Partner Violence Made against Police Officers." *Journal of Family Violence* 20(1): 13–19.

———. 1963. 1963. "Police Discretion: The Ideal versus the Real." *Public Administration Review* 23 (September): 140–48.

Goldstein, Herman. 1967a. "Police Policy Formulation: A Proposal for Improving Police Performance." *Michigan Law Review* 65 (April): 1123–46.

———. 1967b. "Administrative Problems in Controlling the Exercise of Police Authority." *The Journal of Criminal Law, Criminology, and Police Science* 58(2): 160–72.

Grad, Shelby, and Deborah Schoch. 1995. "Cities' Top 25 Lists Show Employees Generously Paid." *Los Angeles Times*. September 9.

Harrison Y, and J. A. Horne. 2000. "The Impact of Sleep Deprivation on Decision Making: A Review." *Journal of Experimental Psychology Applied* 6:236–49.

Horne, J. A., L. A. Reyner, and P. R. Barrett. 2003. "Driving Impairment due to Sleepiness Is Exacerbated by Low Alcohol Intake." *Occupational and Environmental Medicine* 60:689–92.

Killgore, William D. S., Thomas J. Balkin, and Nancy J. Wesensten. 2005. "Impaired Decision Making Following 49 Hours of Sleep Deprivation." *Journal of Sleep Research* 14:1–7.

Killgore, William D. S., Disiree B. Kilgore, Lisa M. Day, Christopher Li, Gary H. Kamimori, and Thomas J. Balkin. 2007. "The Effects of 53 Hours of Sleep Deprivation on Moral Judgment." *Sleep* 30:345–52.

Krull, Kevin R., Landgrave T. Smith, Rajita Sinha, and Oscar A. Parsons. 1993. "Simple Reaction Time Event-Related Potentials: Effects of Alcohol and Sleep Deprivation." *Alcohol Clinical Experimental Research* 17(4): 771–77.

Landrigan, Christopher P., Jeffrey M. Rothschild, John W. Cronin, Rainu Kaushal, Elisabeth Burdick, Joel T. Katz, Craig M. Lilly, Peter H. Stone, Stephen W. Lockley, David W. Bates, and Charles A. Czeisler. 2004. "Effect of Reducing Interns' Work Hours on Serious Medical Errors in Intensive Care Units." *New England Journal of Medicine* 351:1838–48.

Leonhardt, David. 2007. "Economix: Sometimes, What's Needed Is a Nudge." *New York Times*, May 16.

Liberman, A., S. Best, T. Metzler, J. Fagan, D. Weiss, and C. Marmar. 2002. "Routine Occupational Stress and Psychological Distress in Police." *Policing: International Journal of Management* 25:421–39.

Lockley, Stephen W., John W. Cronin, Erin E. Evans, Brian E. Cade, Clark J. Lee, Christopher P. Landrigan, Jeffrey M. Rothschild, Joel T. Katz, Craig M. Lilly, Peter H. Stone, Daniel Aeschbach, and Charles A. Czeisler. 2004. "Effect of Reducing Interns' Weekly Work Hours on Sleep and Attentional Failures." *New England Journal of Medicine* 351:1829–37.

Luenda, Charles, John Violanti, Cecil Burchfiel, and Bryan Vila. 2007. "Obesity and Sleep: The Buffalo Police Health Study." *Policing* 30:203–14.

Mann, Michael B. 1999. "Pilot Fatigue." Statement before the Aviation Subcommittee of the Committee on Transportation and Infrastructure, August 3. Washington, DC: U.S. House of Representatives. http://www.hq.nasa.gov/congress/mann8-3.html.

Marisco, R. 2003. "200 P.A. Officers at Least Doubled Pay with Overtime: Money for Extra Shifts Sets Agency Record." *Newark Star Ledger.* May 14.

McCoy, Candace. 1985. "Lawsuits against Police: What Impact Do They Really Have?" In *Police Management Today,* edited by James J Fyfe. (55–64). Washington, DC: International City/County Management Association.

Miller, Adam, and Rita Delfiner. 2003. "Overtime King: Nonstop Bridge Cop Adds 210G to Salary." *New York Post.* May 15.

Mitler, M. M., D. F. Dinges, and W. C. Dement. 1994. "Sleep Medicine, Public Policy, and Public Health." In *Principles and Practice of Sleep Medicine,* 2nd ed., edited by Meir H. Kryger, Thomas Roth, and William C. Dement (648–56). Philadelphia: W. B. Saunders.

Monk, Timothy H., and Simon Folkard. 1992. *Making Shift Work Tolerable.* London: Taylor & Francis.

Moore-Ede, M. 1993. *The 24-Hour Society: Understanding Human Limits in a World That Never Stops.* Reading, MA: Addison-Wesley.

———. 1995. "When Things Go Bump in the Night." *ABA Journal* (January): 56–60.

Naitoh, P., T. L. Kelly, and H. Babkoff. 1990. "Napping, Stimulant, and Four-Choice Performance." In *Sleep, Arousal, and Performance,* edited by Roger J. Broughton and Robert D. Ogilvie (199–220). Boston: Birkhaüser.

National Aeronautic and Space Administration (NASA). 1999. Hearing on pilot fatigue before the aviation subcommittee of the Committee on Transportation and Infrastructure, U.S. House of Representatives. http://www.afo.arc.nasa.gov/zteam/.

National Sleep Foundation. 1999. *1999 Omnibus Sleep in America Poll.* http://www.sleepfoundation.org/publications/19999poll.html#1.

Powell, Nelson B., Robert W. Riley, Kenneth B. Schechtman, Marc B. Blumen, David F. Dinges, and Christian Guilleminault. 1999. "A Comparative Model: Reaction Time Performance in Sleep-Disordered Breathing versus Alcohol-Impaired Controls." *Laryngoscope* 109 (October):1648–54.

Rajaratnam, S., L. Barger, S. Lockley, B. Cade, C. O'Brien, D. White, and C. Czeisler. 2007. "Screening for Sleep Disorders in North American Police Officers." *Sleep* 30: Abstract Supplement, A209.

Roehrs, Timothy, and Thomas Roth. 2008. "Sleep, Sleepiness, and Alcohol Use." National Institute on Alcohol Abuse and Alcoholism, National Institutes of Health. http://pubs.niaaa.nih.gov/publications/arh25-2/101-109.htm.

Roehrs, Timothy, David Beare, Frank Zorick, and Thomas Roth. 1994. "Sleepiness and Ethanol Effects on Simulated Driving." *Alcoholism: Clinical and Experimental Research* 18 (1): 154–58.

Rosekind, M. R., P. H. Gander, K. B. Gregory, R. M. Smith, D. L. Miller, R. Oyung. 1996a. "Managing Fatigue in Operational Settings 1: Physiological Considerations and Countermeasures." *Behavioral Medicine* 21:157–64.

———. 1996b. "Managing Fatigue in Operational Settings 2: An Integrated Approach." *Behavioral Medicine* 21:157–64.

Slack, D., and M. Cramer. 2006. "82 Officers Punished for Excess Workload." *Boston Globe.* February 17.

Sunstein, Cass R., and Richard H. Thaler. 2008. *Nudge: Improving Decisions about Health, Wealth, and Happiness.* New Haven, CT: Yale University Press.

Thayer, R. E. 1989. *The Biopsychology of Mood and Arousal.* New York: Oxford University Press.

U.S. Congress. *Congressional Record.* 1999. Testimony of M. B. Mann on pilot fatigue before the Aviation Subcommittee of the Committee on Transportation and Infrastructure, U.S. House of Representatives. August 3.

U.S. Department of Justice. Annual. *Law Enforcement Officers Killed and Assaulted.* Washington, DC: U.S. Department of Justice. http://www.fbi.gov/ucr/killed/2006/index.html.

U.S. Department of Transportation, Federal Railroad Administration. 2006. *Validation and Calibration of a Fatigue Assessment Tool for Railroad Work Schedules, Summary Report* (DOT/FRA/ORD-06/21). Washington, DC: NTIS.

Van Dongen, H. P. A., J. A. Caldwell, and J. L. Caldwell. 2006. "Investigating Systematic Individual Differences in Sleep-Deprived Performance on a High-Fidelity Flight Simulator." *Behavior Research Methods* 38:333–43.

Vila, Bryan. 1996. "Tired Cops: Probable Connections between Fatigue and the Performance, Health, and Safety of Patrol Officers." *American Journal of Police* 15(2): 51–92.

———. 2000. *Tired Cops: The Importance of Managing Police Fatigue.* Washington, DC: Police Executive Research Forum.

———. 2006. "Impact of Long Work Hours on Police Officers and the Communities They Serve." *American Journal of Industrial Medicine* 49(11): 972–80.

Vila, Bryan J., Dennis Jay Kenney, Gregory B. Morrison, and Melissa Reuland. 2000. *Evaluating the Effects of Fatigue on Police Patrol Officers.* Washington, DC: U.S. Department of Justice.

Vila, Bryan, Gregory B. Morrison, and Dennis Jay Kenney. 2002. "Improving Shift Schedule and Work-Hour Policies and Practices to Increase Police Officer Health, Safety and Performance." *Police Quarterly* 5(1): 4–24.

Vila, Bryan, and Charles Samuels. Forthcoming. "Sleep Loss in First Responders and the Military." In *Principles and Practice of Sleep Medicine,* 5th ed., edited by Meir H. Kryger, Thomas Roth, and William C. Dement. Philadelphia: Elsevier Saunders.

Violanti, John M., John E. Vena, and S. Petralia. 1998. "Mortality of a Police Cohort: 1950–1990." *American Journal of Industrial Medicine* 33:366–73.

Wesensten, N. J., G. Belenky, and T. J. Balkin. 2005. "Cognitive Readiness in Network-Centric Operations." *Parameters* (Spring): 95–105.

Williamson, A. M., and A.-M. Feyer. 2000. "Moderate Sleep Deprivation Produces Impairments in Cognitive and Motor Performance Equivalent to Legally Prescribed Levels of Alcohol Intoxication." *Occupational and Environmental Medicine* 57: 649–55.

8

Training for the Data-Driven Police Department

Michael D. White

Despite general resistance to change within the profession, policing is by no means static. Changes in law, new and emerging problems, and improvements in technology force police departments to adapt their policy and practice continually. Training is the central means by which police departments respond to change. Training, whether in the academy or in service, provides police officers with the skills required to adapt their work to a changing external environment. For a variety of reasons, however, police training often falls short in adequately preparing police officers for change, whether it involves responding to new problems, such as identity theft, or taking advantage of opportunities presented by new technologies, such as the CompStat model.

The failure of training to keep pace with change is perhaps most evident with the increasing reliance of police departments on computers, crime data, and basic analysis of crime trends. The adoption of CompStat as well as the computerization of all police data more generally (i.e., personnel, training academy, performance evaluations, use of force reports, and citizen complaints) provides a special opportunity for law enforcement agencies to engage in data analysis and investigate important department-related questions. Although data are frequently available for addressing important issues, such as racial profiling and misconduct, police officers—even those in crime analysis, training, and research units—typically lack the technical and analytical skills required to answer those questions sufficiently. In simpler terms, as departments become increasingly computerized and data oriented, police training must keep pace by teaching officers the skills required to meet the objectives of the data-driven police department.[1]

This chapter describes a pilot effort by the New York City Police Department (NYPD) to address this limitation in training through a college-level course that sought to provide officers with the skills to engage in data analysis—and, essentially, to conduct meaningful and sound social research—while on the job. Ideally, changes in police training occur as part of a systematic needs assessment that examines police officer duties and existing training and identifies areas for modification or improvement. Unfortunately, this course—like police training in general—was not developed as part of such a framework. Instead, the training grew out of the personal beliefs and instincts of the NYPD's deputy commissioner of training, Dr. James J. Fyfe. Shaped by Deputy Commissioner Fyfe's unique experiences in both academe and law enforcement, the data analysis training course was offered at the John Jay College of Criminal Justice to 20 police officers during the spring 2004 semester and to 25 officers during the fall 2004 term. This chapter describes how the training course was developed, its organization and content, the officers involved, and the NYPD data that were analyzed. With Kirkpatrick's training evaluation model as a guide (*reactions, learning, behavior,* and *results*), the chapter describes training outcomes, including officer assessments of the course (*reactions*), officer performance (*learning*), and findings from analyses (1959a, b; 1960a, b). Results from a follow-up survey sent to officers five months later are also presented (*behavior*). The results are considered in the context of a more general call for increased relevance in police training, both academic and in service. The chapter concludes with a discussion of how this training model represents a "middle ground" that can be applied to other issues in policing.

Increasing the Relevance of Police Training

Central to the issue of police training—and its relevance—is the debate over whether the occupation is a *craft* where the primary skills are learned through on-the-job training, or a *profession,* where skills are first passed onto recruits through an academically oriented academy curriculum and supplemented by later field experience (i.e., similar to medical school and residency). In police lore, we often hear of the seasoned veterans telling the rookies that the first thing they need to do is forget everything they just learned in the academy. Police officers traditionally argue that classroom training—both academic and in service—does not prepare officers for the street because policing is a craft "in which learning comes exclusively through experience intuitively processed by individual officers" (Bayley and Bittner 1984, 35). In other words, learning the skills necessary to become a good police officer comes exclusively from experience on the job (Bayley and Bittner 1984; see also Wilson 1968). From this perspective, police officers are viewed as skilled laborers who bring specialized skills and training to their trade, much like plumbers and electricians (Bumgarner 2002; Crank 1990; Stinchcombe 1980).

Many scholars and police leaders argue, however, that policing possesses the key features of a profession, including a specialized body of knowledge and skills, accreditation through a professional organization, an orientation toward clients or service, considerable discretion given to members, and a primary objective other than profit (Capps 1998; Crank, Payn, and Jackson 1993; Radelet and Carter 1994). Efforts to professionalize policing place a premium on education, and classroom training (and college education) served as a foundation of the early professionalism movement led by August Vollmer (Walker and Katz 2002). The increasing emphasis on college education for police officers is based on the assumption that the occupation is a profession where the skills and knowledge necessary to do the job successfully can be learned in a classroom setting, not solely through on-the-job training.[2]

Although there is little agreement on whether policing is a craft or a profession, most agree that current classroom training has significant limitations and often leaves officers ill prepared for actual police work (Berg 1990; Dantzker 2000a, b; Doerner, Horton, and Smith 2003; Edwards 1993; Ness 1991; Stinchcombe and Terry 1995). Several scholars argue that reducing the gap between classroom training and police work on the street simply requires developing more relevant training programs. Bayley and Bittner argue that, even if policing is a craft where formative experiences occur on the street, learning can be "accelerated and made more systematic" by relevant training: "What is needed in police training . . . is frank discussion, with case studies of the realities of field decision" (Bayley and Bittner 1984, 55). Several scholars have heeded Bayley and Bittner's advice and devised special approaches for teaching police officers. Memory (2001) applied this rationale to teaching problem-solving skills to patrol officers. Pollock and Becker (1995) used a similar approach to teaching ethical issues to police (see also McKenzie's 2002 discussion of distance learning).

A Model for Evaluating the Impact of Training

More than four decades ago, Kirkpatrick (1959a, b; 1960a, b) introduced a four-level evaluation model that has enjoyed widespread popularity in both the public and the private sectors for nearly half a century and has served as the conceptual framework for measuring the effectiveness of training. Kirkpatrick's model includes four measures or steps of effectiveness:

1. *Reactions:* trainees' views or attitudes toward the training (i.e., did they value it?)
2. *Learning:* the degree to which the information is understood and internalized by trainees
3. *Behavior:* the degree to which the newly acquired information is used on the job
4. *Results:* the degree to which organizational outcomes or goals are achieved

The longstanding popularity of Kirkpatrick's model stems in large part from its simplicity and from its utility in thinking about how to operationalize the effectiveness of training.

A number of scholars over the years have questioned the validity of Kirkpatrick's model, however. Some have suggested modifications to the model, for example, adding a fifth level to reflect organizational success criteria, such as economic benefits (Hamblin 1974), social value (Kaufman and Keller 1994), or return on investment (Holton 1996; Phillips 1996). Others have argued that the problems with Kirkpatrick's model are more fundamental. Alliger and Janak (1989) outline three problematic assumptions of the Kirkpatrick model: (1) the levels are arranged in ascending order of information provided; (2) the levels are causally linked; and (3) the levels are positively correlated. They then argue that none of the assumptions are supported by research. Holton (1996) states that the Kirkpatrick model is actually a taxonomy or classification of outcomes, not a researchable evaluation model. Holton (1996) offers an alternative model with three outcomes—learning, individual performance, and organizational results—with individual ability, motivation, and environment as influences on those outcomes.

In short, there has been considerable emphasis on the importance of assessing training effectiveness, and the private sector, in particular, has embraced and internalized this message. Police training, unfortunately, has rarely been evaluated for its effectiveness. Although it is assumed that training (especially in the academy) provides the fundamental skills necessary to be a good police officer, the empirical support for this assumption is scant. The "hodge-podge" nature of police training (academy, field training, and the like), in fact, suggests an awareness of its limitations among those in the profession. Still, both the original Kirkpatrick model and its progeny suggest that there are multiple levels of effectiveness to consider, and the Kirkpatrick model, in particular, serves as a solid foundation and launching point for asking good questions about police training: What did the officers think about the training? Did learning occur? Did learning result in behavioral change? What are the implications of that behavioral change?

The NYPD and the Emergence of CompStat: Implications for Police Training

CompStat, developed in the 1990s in New York, is based on the notion that police have the capacity to affect crime and that, by controlling serious crime, they will be better able to maintain order, address community issues, and promote public safety. CompStat is based on five principles (McDonald 2002, 10)[3]:

- Specific objectives
- Timely and accurate intelligence
- Effective strategies and tactics
- Rapid deployment of personnel and resources
- Relentless follow-up and assessment

CompStat clearly represents a fundamental shift in how police do business. The last principle, follow-up and assessment, is arguably the most innovative aspect of CompStat, given that the traditional model of policing trains officers to deal with each situation as quickly as possible to make themselves available for additional calls (with no real emphasis on later evaluation of whether their "intervention" had an impact). Timely analysis of data, under CompStat, becomes the foundation for police management and operations—the "engine" that drives the department (McDonald 2002, 1). CompStat, credited by many as the primary cause of the significant decrease in crime in New York City, has been adopted by numerous departments around the country (Weisburd et al. 2003).

The CompStat model includes the basic elements of social science research—identifying an objective, collecting and analyzing data, implementing a targeted strategy, and assessing its impact. The operational elements of the strategy are quite simplistic and typically involve comparisons of computerized maps over time (i.e., has the number of "pins" decreased since the department implemented its targeted strategy?). In methodological terms, the department typically engages in a weak quasi-experimental research design, where an intervention is employed and the dependent variable is examined before and after implementation with no control or comparison group (Taylor 1994). Setting aside the discussion of methodological rigor, the key issue is that the collection and analysis of data have become centrally important to the police department.

Relevant Training in Data Analysis

Despite the critical role of data and analysis for the NYPD (and other departments that have adopted the model), most officers—with the exception of a few assigned to specialized research units—have not been trained and do not possess the necessary skills to take advantage of the available data to address important issues facing the department (i.e., moving beyond weak quasi-experimental research). In 2002, James J. Fyfe, a leading police scholar and distinguished professor of law, police science, and criminal justice administration at the John Jay College of Criminal Justice, was appointed as the first deputy commissioner of training for the NYPD. Dr. Fyfe, because of his background as a scholar and researcher, was acutely aware of both the more general disconnect between classroom training and real-world policing and specifically of the potential for improving the department's capacity for data analysis through more relevant training. Dr. Fyfe believed that many of the current controversial issues affecting the NYPD—use of force, racial profiling, and value of academy training, for example—could be investigated thoroughly by the department itself, if personnel could be trained in the required technical skills. More broadly, the last principle of CompStat, follow-up and assessment, could be greatly enhanced if appropriate training provided officers with more sophisticated analytical abilities.

In fall 2003, Dr. Fyfe asked the author to create a new training course that would teach advanced analytical skills using SPSS to selected members of his staff.[4] Clearly, this training was not to be a typical in-service program. The success of the proposed training hinged on the ability to get buy-in from the officers assigned to participate. The college-level course described in this chapter reflects the spirit of finding middle ground and adopts the perspective that, for the training to be successful, it must be taught in a way that is relevant for the police. The deputy commissioner of training and the author devised an approach that optimized the likelihood of officer buy-in. This approach included handpicking officers who were most likely to find the training relevant to their work, analyzing real NYPD data, engaging in work that could potentially have policy implications for the department, and offering college credit for participation (at no cost to the officers). Dr. Fyfe chose to implement the training on a limited scale involving only his staff for several reasons:

- The training was not developed through a needs assessment or job task analysis; instead, it was developed based on his own personal experiences and beliefs.
- He was reasonably sure the skills would be relevant to those working directly for him.
- He felt he was in the best position to assess the value of the training— specifically, did the officers learn the material? Did the officers employ their newly acquired skills in the field? And was the department realizing dividends from their enhanced performance (the *learning, behavior,* and *results* levels of Kirkpatrick's model)?

The Training Course: Computer Applications for Police Managers

The Officers

Dr. Fyfe handpicked the officers for the course, including staff from the Training Academy and Office of the Deputy Commissioner of Training.

In all, 20 officers were assigned to the training course in spring 2004 and 25 in fall 2004. Most were male (only 10 females out of the 45 officers) and approximately two-thirds were white, non-Hispanic. Officer rank varied significantly and included patrol officer, sergeant, lieutenant, captain, deputy inspector, and inspector.[5] There were also civilian personnel in the class.

Designing the Training Course: Content and Data

The course, at Dr. Fyfe's request, was intended to provide officers with the fundamental skills for engaging in statistically and methodologically sound research. The training was divided into three basic blocks. Although all the officers in the course were comfortable with computers, none had been exposed to SPSS. The initial training block consequently focused on the basic operation of SPSS: opening files, creating and saving data, data entry, running frequencies and cross-tabs, and interpreting output.[6] The second block of the course involved more in-depth use of SPSS, including recodes, data transformations, and simple correlational analyses (i.e., Pearson's r, chi-square, t-tests). The final block of the course introduced officers to regression analysis, including multiple linear and logistic regression.[7]

Dr. Fyfe provided four datasets to be analyzed:

- Background and training academy performance data for the July 2002 recruit class ($n = 2,473$).
- Background and training academy performance data for the July 2003 recruit class ($n = 1,556$).
- All firearms discharge and assault reports for 2003 ($n = 1,697$).
- All TASER incidents for 2003 ($n = 91$).

None of the data sets had been analyzed in any systematic way by the NYPD before the course. Dr. Fyfe, in fact, envisioned that the training course would play a supplemental analysis role for the department, thereby accomplishing two objectives at once (teaching data analysis to officers and doing so with previously unexamined data). The training was designed to be open-ended, in that officers would identify the specific research questions that interested them and then conduct analyses to address those questions.

The recruit data for the 2002 and 2003 classes were of particular interest because the 2002 training class was the last class to receive the "old" training curriculum and the 2003 class was the first to receive the new, updated curriculum.[8] Each data set included basic background and demographic information, as well as scores for the various academy tests and final outcome information (graduated or not). Specific issues that were examined included performance by race, gender, and age; the relationship between college education and academy performance; the relationship between reading level and performance; and differences in performance between 2002 and 2003 recruits.

The firearms discharge and assault form is completed every time an officer is assaulted, whether injured or not, or discharges his or her firearm. The form is typically just one page, including basic incident, suspect, and officer information, as well as a brief narrative of the encounter. Firearms discharges include the same one-page form as well as the entire shooting investigation. Of the nearly 1,700 forms for 2003, 71 incidents involved a firearms discharge. Specific issues examined included characteristics of suspects and officers, characteristics of incidents, predictors of officer injury, and predictors of whether the incident would escalate to a firearms discharge. The Taser deployment form is a similar one-page report, collecting a variety of information on the officer, suspect, and Taser use through a "check the appropriate box" format and short narrative section. Work with the Taser data focused on simple descriptive analysis of officers, suspects, and the nature of incidents (i.e., level of threat to the officer, suspect, and others).

Measuring the Effectiveness of the Training

Success or effectiveness of the training can be measured in a number of ways, based on the Kirkpatrick model. The simplest measures of effectiveness involve the officers' perceptions of the training and their performance in it (each officer was assigned a grade at the end of the training, much like a college course). These measures represent the *reactions* and *learning* steps in Kirkpatrick's model, respectively. Another measure of success is the discovery of important or interesting findings. Officers were also asked to complete a follow-up survey five months after the course ended, indicating whether they were applying the skills taught in the training to their work at the department. This survey sought to tap into Kirkpatrick's third level, *behavior*.

Officers' Assessments of the Training, or Kirkpatrick's *Reactions* Step

Officers were asked to complete a course evaluation at the end of the training. The author constructed an evaluation specifically for the data analysis course.[9] The first part of the form included six statements and asked officers to indicate their level of agreement with each statement: strongly disagree (1), disagree (2), not sure (3), agree (4), and strongly agree (5). Table 8.1 shows the mean score for each statement by semester and overall.

The statements asked officers to assess the relevance and value of the training for their work in the department, whether the course improved their understanding of data and analysis, and whether it should be offered regularly. Table 8.1 shows that overall mean scores on all six items are above 4.0 (agree), with a low of 4.04 and a high of 4.78. Mean scores in the spring semester for four of the six statements are above 4.5, indicating a strong level of agreement with improved understanding of the material, the importance of the skills learned, the practical importance of the analyses conducted, and the need to offer the course again. The mean score for each item dropped in the fall semester, however. The

Table 8.1. Statements and Mean Scores from the *Computer Applications for Police Managers* Course Evaluations, Spring and Fall 2004

	Spring (n = 11)	Fall (n =15)	Total (n = 26)
I believe this course was relevant to my work in the NYPD.	4.36	4.13	4.23
I believe this course will help me in my position in the NYPD.	4.09	4.00	4.04
I believe the analyses we conducted in class have practical implications for the NYPD.	4.73	4.44	4.56
After taking this course, I believe I have a better understanding of data, analysis, and their value for the NYPD.	4.91	4.69	4.78
I believe it is important to have officers in the NYPD who possess the skills taught in this class.	4.55	4.38	4.44
I believe this class should be taught to NYPD personnel on a regular basis.	4.55	4.13	4.30

Source: Author.

reasons for the drop-off are not known, although potential explanations involve differences in the officers and their background (i.e., differences in rank or computer expertise), the instruction, and the course material (although the content and format were essentially the same across semesters).

Officers were also asked three open-ended questions: What was the best aspect of the training? What was the worst aspect of the training? Do you have any specific recommendations for improving the training? Written responses were mostly positive, as shown by selected comments in table 8.2. Responses regarding the best aspect of the training tended to focus on the

Table 8.2. Selected Responses to Open-Ended Questions from the *Computer Applications for Police Managers* Course Evaluations, Spring and Fall 2004

What was the best aspect of the training?
- "learning how to analyze data"
- "learning the program SPSS and being able to apply NYPD data"
- "having the opportunity to take part in a program that may potentially help the department in improving policy making methods"
- "using data that are relevant to police work"
- "some of the work was in a group environment"
- "class comprised entirely of NYPD personnel in units with a common interest in the course data"
- "the instructor was very knowledgeable in law enforcement–related studies"

What was the worst aspect of the training?
- "the coding of data from the FADR"
- "not enough time to give course my full attention"
- "none"
- "realizing the NYPD will not use analyses this in depth to improve its functioning, delivery of service, or training"
- "analyzing the outputs of the computer program was at times confusing"

Do you have specific recommendations for how the training could be improved?
- "no—it will just be more informative as the amount of data used increases (i.e., more than two classes of recruits, more than one year of firearms reports)"
- "nothing to report"
- "no"
- "handouts of output identifying the various elements of the output"
- "Having persons in decisionmaking capacities attend and learn how useful this information could be to the NYPD, and use the data to shape policy and training"

Source: Author.

data that were examined and their relevance or implications for the NYPD. Responses to the questions on the worst aspect of the training and recommendations for improving the course tended to involve the workload for the course and the complexity of the SPSS program.

Meeting Course Requirements, or Kirkpatrick's *Learning* Step

Officers were asked to complete four take-home assignments and two in-class exams as part of the training. Officers performed well on assignments and exams, as reflected in final grades. Final grades for the 15 students who completed the spring semester were as follows: A (5), A- (4), B+ (2), B (2), B- (1), and C (1). Final grades in the fall were A (14), A- (2), B+ (2), and B (3). This is clearly not the typical bell curve. Then again, these were not typical students. They were upwardly mobile professionals who had a vested interest in the content of the course and in performing well. Also, although the course functioned much like a college class, it was conceived of and implemented as an in-service training. Recall that the students had been handpicked by their commanding officer to participate and would ultimately be accountable to him if they performed poorly. In short, the training appeared to achieve the *learning* step in Kirkpatrick's model.

Key Findings from the Analyses

Analyses conducted in class and as part of take-home assignments produced a number of interesting findings, with potential practical implications for the NYPD and theoretical implications for the field. Several of the findings described below led to lively discussions in class (and later back at the office) about how particular issues and problems could be addressed, changed, and improved.

2002–2003 Recruit Data
- Male recruits had significantly higher reading levels and entrance exam scores than female recruits (both classes).
- White, non-Hispanic recruits had significantly higher reading levels and entrance exam scores than African-American and Hispanic recruits (both classes).

- Male recruits scored higher on exams than female recruits, and whites scored higher than minorities. Differences in reading level, not race and gender, explained the differences in performance (both classes).
- Recruit age was negatively associated with performance in the academy: as age increased, performance decreased (both classes).
- The number of college credits a recruit had earned before entering the academy was not related to performance in the academy (2003 class only).
- Members of the NYPD Cadet Corps did not perform significantly better than other recruits (2003 class only).[10]
- Because the curriculum changed dramatically, it was difficult to compare the outcomes between 2002 and 2003 recruits. However, analyses did show some differences:
  - Mean exam scores increased notably in the 2003 class for all recruits (male, female, white, Hispanic, African American, and Asian).
  - The attrition rate dropped in the 2003 class, especially among minority recruits.
  - In the 2002 class, male recruits scored significantly higher than female recruits on the final exam. In the 2003 class, males and females scored equally on the final exam.
  - One of the problems identified with the old curriculum was that the exams were too reading intensive (i.e., long reading comprehension–type questions that were timed), which negatively affected minority recruits (who generally possessed lower reading levels than white recruits). The new curriculum sought to create a less reading-intensive format. Findings indicate that the percentage of variance in final exam performance explained by recruit reading level dropped from 25 percent in 2002 to 16 percent in 2003.

2003 Data on Firearm Discharges and Assaults on Officers

- A number of officers (4 percent of cases, $n = 59$) filled out the form improperly, when they received an injury that did not involve an assault by a suspect (i.e., accidental injury) or when they were not injured at all. Officers indicated that the department may need to schedule retraining on when it is appropriate to complete the form (and when it is not).

- The typical incident involving a firearms discharge or assault on an officer:
  - Occurred outside (63 percent)
  - Involved a patrol officer (77 percent)
  - Involved a white male officer (88 and 63 percent, respectively)
  - Involved an on-duty officer attempting to make an arrest (97 and 49 percent, respectively)
  - Had more than one officer present (83 percent)
  - Involved one suspect who was nonwhite (88 and 85 percent, respectively) and male (88 percent)
- Incidents involving firearms' discharges were similar to incidents involving assaults on officers, with a few notable exceptions:
  - Incidents involving a gun discharge were more likely to involve a male officer (96 versus 88 percent) and a male suspect (100 versus 88 percent).
  - Incidents involving a gun discharge were more likely to involve a robbery (16 versus 5 percent).
  - Incidents involving a gun discharge were less likely to involve a white suspect (5 versus 15 percent).

2003 Taser Data

- Suspects
  - Most suspects were male (86 percent), minority (46 percent black; 24 percent Hispanic), and older (mean age was 36).
  - Nearly all (98 percent) suspects were classified as "emotionally disturbed," and 14 percent were intoxicated.
  - 98 percent were taken to a hospital after the incident; only 28 percent were arrested.
  - 89 percent were exhibiting violent behavior; 37 percent were armed with a weapon.
- Officers
  - 95 percent of officers were assigned to the Emergency Services Unit (ESU).[11]
  - 42 percent were patrol officers; 48 percent were detectives; 10 percent were supervisors.
  - In nearly all cases, both a supervisor and backup officers were present (95 and 91 percent, respectively).

- Taser deployment
  - In 75 percent of the incidents, the Taser was deployed only once.
  - Median time to incapacitation was five seconds.
  - 74 percent of officers said the Taser performed satisfactorily.
  - 100 percent of cases were deemed to fall within departmental policy for Taser deployment.

Results from the Follow-Up Survey

Officers were asked to complete a short follow-up survey five months after the training ended (November 2004 and May 2005) indicating, among other things, whether they were using the skills taught in the course in their work and whether the training had helped them in their jobs. The survey was structured like a course evaluation, using a Likert scale to indicate their level of agreement with nine statements. Table 8.3 shows the statements and the mean responses for each overall and by class.[12] Officers felt strongly that the class had improved their understanding of data and analysis (4.67 overall), that the skills taught in the training could improve the department's ability to analyze data (4.42 overall), and that the findings from the class could potentially influence policy, practice, and training in the department (4.17 overall). Officers felt less strongly about the potential impact of the training on CompStat and the importance of their teaching the skills to others in their office (3.83 and 3.67, respectively). There is a notable drop-off again among responses from officers in the second course. Officers in the second course indicated that the training improved their analytical skills (4.33) and that it could positively influence the department (4.0 for both ability to influence training, policy, and practice and ability to improve the department's analytical capabilities), but scores on other items were quite low: 3.17 and 2.83 for whether the skills are useful in their work and whether it affected their job performance, respectively. These findings suggest that officers in the second training cohort acquired new skills and saw value in those skills but that the training may not have been as relevant for their particular jobs (compared to officers in the first training).

Experts in training evaluation generally recognize surveys of trainees as a weak measure of Kirkpatrick's *behavior* step. Better measures include

Table 8.3. Statements and Mean Scores from the *Computer Applications for Police Managers* Follow-Up Survey, Spring and Fall 2004

	Spring ($n = 6$)	Fall ($n = 6$)	Total ($n = 12$)
The skills I learned in class have been useful in my work at the NYPD.	4.33	3.17	3.75
My job performance has been positively affected by taking the data analysis course.	4.33	2.83	3.58
I believe it is important to teach or demonstrate the skills I learned in class to others in my office.	3.67	3.67	3.67
The analysis of NYPD data in the class has led to discussions at work about training, policy, and practice.	4.17	3.50	3.83
The analyses we conducted in class have the potential to influence training, policy, and practice of the NYPD.	4.33	4.00	4.17
The skills taught in the course can help improve the department's ability to analyze police data.	4.83	4.00	4.42
The skills taught in the course can help improve CompStat.	3.83	3.83	3.83
I believe it is important to have officers in the NYPD who possess the skills taught in this class.	4.33	3.33	3.83
The course gave me a better understanding of data, analysis, and their value for the NYPD.	5.00	4.33	4.67

Source: Author.

interviews with supervisors who can offer independent assessments of change in performance, researcher observations of fieldwork, and examinations of formal performance evaluations. All of the officers participating in the training worked directly for Dr. Fyfe, and the author originally intended to interview Dr. Fyfe about each officer to get individual assessments of training effectiveness (i.e., his assessment of each officer's *behavioral* change). Given the logistical problems associated with observing officers in the workplace as well as gaining access to their personnel files (to review performance evaluations), the interview with Dr. Fyfe held the greatest potential for assessing effectiveness at the *behavioral* and *results* steps. Sadly, Dr. Fyfe passed away before this additional work could be completed.

Discussion

In the context of a more general call for relevant police training, the New York City Police Department sought to enhance its training in data analysis by developing a college-level course using SPSS and police data. Initial indications from the analyses presented here suggest that the training was well received, that it enhanced officers' analytical skills, and that many of the officers were applying those skills in their work. There is persuasive evidence that effectiveness at the *reactions* and *learning* steps of the Kirkpatrick model was achieved and some support that success at the *behavior* stage also occurred. The remainder of the chapter is devoted to a discussion of the advantages of developing such a course, as well as the potential for broader application of this middle-ground model of police training. Before that discussion, however, it is important to review the limitations of this chapter.

Clearly, the generalizability of the findings is limited, for several reasons. First, the extent to which this experience provides useful information to other police departments seeking to develop similar training remains unclear (i.e., external validity). Certainly, this experience is a unique one, given the size of the NYPD and its long-term partnership with John Jay College. Would the same challenges arise in Chicago, San Francisco, Boston, or Orlando? Would the experience in New York be illustrative for partnerships among small departments and colleges? The answers to these questions remain unknown.

Second, the article describes two sections of the training course only, involving just 45 officers. Experience in subsequent training sessions with different officers could produce different results. The perceived value of the training will also vary based on the assignments of those who participate. Third, only 12 of the 36 officers who finished the course completed the survey, raising concerns about selection bias with regard to the follow-up findings (in addition to the traditional limitations of self-report surveys). Last, the author chose to use Kirkpatrick's model of training effectiveness as a guiding framework because of its widespread popularity, although as stated earlier, the model has its limitations. In addition, while the author was able to produce good measures of earlier steps in the model (*reactions* and *learning*), the follow-up surveys are a relatively weak measure of the later stages. Logistical and resource limitations, as well as Dr. Fyfe's death, prohibited more in-depth analysis of these later steps.

The Benefits of Training Officers in Data Analysis

The data analysis course described here offers a number of advantages to both the police department and the officers involved. From the police department's perspective, a core group of its officers received training in an increasingly important and expanding area of department business. Police departments today are expected to do more than traditional reactive patrol and respond to calls for service. Community and problem-oriented philosophies of policing, as well as more data-driven approaches, demand that departments be proactive, flexible, and responsive to community needs. For both departments and individual officers, basic knowledge of the social science research process, data, and analysis offers an opportunity to be better informed, to be better able to respond to crime trends and community concerns, to become better problem solvers, and to make decisions based on rational, objective analysis rather than on subjective judgment and gut instinct.

Moreover, particularly in the wake of controversial police-citizen encounters or scandals, departments are often placed under tremendous pressure by other government agencies (local, state, and federal), advocacy groups, and communities to demonstrate their performance and justify the actions of their officers. A department that has a core group of officers trained in data analysis has the ability to conduct its own research (either on short notice or as part of an ongoing process) to respond to particular issues and crises. A department accused of racial profiling or ignoring citizen complaints, for example, could carry out an internal analysis of data to investigate the issue and refute or substantiate those claims. Departments could also use data analysis to examine other relevant issues such as officer performance, predictors of good and bad performance, the development of an early warning system, use of force, and the impact of specific policies.

The NYPD under CompStat has become the prototypical data-driven police department. The core of the CompStat model involves developing interventions to address specific problems and assessing the impact of those interventions. In different terms, the foundation of the model that many argue represents a revolution in policing involves independent and dependent variables and quasi-experimental research. CompStat-like models are only enhanced when the final component—follow-up and assessment—includes in-depth, empirical analysis of data, including univariate, bivariate, and multivariate techniques.

The Potential for Broader Application
of This "Middle Ground" Training Model

This training was developed and implemented in the context of Bayley and Bittner's (1984) call (and others more recently) for more relevant police training—a middle ground in the debate over whether policing is a craft or a profession. This course was conducted in the classroom, where the training disconnect is typically greatest, but the course content, the officers who participated, the data that were analyzed, and the partnership with John Jay were carefully crafted in a model intended to reflect the spirit of Bayley and Bittner's challenge. The training model tapped the expertise—and resources—of a college, offered the training in the form of a college-level class, but was structured in a way that sought to make the material relevant, interesting, and useful for police.

Given the initial indications of success, some discussion of the key elements of the training approach and its potential application to other areas of policing is warranted. The key elements of the training model include partnership with a college or university, flexibility, relevant content, carefully selected personnel, and the college setting:

- First, Dr. Fyfe sought out John Jay for this training because he felt that no one in the NYPD had the expertise or time to teach this course, a situation similar to that in the vast majority of police departments, which highlights the importance of the college-police partnership.
- Second, both the police department and the university must be flexible. The department must be willing (and able) to free up officers to attend weekly training, a longer and more intense commitment than typical in-service trainings. The professor may need to be more flexible with the officers than with traditional undergraduates, as officers may have to miss class because of special assignments and manpower shortages or other atypical circumstances. The university and police department should develop a way to offer the training with no cost to the participating officers. This approach may represent a real challenge because the model, as conceived here, has clear resource implications for the university (professor's time, books, computers, software, and the like).
- Third, the training course described here is unique because of the availability of NYPD data. The recruit, Taser, and firearms and assault data allowed the author to structure the course in a way that

not only maximized interest among the officers but served to answer basic questions for the police department. Officer interest in the course would have no doubt waned considerably had the author used the standard social science survey data or some other less relevant dataset.

- Fourth, selecting the appropriate officers for the course is important for success. Officers assigned to training and academy units, as well as those in research and crime analysis assignments, are likely the best candidates for the data analysis course because they are most likely to find the course material relevant to their work.[13] Because of the department's size, there was no shortage of officers to assign to the training. Smaller police departments, however, may be unable to send enough officers to sustain the training course. If one department cannot send enough personnel to support a class, perhaps other surrounding departments could be contacted to also send officers.

- Fifth, and last, the course is most likely to be successful if taught in a university environment for college credit. Holding the class at the university makes available the resources of the university. Most police departments simply do not have a room with twenty personal computers, all with SPSS or a similar statistical package. In addition, officers taking the class should receive college credit, and, if at all possible, the class should place no financial burden on the officers, making it more attractive to police personnel.

The initial application of this training approach involved a focus on data and analysis, but it has the potential for employment in a wide range of police training areas. Partnerships with universities or other public and private sector agencies and businesses could be developed in many other training areas:

- *Mental illness:* partnering with psychiatrists and psychologists either in private practice or from a university
- *The homeless:* partnering with social service agencies and shelters
- *Domestic violence:* partnering with universities, victim advocate agencies, and battered women's shelters
- *Computer crime and identity theft:* partnering with private security firms and the computer industry (especially their security personnel)
- *Terrorism:* partnering with universities, private security, and government

- *Management practices:* partnering with the private sector and universities (business faculty)
- *Performance evaluation:* partnering with the private sector
- *Communication:* partnering with universities and the private sector

The issues and challenges may vary with each of the aforementioned areas—as may the degree of success of the training—but many of these police issues are among those where academy or classroom training is typically seen as unrealistic and irrelevant. Application of this training model—whether it centers on a police-university partnership or some other collaboration—would represent a move toward more practical and relevant training. Finally, application of any new training, this approach included, should be accompanied by careful assessment and evaluation to ensure it is achieving its intended objectives. Kirkpatrick's model (and others) has been widely used to assess training effectiveness in other settings, and it offers a solid foundation for police training as well. Given that training at its foundation seeks to provide police officers with the skills necessary to perform their duties, more relevant training should ultimately produce better performance on the street, and each training modification should be examined in that context.

Acknowledgments

The author would like to thank the late Dr. James J. Fyfe, deputy commissioner of training, New York City Police Department and distinguished professor at the John Jay College of Criminal Justice, and the 45 New York City police officers who participated in the training.

NOTES

1. James J. Fyfe, personal communication, August 28, 2004.

2. Although research on the impact of college education on officer performance is mixed, the arguments for requiring a four-year degree are compelling (i.e., officers possess better communication and problem-solving skills; see Walker and Katz 2002).

3. This review is not intended as a complete discussion of the CompStat model. Rather, it serves as an illustration of the central role of data and data analysis in the NYPD. For a more detailed discussion of CompStat, see McDonald (2002).

4. SPSS is available in a variety of NYPD offices at both One Police Plaza (headquarters) and the Training Academy. The decision to partner with John Jay for the train-

ing arose from the existing relationship between Dr. Fyfe and the author and the fact that Dr. Fyfe knew of no one in the department who had the skills or time to run the training in house.

5. The first cohort of officers tended to be of higher rank (Dr. Fyfe's immediate staff), while the second cohort included a greater number of line staff from the academy and commissioner's office. All worked directly under Dr. Fyfe, however. Note that only 36 of the 45 officers assigned to the training course actually completed it.

6. The initial block also reviewed key methodological issues, including the research process, why research is important for police, levels of measurement, theory, independent and dependent variables, sampling, different research approaches, and benchmarks of scientific quality (validity and reliability).

7. This block was *not* intended to give officers a comprehensive understanding of the technical aspects of regression. Rather, officers were given broad discussion of the theory behind regression, how it is employed in social science, and its limitations.

8. The initial, primary task for the Office of the Deputy Commissioner of Training involved an intensive, "top-to-bottom" review of the recruit curriculum, which had not been revised in 30 years. The review and modifications were completed in 2003, resulting in a completely revamped curriculum that employs a more interactive, less lecture-based approach (i.e., emphasis on role playing and scenarios), with updated training content and improved continuity.

9. The evaluations were anonymous, as there was no way to trace any particular form to a given officer. Evaluations were completed at the end of class, after the author left the room. The evaluations were taken back to Dr. Fyfe's office by one of the officers and kept there until after final grades had been submitted by the author. Officers were told that their responses on the evaluation form might be used in a scholarly article. If an officer approved of his or her evaluation being used in the article, he or she was to indicate so by marking an x in the bottom left corner of the top page. One officer did not mark an x, and his or her evaluation has been excluded from the analysis.

10. The NYPD Cadet Corps is similar to the national Police Corps program. Selection to the Cadet Corps is very competitive, and cadets are viewed as "the best of the best." Cadets are reimbursed for college tuition but must serve a minimum number of years with the NYPD.

11. The NYPD has issued Tasers only to officers assigned to the Emergency Service Unit (ESU). Each precinct also has a Taser that can be signed out by a supervisor. Most ESU calls involve "emotionally disturbed persons." The department has very strict guidelines for use of the Taser, and supervisors review each case for appropriateness.

12. The follow-up survey was self-administered and sent via e-mail to each officer. Once completed, the officers e-mailed it back to the author. Of the 36 officers completing the class, 12 completed the follow-up survey, for a 33 percent response rate.

13. The professor must also be comfortable teaching police officers. Frankly, teaching multiple regression to police officers is different from teaching traditional college students. Also, the presence of 20 guns in class would be a new—and in some cases, troubling—experience for many college professors. In short, selecting the right professor is just as important as selecting the right officers.

REFERENCES

Alliger, George M., and Elizabeth A. Janak. 1989. "Kirkpatrick's Levels of Training Criteria: Thirty Years Later." *Personnel Psychology* 42 (2): 331–41.

Bayley, David H., and Egon Bittner. 1984. "Learning the Skills of Policing." *Law and Contemporary Problems* 47:35–59.

Berg, Bruce L. 1990. "Who Should Teach Police: A Typology and Assessment of Police Academy Instructors." *American Journal of Police* 9(2): 79–100.

Bumgarner, Jeff. 2002. "An Assessment of the Perceptions of Policing as a Profession among Two-Year and Four-Year Criminal Justice and Law Enforcement Students." *Journal of Criminal Justice Education* 13(2): 313–34.

Capps, Larry E. 1998. "CPR: Career-Saving Advice for Police Officers." *FBI Law Enforcement Bulletin* (July): 14–18.

Crank, John P. 1990. "Police: Professionals or Craftsmen? An Empirical Assessment of Professionalism and Craftsmanship among Eight Municipal Police Agencies." *Journal of Criminal Justice* 18:333–49.

Crank, John P., Betsy Payn, and Stanley Jackson. 1993. "The Relationship between Police Belief Systems and Attitudes toward Police Practices." *Criminal Justice and Behavior* 20:199–221.

Dantzker, Mark L. 2000a. "Police Academies and Their Curriculum: Beginning the Exploration." *Police Forum* 10(2): 8–11.

———. 2000b. "Comparing Police Academy Curricula: Toward a National Curriculum." *Police Forum* 10(3): 4–7.

Doerner, William G., Christy Horton, and Jimmy L. Smith. 2003. "The Field Training Officer Program: A Case Study Approach." In *Police and Training Issues,* edited by M. Palmetto. Upper Saddle River, NJ: Prentice-Hall.

Edwards, Terry D. 1993. "State Police Basic Training Programs: An Assessment of Course Content and Instructional Methodology." *American Journal of Police* 12(4): 23–45.

Hamblin, Anthony C. 1974. *Evaluation and Control of Training.* Maidenhead, U.K.: McGraw-Hill.

Holton, Elwood F. III. 1996. "The Flawed Four-Level Evaluation Model." *Human Resource Development Quarterly* 7(1): 5–21.

Kaufman, Roger, and John M. Keller. 1994. "Levels of Evaluation: Beyond Kirkpatrick." *Human Resource Development Quarterly* 5(4): 371–80.

Kirkpatrick, Donald. L. 1959a. "Techniques for Evaluating Training Programs." *Journal of ASTD* 13(11): 3–9.

———. 1959b. "Techniques for Evaluating Training Programs: Part 2—Learning." *Journal of ASTD* 13(12): 21–26.

———. 1960a. "Techniques for Evaluating Training Programs: Part 3—Behavior." *Journal of ASTD* 14(1): 13–18.

———. 1960b. "Techniques for Evaluating Training Programs: Part 2 Results." *Journal of ASTD* 14(2): 28–32.

McDonald, Phyllis P. 2002. *Managing Police Operations: Implementing the New York Crime Control Model CompStat.* Belmont, CA: Wadsworth.

McKenzie, Ian K. 2002. "Distance Learning for Criminal Justice Professionals in the United Kingdom: Development, Quality Assurance and Pedagogical Properties." *Journal of Criminal Justice Education* 13(2): 231–51.

Memory, John M. 2001. "Teaching Patrol Officer Problem Solutions in Academic Criminal Justice Courses." *Journal of Criminal Justice Education* 12(1): 213–30.

Ness, James J. 1991. "The Relevance of Basic Police Training: Does the Curriculum Prepare Recruits for Work? A Survey Study." *Journal of Criminal Justice* 19(2): 181–93.

Phillips, Jack J. 1996. "Measuring the Results of Training." In *Training and Development Handbook,* edited by Roger L. Craig and Lester R. Bittel. New York: McGraw-Hill.

Pollock, Joycelyn M., and Ronald F. Becker. 1995. "Law Enforcement Ethics: Using Officers' Dilemmas as a Teaching Tool." *Journal of Criminal Justice Education* 6(1): 1–20.

Radelet, Louis A., and David L. Carter. 1994. *The Police and the Community.* New York: Macmillan Publishing Company.

Stinchcombe, Jeanne B. 1980. "Beyond Bureaucracy: A Reconsideration of the Professional Police." *Police Studies* 3:49–60.

Stinchcombe, Jeanne B., and W. Clinton Terry III. 1995. "A Study of State Certification Exam Results for Florida Police and Correctional Recruits in Relation to Grade-Level Equivalency." *Criminal Justice Policy Review* 7:223–43.

Taylor, Ralph B. 1994. *Research Methods in Criminal Justice.* New York: McGraw-Hill.

Walker, Samuel, and Charles M. Katz. 2002. *The Police in America: An Introduction.* New York: McGraw-Hill.

Weisburd, David, Stephen D. Mastrofski, Ann Marie McNally, Rosann Greenspan, and James J. Willis. 2003. "Reforming to Preserve: CompStat and Strategic Problem Solving in American Policing." *Criminology and Public Policy* 2:421–56.

Wilson, James Q. 1968. *Varieties of Police Behavior.* Cambridge, MA: Harvard University Press.

About the Editor

Candace McCoy is a professor of criminal justice at the Graduate Center of the City University of New York, where she teaches in the doctoral program of John Jay College of Criminal Justice. McCoy researches and publishes frequently on topics related to courts, including prosecution and sentencing, and applies law and society approaches to the study of criminal justice system operations. She has published articles in a variety of journals, conducted evaluations of many innovative court-related programs, and has consulted widely with government and nongovernmental organizations. She received the American Society of Criminology's Herbert Block Award for distinguished service to the profession in 2003.

About the Contributors

James J. Fyfe worked as a professor, police official, court expert witness, and media commentator in a remarkable career spanning four decades. His scholarly research, service on independent commissions and government advisory boards, and work as an expert witness in over 500 civil rights cases showed his tireless devotion to improving the policing profession. He began his career as a patrol officer with the New York City Police Department, left the force to take on a career in teaching and research, and returned 25 years later as deputy commissioner for training. He was a beloved professor at American University, Temple University, and the John Jay College of Criminal Justice. The authors in this book were all students or associates of Fyfe and dedicate the book to his memory.

Lorie Fridell is a professor of criminology at Florida State University. Throughout the 1990s, she served as the research director for the Police Executive Research Forum in Washington, D.C. Dr. Fridell has 20 years of experience conducting research on law enforcement. Her primary research areas are the police use of force and violence against police. She also writes, consults, and trains in the area of racially biased policing. She has written or edited six books and numerous articles and chapters on these topics.

David Klinger is a professor of criminal justice at the University of Missouri–St. Louis. He is currently on leave to serve as senior researcher with the Police Foundation in Washington, D.C. Klinger's academic specialty is the study of police use of force, particularly deadly force, as well as police response to domestic violence. His book *Into the Kill Zone* won the "best book" award for 2002 from the Police Division of the Academy of Criminal Justice Sciences. His research interests include many issues in crime and justice, with an emphasis on the organization and actions of modern police. He has published scholarly manuscripts that address arrest practices, the use of force, how features of communities affect the actions of patrol officers, and terrorism.

Justin Ready is an assistant professor of criminal justice at Arizona State University. He has served as a lead researcher on several projects evaluating the effects of police initiatives to reduce crime in urban "hot spots," funded by the Police Foundation in Washington, D.C. His interests include urban policing strategies, crime displacement, and environmental criminology.

William Terrill is an associate professor in the School of Criminal Justice at Michigan State University. He has directed several federally funded research projects, including a present study examining police use of force policies in eight cities across the country. Professor Terrill has published numerous scholarly articles on policing, mainly in the area of police use of force practices, as well as a book titled *Police Coercion: Application of the Force Continuum.*

Bryan Vila is a professor of criminal justice at Washington State University at Spokane. Prior to becoming an academic, he served as a law enforcement officer for 17 years—including nine years as a street cop and supervisor with the Los Angeles County Sheriff's Department and six years as a police chief helping the emerging nations of Micronesia develop innovative law enforcement strategies, and two years as a federal law enforcement officer. He has published four books, including *Tired Cops: The Importance of Managing Police Fatigue* (2000) and *Micronesian Blues* (2009).

Samuel Walker is a professor emeritus of criminal justice at the University of Nebraska at Omaha. He has published widely, including 12 books on police accountability, the control of discretion in the criminal justice system, and civil liberties topics, including *Sense and Nonsense about Crime* and the best-selling textbook *Police in America*. Professor Walker has served as a consultant to the Civil Rights Division of the U.S. Department of Justice and to local governments and community groups in a number of cities across the country on police accountability issues. His current research interest is the effect of citizen participation and oversight in police operations.

Michael D. White is an associate professor in the School of Criminology and Criminal Justice at Arizona State University. He researches the effectiveness of police administrative practices as well as a variety of criminological topics. He served as director of the office of police research and evaluation at John Jay College of Criminal Justice before moving to Arizona State in 2008.

Index